A Ned Rorem Reader

A Ned Rorem Reader

≀

Ned Rorem

≀

Foreword by J. D. McClatchy

≀

Yale University Press

≀

New Haven & London

Designed by Nancy Ovedovitz and set in Scala type by Tseng Information Systems.
Printed in the United States of America by R. R. Donnelley & Sons,
Harrisonburg, Virginia.

Library of Congress Cataloging-in-Publication Data
Rorem, Ned, 1923–
A Ned Rorem reader / Ned Rorem ; foreword by J.D. McClatchy.
p. cm.
ISBN 0-300-08984-8 (alk. paper)
1. Music—History and criticism.   I. Title.
ML60 .R78425   2001
780'.92—dc21   2001033334

A catalogue record for this book is available from the British Library.

The paper in this book meets the guidelines for permanence and durability of the
Committee on Production Guidelines for Book Longevity of the
Council on Library Resources.

10 9 8 7 6 5 4 3 2 1

Contents

Contents   vii

—Why am I writing this book?

To revive a tottering conviction, long ago banished to a dim
corner of my room, that if we could Only Connect the world
would have meaning. But what's the meaning of connect? And
isn't the sense of life just as full or empty when alone? Nothing
can penetrate the sumptuous solitude of Everyman, yet I have
a frantic urge (many people I know do not, including
composers and writers) to *leave* something.

Foreword

J. D. McCLATCHY

Of course there have been writers who composed. Jean-Jacques Rousseau struggled all his life to write opera, had a success with *Le devin du village* in 1752, but concluded that opera couldn't be written in the French language and sought instead the consolations of philosophy. Samuel Butler, Ezra Pound, and Paul Bowles tried their hands at opera too. Gerard Manley Hopkins wrote songs, and Lord Berners ballets. It's just that their words have rightly overshadowed their notes. E. T. A. Hoffmann even wrote eleven operas of his own, but his greatest contributions to the history of music were the tales he wrote that other composers set. It's more likely that what the French call *bicéphals* —two-headed prodigies—are to be discovered the other way around. From Hector Berlioz to Igor Stravinsky, there have been composers with spirited literary styles and the energy for anecdote and argument. The letters of Mozart and Richard Strauss remain vivid. The criticism of Schumann, or the memoirs of Ethel Smythe bear study. American composers—Deems Taylor, Roger Sessions, Virgil Thomson, Leonard Bernstein—have been particularly versatile. Even so, most composers find writing to be a chore. To finish a newspaper article, Berlioz had to lock himself in his room for three anguished days while his pistols "looked at me with round eyes" until he had "succeeded, I know not how, in writing I know not what on I know not whom." Stravinsky just hired Craft.

But no writer has composed, and no composer written, better than Ned Rorem. Not that Rorem would think of himself as having two heads. He is a composer who writes: one head with other things on its mind. At first, he kept watch, and notes—knowing all along, as any diarist does, that he was writing down details of his life abroad from 1951 to 1955 so that they could one day be written up. The publication of his first book, *The Paris Diary,* in 1966, created the sort of scandal any writer yearns for. Its pithily elegant entries were filled with tricks turned and names dropped—Cocteau, Poulenc, Balthus, Dalí, Paul Bowles, John Cage, Man Ray, and James Baldwin, along with the rich and titled, the louche and witty. Reviewers seemed either shocked or ecstatic; Janet Flanner was both—she called it "worldly, intelligent, licentious, highly indiscreet." Buoyed by uproar, Rorem the following year published *The New York Diary,* which took the story up to 1961 and deepened his self-portrait as an untortured artist and dashing narcissist. Three hefty further installments appeared, *The Final Diary* in 1974, *The Nantucket Diary* in 1987, and *Lies* in 2000, which carry the account of his nights and days right up to the present.

If parody is the final form that praise takes, Rorem was soon enough, and uncomfortably, offered a dubious accolade. In 1975 the poet Howard Moss, several of whose poems Rorem had in the past set to music, published in *The New Yorker* a hilarious send-up called "The Ultimate Diary." Its little gilded barbs were dipped in a poisonous wit:

MONDAY

Drinks here. Picasso, Colette, the inevitable Cocteau, Gide, Valéry, Ravel and Larry. Chitchat. God, how absolutely dull the Great can be! I know at least a hundred friends who would have given their eyeteeth just to have had a *glimpse* of some of them, and there I was bored, incredible lassitude, *stymied*. Is it me? Is it them? Think latter. Happened to glance in mirror before going to bed. Am more beautiful than ever.

THURSDAY

Half the Opéra-Comique seems to have fallen in love with me. I cannot stand any more importuning. Will go to Africa. How to break with C? Simone de Beauvoir, Simone Signoret, Simone Weil and Simone Simon for drinks. They didn't get it!

Behind the satire, though, lurk more serious matters. Edgar Allan Poe once wrote that the ambitious man's "road to immortal renown lies straight, open, unencumbered before him. All that he has to do is write and publish a very little book. Its title should be simple—a few plain words—'My Heart Laid Bare.' But—this little book must be *true to its title*. No man dare write it. No man *could* write it, even if he dared. The paper would shrivel and blaze at every touch of the fiery pen." Yes, there's a strong dose of self-absorption to Rorem's diaries, but there's also an honesty—touched up, as any on-the-spot notation must be, to give it the tone of even more spontaneous ingenuity. Documenting oneself poses as a kind of writing that is both artless and knowing. The intimate journal, as distinct from autobiography, has never especially appealed to American writers, as it has to the French, though both nationalities are high on self-promotion.

Perhaps it took living for a spell in Paris to help Rorem cultivate the turn of mind that gazes at the world through the narrow lens of a diary. He'd kept one briefly as a child, and again as a young man. Soon after he moved to Paris in 1949, he resumed a chronicle of his composing, calling it *Journal de mes mélodies* in imitation of Francis Poulenc. He started it in French, soon reverted to English and began to deal with more mundane matters. In 1959, back in America and staying for the summer at Yaddo, he met the author Robert Phelps who, with his wife, was also a guest at Yaddo. Because Phelps was a Francophile and a "born fan," Rorem read to him from his diary. He may as well have been Scheherezade. Phelps was captivated. He was working then as a reader for the publisher George Braziller, who signed on the book at once. Phelps insisted it would be best if he edited the book, and Rorem, delighted at the prospect of his first publication, agreed. Phelps selected his favorite bits, removed their dates, and rearranged them. Not until *The Final Diary* was Rorem his own editor.

"My music is a diary no less compromising than my prose," he has written. "A diary nevertheless differs from a musical composition in that it depicts the moment, the writer's present mood which, were it inscribed an hour later, could emerge quite otherwise." The diary's ebb and flow of moods and events, its staircase repartee, though it has consistently been the foundation of all his writing, has often yielded to work meant to stand on more permanent footing. A prominent death or an important performance may have prompted a magazine editor's commission. A deadline looms for a lecture date or record review. Throughout his career, Rorem has taken the time to gather his more considered thoughts. All along he has been contributing occasional essays, profiles and ruminations to magazines, and collecting the best of them into other books—*Music from Inside Out* (1967), *Music and People* (1968), *Critical Affairs* (1970), *Pure Contraption* (1973), *An Absolute Gift* (1978), *Setting the Tone* (1983), *Settling the Score* (1988), *Other Entertainment* (1996), along with a memoir of his early years, *Knowing When to Stop* (1994). If his life is the subject of his diaries, his taste is the stuff of his essays. And unlike the vagaries of life, Rorem notes that "since adolescence, although my cultural vocabulary has changed, my taste has remained the same." His essays are composed like scores. The same hallmarks we listen for in Rorem's music will be found in his essays as well: indirection, instinctive grace, intellectual aplomb, a lyrical line. The essays are rarely through-composed. As if putting together a song-sequence, Rorem prefers the discrete installment, the short take. His ideas accumulate rather than develop. If he thereby talks around a subject sometimes, rather than tackling it head on, he does so in ways that are consistently surprising and illuminating.

"Don't look back," said Cocteau, "or you risk turning into a pillar of salt—that is, a pillar of tears." Rorem's elegiac reminiscences, which have a distinct novelistic flavor, will seem to some a miniature Père Lachaise where so many of his celebrated friends and acquaintances lie at rest. In its splendors and miseries, it seems a vanished world. In retrospect he was its Audubon, an American dauphin in disguise, a tender draughtsman taking aim. His memories are all elegiac, and his opinions may seem defensive. It would be wrong to overlook the shoulder for the chip. His ideas are strongly held and vividly argued. And as contemporary music's *philosophe,* he is no more American than in his breezy originality, his contrarian defense of traditions too readily scorned during the tumultuous upheavals of twentieth-century music. With Stravinsky, he'd say "I don't like that which resembles nothing." The work of Rorem's prose has been to reveal and celebrate the *something* from which the best in our culture derives its energy and significance. It is from this congeries of impulses and convictions, this rich trove of diaries and essays, the most extensive and intimate account we have of any composer's mind and heart, that *A Ned Rorem Reader* is drawn.

For a Quaker, Rorem has evidently quite often been moved by the spirit to speak. His voice in the pages that follow is a distinctive one, and remains his best tribute to France. Rorem's France is that of the 1950s—glamour on the cheap, parties crowded with sacred monsters, above all a genuine artistic fervor in the air. (I suspect it will turn out that the 50s, along with the 20s, were the two most creative decades in the Paris and New York of the twentieth century.) Rorem praises the French, but wouldn't want to be French. Being an American allows him a freedom—to praise the French, say—unavailable in Paris. Besides, he prizes his *difference* above all. But from the French he learned a style: as sleek and epigrammatic as a courtier, its logic leaving behind the faint perfume of polish. He likes to assert and vanish, prefers paradox and provocation, looks for what truth can be found in the space between two contradictory ideas. In this he is both a romantic and a realist. The romance, of course, is not only with the French temperament but with himself as its personification. His lifelong romance is a troubled one—which is why his meditations on loneliness and vanity are especially striking. Both feelings stem from what he elsewhere in this book calls "the small sad need of wanting to be loved." It is a need that accounts for the best and worst of our actions, and for all of art. It is curious to see how, unlike Virginia Woolf's, Rorem's diaries demonstrate little interest in the unfolding landscape, the passing weather, the blur of natural details. He starts with his body (the poet George Seferis once noted in *his* diary that "in essence, the poet has one theme: his living body") and hovers over the self, its little triumphs and long trials. This is precisely where the cosmopolitan romance crosses over into a more familiar American realism. At the pond's edge, after all, Rorem is as much a Thoreau as a Narcissus, a naturalist whose minute observations of the complex interchanges of self and world are canny. Voltaire said that illusion is the first of all pleasures, and it is Rorem's music that is illusory. "I compose for my own necessity," he says, "because no one else makes quite the sound I wish to hear." The instant gratifications of Rorem's music, its throbbing, swooning plangencies, are a private pleasure the rest of us are privileged to share. But his writings have another ambition. Their exquisite honesty, startling in its acuity, takes realism to a rare pitch. Nothing is hidden, nothing is spared. The accounts included here of a mescaline trip with friends and of his nights at the baths have the precision of both the clinical report and the boulevard farce. "Ned Rorem" is just another phenomenon to be analyzed, and the fears and pretensions disclosed make him at once more remote and more sympathetic. One looks back to Montaigne for that kind of difficult self-examination.

Rorem's appetite for music is remarkable, from Bartók to the Beatles. But then one notices he rarely writes about the Great Masters. That *L'Enfant et les sortilèges* is "the most beautiful music ever written" is a judgment almost casually tossed out. But where one would be curious about his thoughts on Bach and Mozart, Beethoven and Verdi, he walks around such giants. His preference for all things French suggests such a swerve, of course, but it may also be that startling opinions are more easily held of smaller talents. And it is Rorem's strong, pungent opinions that are this book's glory. I don't know of any writer who has more of them—judgments really, everything compared and consigned, often before it's even been fully described. Some are autobiographical, as when he reveals that he "filched for my vocal writing the lilt and ebb of Billie Holiday's whine no less than the clean sweep of Schumann or Chabrier." His musical opinions can be scolding or scandalous, but are usually dead-on, as when he notes that "Virgil Thomson's composing gift has never relied on interesting ideas, but on the uses to which dull ideas can be put" or sneers that "bel canto emphasizes the gargoyles more than the cathedral." And who else would concoct a stylistic similarity between Copland and Ravel? Bracing too are his icy generalizations: "Perfection is a realistic goal, greatness is not." "Originality is a hollow virtue; everything's new under the sun." "On its lowest plane the pictorial is more accessible than the sonorous—the eye is a less complex instrument than the ear—so there are more painters around than composers." One hardly even stops to think whether these remarks are true, because of our sudden delight in having the stale givens upended.

It may be that both Rorem's music and his writing are driven by silence, and all that silence encompasses . . . death . . . the future . . . . Silence is both his friend, the prompt of music, and his enemy, that void he wants words to fill. But I'd like to think that, for all their slippery distractions and silvery harmonies, Rorem's work is of a piece, and in service to what Proust called the *inner task*. Most of us, said Proust, instinctively give precedence over the inner task that we have to perform to the outward role which we are playing. But not the true artist. It is he who knows "we have to rediscover, to make ourselves fully aware of that reality, remote from our daily preoccupations, from which we separate ourselves by an ever greater gulf as the conventional knowledge which we substitute for it grows thicker and more impermeable, that reality which it is very easy for us to die without ever having known and which is, quite simply, our life." Rorem's inner task has been, above all, to compose. But it has also been his passion for full awareness, his need to cut through the brambles of mere convention, to kiss awake that sleeping beauty, Life.

Reading Rorem's work puts me in mind of another observation by Proust: "In reality, every reader is, while he is reading, the reader of his own self. The writer's work is merely a kind of optical instrument which he offers to the reader to enable him to discern what, without this book, he would perhaps never have perceived in himself." Notice that Proust says not *for* himself, but *in* himself. *A Ned Rorem Reader* is just such a precision-jeweled optical instrument, and our author's self-dramatizations are finally ways for us to take ourselves by surprise. Properly read, Rorem is one of Emerson's representative men. However we read him, however we may delight in or resist the panache, however harrowing or enthralling we find the self-portrait, in the end we realize that what we have to discover here is nothing less than ourselves.

I first met Ned Rorem over twenty years ago. I even know the precise date: February 13, 1979, at a dinner party given by the novelist Edmund White. I know because I read about it years later in Rorem's diary. (I might have anticipated the entry; after that dinner, while guests were fetching their coats, Rorem came over to me and asked, "How exactly do you spell your name?") In 1974 the composer bought a slumping bungalow on Nantucket, which he keeps as a retreat. But I think of him at his most characteristic in his Upper West Side apartment in New York City. In the years since we first met, I've enjoyed dozens of occasions there, either with a handful of guests for high tea and a new recording, or *à deux* to gossip away an idle afternoon. Dominating the living room is the Steinway at which he works. It's heaped with scores. Books and recordings are piled everywhere, and line the walls of the apartment's other rooms. His furniture is unstylish, but there are paintings to admire—by Leonid Berman, say, and by his friends Jane Freilicher, Jane Wilson, Gloria Vanderbilt, Robert Dash, Joe Brainard, and Nell Blaine. There are several drawings by Cocteau hung near the piano, and at the other end of the room are some of the many portraits of Rorem by the likes of Larry Rivers and Maurice Grosser. Born in 1923, he has the sort of looks men used to try for with injections of animal glands. He's trim, handsome, energetic, voluble. He might be coming out of the kitchen right now. He has a tray with teapot and cups and a plate of petits fours. On his face is a sly look. He's eager to tell you a delicious absurdity that wants needling, or his new take on twentieth-century opera. Settling into this *Ned Rorem Reader* as into an armchair, you have now the chance to listen in on an extraordinary conversation about music and life, a conversation that he's been having with himself for half a century, one that remains as effervescent and astonishing as it was when it all started.

Preface: Two Hats

What is the difference between European and American professionals? Europeans are general practitioners, Americans are specialists. A Parisian doctor who inspects your ears will also be glad to diagnose your arthritis, prescribe for your stomach, and set your broken arm; in the evening you may run across him at a party for a diva where there will also be butchers and bakers and candlestick makers. A New York doctor who inspects your ears will send you across town for your other complaints; nor will you find him at the diva's party—he hobnobs only with physicians.

The same obtains in the arts. A French composer, to make ends meet, must write not only string trios and symphonies, but backgrounds for films, chansons for Piaf, and mood-setters for plays by everyone from Aeschylus to Anouilh, while his social life is all-inclusive. An American composer who writes string trios might also write symphonies, but won't touch the theater, much less the human voice, and his society is almost strictly musical.

The sole area where these generalities are reversed is that of recital singers. Young German or Italian or French sopranos and baritones master the literature of their land first and foremost, often to the exclusion of all other literature; they are proud of their native tongue, in song as in speech. The same obtains to their listeners: German audiences, nursed on *lied*, hear with head in hands; in Italy even the barber and grocer know their *bel canto* backwards; and the French public, while preferring visual arts to aural, are nonetheless content in their assurance that no music exists beyond their frontiers. Young American singers, meanwhile, learn to sing, albeit unsteadily, in every language but their own. Americans know they're better than the rest of the world in bombs and budgets, but retain a vague inferiority vis-à-vis the musical arts, still feeling that European repertories, not to mention European conductors, are better than ours.

For Americans there is always the suspicion that to practice more than one trade is superficial. "Think what he could do if he didn't spread himself so thin!" people used to say about Leonard Bernstein, who, as we know, never got very far. Did such people consider the jacks-of-all-trades abroad, from Leonardo and Michelangelo to Jean Cocteau and Noel Coward? True, America at the end of the last century did fashion two-faced monuments like the poet Wallace Stevens, publicly an insurance attorney; the composer Charles Ives, also publicly in insurance; and the poet William Carlos Williams, who earned his living as a pediatrician. Their words and music were closeted behind mundane professions. They could not exist today.

I am a composer who also writes, not a writer who also composes. The distinction lies not in how I spend my time but in how I subsist. Born in 1923, I was very early entranced with all the arts, as much a doer as a consumer. If I showed little gift as a painter, I did scribble tragic poems and garish novellas, practiced the piano (mostly what was then termed "modern music"—Debussy, Poulenc, John Alden Carpenter)—until I was good enough to improvise my own notions, then to inscribe them. My parents, albeit liberal WASPs in a capitalist culture, had mixed feelings about an artist in the house—how would he earn a

living!—but remained unstintingly supportive. It was a matter of toss-
ing a coin between whether I'd pursue formal studies in words or in
music. Music won.

Nevertheless, I hesitated to remove the other hat. I kept a journal
all those years, and occasionally wrote an essay for some specialized
magazine. But not until 1965, with the publication of *The Paris Diary*
when I was forty-one, did I become a professional author. Within three
months I received more mail about this one book than I had received
about all my music in the preceding twenty years. Priorities began to
shift. If total strangers were going to read me, then perhaps I'd better
make the prose less rhapsodicly self-indulgent and more firmly objective. As for the music, which had hitherto been (so I imagine) elegant,
pristine, well-chiseled, I consciously tried for more . . . well, for more
ugliness, more space and more madness. And so, the Good Ned of Notes
entered a destabilizing mirror while the Naughty Ned of Verbs exited.
The two changed places permanently and, with benign schizophrenia,
have run on parallel tracks ever since. They seldom meet.

Except for Paul Bowles, am I the only composer splitting his time
between words and music? Other composers do write prose (Schumann, Berlioz, Debussy, Thomson), but the prose has always been
about music—their own or other people's. Bowles's prose is plotted
stylized fiction serving quite another purpose. And yes, other composers do write fiction (Wagner, Mussorgsky, Menotti, Blitzstein), but
their fiction is for singing, for librettos, in service to their primary
craft. (Interestingly, when poets compose, as Hopkins, Pound, Paul
Goodman have done, the result invariably falls flat. Lionel Barrymore
too wrote music, so did Hitler. That's another story.) My prose, like
Bowles's, is not consciously related to music, except when I'm review-
ing; it follows some other urge, impossible to define except through its
very expression.

It is a truth universally acknowledged that the entire solar system is
torn between two esthetics: French and German. Virtually everything

is one or the other. Blue is French, red is German. No is French, yes is German. Formal gardens are French, oceans are German. The moon is French, the sun German. Gay men are French, lesbians German. Crows feet are French, pigs knuckles German. Wolff on his good days is French, Berlioz is forever German. Balinese are French, Hawaiians are German. Jokes are French, the explanation of jokes is German. If French is to be profoundly superficial, like Impressionism, which depicts a fleeting vision of eternity, then German is to be superficially profound, as when Bruckner digs ever deeper into one narrow hole. If you agree with all this, you're French. If you disagree, you're German.

Since Americans are German while Europeans are French, am I then a Frenchman trapped in a German body? If prose is German while music is French (although subdivisions of prose, like essays, are French, while subdivisions of music, like symphonies, are German; and Schubert, say, though anatomically Austrian, was, in his economy, French-ish, while Franck, though biologically Belgian was, in his profligacy, Germanic), then am I, according to my own definition, half and half?

Let me put on my thinking cap. But which one? For I do wear two of them, but never at the same time.

PART 1

Diaries and Musings

In the strain of resurrecting geographies and histories
and liaisons of yore, the core gets lost. What was I *thinking*
while in Twig, or Yellowstone, or at the world's fair? What was I
thinking in the arms of those strangers—or at the announcement of German encroachments—beyond how to protect my
own skin? Most of the time I was thinking about music, or
writing it, or reading and dreaming about it. The issue of that
thinking was, ten years, forty years after, more thinking and
reading and writing, while the world proper grew increasingly
invisible to me, and I to it. That is the pith of an artist's life.

So his biography contains everything but the essential.

The Art of the Diary

J. D. McCLATCHY

Children, it seems to me, have no capacity to distance themselves from their own lives, and so no sense of reflection. All of that starts to well up—in the form of Great Ideas and Deep Feelings—in the teenager. But for the record, did you start keeping a diary as a child?

NED ROREM

Don't be too dismissive of children. While it's true that few children are artists, all artists are children. And insofar as artists adopt the grown-up stance that blinds them to the wide-open perceptions of their childhood, they cease being artists. That said, I'm not much interested in children before they're twenty-one. And yes, their diaries— even Anne Frank's or Daisy Ashford's—are not repositories of Great Ideas. What are Great Ideas anyway, and are mature artists interested in them? Most of my writer-friends gossip when they get together, and reserve their nuance for the page. Deep Feelings were expressed in the college dorm. Not that we don't suffer after fifty, but the suffering is more often about health and death than about Love and Abandonment.

I did keep a diary in 1936, age twelve, for three months when our family went to Europe. Except for frequent references to Debussy and Griffes, it focuses breathlessly on American movies seen in Oslo, or tourists we met on boats. No shred of lust, much less of intellect or guile. Admittedly, words are never put on paper, be it *War and Peace* or a laundry list, without thought of other eyes reading them, even though those eyes might just be one's own at another time. But I didn't think of myself as an author. Ten years later I began a literary diary and kept it up until I went to France in 1949. It's filled with drunkenness, sex and the talk of my betters, all to the tune of André Gide.

J. D. McCLATCHY

Your Quaker upbringing—did that encourage early habits of introspection?

ROREM

I didn't really have a "Quaker upbringing." My mother's younger brother was killed in the First World War at the age of seventeen. She never got over the trauma. When they were married in 1920 my parents (she a Congregational minister's daughter, he a Methodist) looked around for a group that would work for peace, internationally, and not just in time of war. The Society of Friends was the answer. They weren't concerned with the God part (I'm not sure they even believed in God), only with the peace part. Thus my older sister, Rosemary, and I were raised as pacifists, to think that there is no alternative to peace. Which I believe. Whether I'm right or wrong, I'm not ashamed of it. . . . So I was not raised piously, much less in silence. We were taken regularly to all the best concerts and plays that came to Chicago. My background was far more structured by the cultured and caring intellect of my parents than by the strictured structure of the stricter Quakers.

J. D. McCLATCHY

What prompted you to start that diary in 1946?

ROREM

Prior to entering Juilliard in the fall of 1945, it was necessary to take some liberal-arts courses to qualify for a degree as distinct from a diploma. So I went to summer school at NYU in Washington Square. During the first class in English literature, our instructor happened to say, "Happiness, then, is an answering after the heart." On the way home I bought a 5" × 9" ruled hardcover notebook and began a diary with the phrase—a phrase that today seems both corny and unclear. Also, knowing that David Diamond kept a diary was an incentive. Diamond was an example—one I emulated perhaps—of a disciplined composer (who could account for every note) trapped in a self-destructive body. The style of that early diary (my diaries are really journals, since they're hardly daily—although *journal* means daily too, doesn't it?) was often like Diamond's, or like the books he read, *Moby-Dick*, *The Heart Is a Lonely Hunter*. Probably I took to the form because it was a crazy, open-ended contrast to my rather Spartan music. The entries are all about screwing, drunkenness, suicidal urges . . . the usual. If they ring true at all, it's the truth of the young. I left the book lying around. Once a piece of rough trade stole it and tried to blackmail me. He felt we could make a killing together in royalties! I got the book back, but that's another story.

Incidentally, I kept the diary in longhand for the next twenty years, until I realized it might be published.

J. D. McCLATCHY

You left for France in 1949. That would be incentive enough to continue keeping your diary, but was there a moment when you became more self-conscious about doing so?

ROREM

When I left for France in May of 1949, the visit was to have lasted three months, so I didn't bring my diary. I ultimately remained eight years. On realizing that I'd never come back to America, I wrote Morris

Golde and asked him to ship all my previous journals to Hyères, where I was living chez Marie-Laure de Noailles. One morning she came into my room and handed me a pretty little carnet with several hundred empty pages, saying: "Here, write. Even if you feel bad before and after, *while* you're writing your cares are transferred." She kept her own diary every night before bed, faithfully, drunk or sober. It mainly related facts of the day. Mine—which for several months I kept in French, then reverted to English, which was, of course, more *me*—related states of mind as well as of body, and was probably modeled on Julien Green's journal. Green, who had become an intimate friend (the friendship exploded fatally a year later), was as strong a literary influence on me as Paul Goodman had been during my adolescence. And yes, probably I was thinking of other eyes than my own as I penned the pages.

Marie-Laure and Green were the same age (she was born in 1902, he in 1900), but opposites. She: French, half-Jewish, unimaginably rich, Catholic but communist and a nonbeliever, odd-looking but forceful, like George Washington in a Dior gown, vastly cultivated, sophisticated (but like many sophisticated females of the period, more innocent than she pretended about sex), self-consciously bohemian, liking queer men, including her very closeted husband, the Vicomte de Noailles, who was her best friend but whom she seldom saw, and to whom a marriage had been arranged when she was twenty, thus making her noble (the Noailles go back to Louis XIII) and still richer. She was a rather gifted writer and a very gifted painter, but, like many of the rich, undisciplined with pen and paintbrush. She was powerful and famous too, and launched me, sort of. Otherwise I may have returned here sooner. Julien, meanwhile, was American (but raised in France) and the truest bilingual I've ever known. A True Believer, Catholic convert, writer of a strange and passionate passivity, if that makes sense. His force came through a sort of hypnotism. He loved me, and I was infected with the casual cruelty of the young. He felt, probably, that my remarks about God were frivolous, and that I made mockery of his sexual leanings.

He came to Hyères for a one-day visit in 1951, and seeing the two of them together was odd—especially since, exceptionally, the vicomte was also there. They were all so *respectful* of each other, yet their only interest in common (beyond the considerable one of art) was me. This went to my head.

J. D. McCLATCHY

The anecdote that opens *The Paris Diary*—was it meant to be emblematic? It goes this way: "A stranger asks, 'Are you Ned Rorem?' I answer, 'No,' adding, however, that I've heard of and would like to meet him." Was that meant to point toward some underlying theme of self-discovery, or self-making? Or worse, some condition that calls for a negation of the self, or a devotion to the diary as a substitute for the self?

ROREM

Your question ignores this fact: *The Paris Diary* is the only one of my fourteen books that was edited by someone else. Being my first book, all suggestions were accepted. Not a word is changed from the manuscript, but Robert Phelps radically shifted the order of entries. Thus that first remark was originally embedded somewhere in the center. To change place is to change meaning, even when that which is changed remains unchanged, so to speak. Would you have posed your question about that entry if it were elsewhere?

J. D. McCLATCHY

Fair enough. Now, however the entries were rearranged in the end, what first prompted you to record a particular event or idea? The amusing remark? The annals of star-fucking? Or were you, in prose, marking your growth, as with a ruler and pencil on the kitchen wall?

ROREM

Hmm . . . Does the diary, in fact, record events and ideas and amusing remarks? It's a long time since I've reread it. Probably I wrote what I wrote because, although I've always known that nothing in the universe really counts, and that when we're gone we're gone, I still have a terror of being lost, of becoming as anonymous as an Assyrian slave, or even as an Elizabethan poet, whose works, to be sure, are recalled, but not his body—not, say, Marlowe's scalding male flesh. As for star-fucking (your term), I've never practiced that. Of the three thousand people I bedded between 1938 and 1968, only four were famous, and it wasn't my doing. (They're listed in *Knowing When to Stop.*) I can't sleep with the famous, it's an ego clash. But if many of my friends have rec-ognizable names, I know them not for their fame but for what made them famous, their music, or books or pictures. I'd rather have first-rate acquaintances than not. I don't know any baseball players (though they're sexier than, say, dress designers) because we have nothing in common.

J. D. McCLATCHY

Does one have to be a narcissist to keep a diary?

ROREM

Am I really more of a narcissist than other artists? Or do I just admit it more readily? Certainly I'm not hot for myself. I'm not my own type. Nor does the diary use the word *I* more than do most contemporary poets. Jorie Graham, for instance, or Frank O'Hara, or indeed yourself, sprinkle the page with *I*. Marie-Laure used to say that I was more inter-ested in a state of body than a state of mind (*un état de corps, non pas un état d'âme*). But how can I know? We live inside ourselves, by defi-nition, and none of us can see ourselves as others see us. Inasmuch as every work of art, whether vertical or horizontal, has a beginning, middle and end, a diary cannot by its nature qualify, though certainly a good diary hits the mark more convincingly than a dull, but expertly penned, novel. But who makes the definitions?

J. D. McCLATCHY

Speaking of which, Auden defined the narcissist as the hunchback who gazes at his image in the water and says, "On me it looks good."

When I asked you about the diarist's narcissism, I didn't just mean the recurrence of *I*, but the self-absorption: whatever happens to the self is deemed of interest to others.

ROREM

Well, yes. Auden was right even when he was wrong. Cocteau said, *"Je suis le mensonge qui dit la vérité."* All art is a lie, insofar as truth is defined by the Supreme Court. After all, Picasso's goat isn't a goat. Is the artist a liar, or simply one for whom even a fact is not a fact? There is no truth, not even an overall Truth.

J. D. McCLATCHY

Was there something about the French turn of mind and phrase that influenced the way you recorded things then?

ROREM

Yes, but I never said to myself, "I shall now make a French-type entry." I was, after all, living among the French, some of the smartest, and was still young enough to emulate my elders. Also, there is such a thing as writing French in English: Janet Flanner, for instance, or Virgil Thomson. Their English is economical. Illustrative, and terse in the sense of the *mot juste*—yet the *mot* was inevitably Anglo-Saxon. Virgil used to tell fledgling critics on the *Tribune*, "Don't say she had faulty intonation, say she sang out of tune. The best English doesn't use Latinate nouns." German in English? Probably Faulkner, who takes forever to get to the point. Or even, ironically, Proust. Julien Green wrote English in French; at least his subject matter was often about American Protestant misers, described in the tongue of Mallarmé. Very disconcerting.

J. D. McCLATCHY

When it first appeared, *The Paris Diary* was nothing if not a *succès de scandale*, though those were more shockable times. Were you deliberately naughty *pour épater les bourgeois*?

ROREM

I doubt it. When prepublication extracts from *The Paris Diary* first appeared, most notably in this very magazine [*The Paris Review*], I was stunned when people found it outrageous (more for the narcissism than the queerness, although the latter was invariably stressed in straight reviews), because anything we do, when seen in multiple reproduction, is no longer ours. You know how it feels to see your poem in *The New Yorker*? Imagine how it feels to sit in a box and hear your music played. Especially played badly.

J. D. McCLATCHY

Can you recall now an incident you wish you'd recorded and didn't, and one that's included in the published diary but you wish were not?

ROREM

There's nothing recorded that I regret, though I have remorse about certain entries and have lost friends. As for what I didn't record, that can always be remedied in a memoir.

J. D. McCLATCHY

By the end of *The Paris Diary* (or the end that was concocted for it), you sound both satisfied and sated. Or perhaps the word I want is more *American,* in the sense that Gertrude Stein declared Paris is where "Americans can discover what it means to be American." When you return to the States in 1955 and pick up with *The New York Diary,* perhaps you sound a little French—or at least a little out of place. Did that second diary begin with an odd sense of *dépaysement?*

ROREM

You're asking me to ascribe motivations decades after the fact. A diary is, by definition, on-the-spot reporting, even when most introspective. I cannot today be sure that I recall a certain incident purely, rather than what I've *written* about the incident. Thus I cannot know today what made me start the damn book in the first place. I do know that there's less responsibility—less urge to chisel and ply and plot —than when writing a poem or play or novel or, indeed, a song or symphony. Diaries have no beginnings, no endings. They are per-petual middles. But of course I state this only now, with the percep-tion of hindsight, and hindsight is always skewed. Which is why those seminars of Anaïs Nin (Anus Ninny, as Phelps called her) were sheer blather. There are as many shapes to a diary as there are diarists, whereas a sonnet or sonata is always a sonata or sonnet. Oh, maybe not . . . I'm less caught up by our discussion this hour than by concern for the health of my beloved Jim Holmes. He is my diary. You are my sonata. Oi!

J. D. McCLATCHY

The first three diaries have no index, where one could cruise for one's enemies and friends. It's maddening! Was it deliberate?

ROREM

My memory of the reason is clear. Though now that you ask—not so clear. Joe Adamiak, my boyfriend in 1965 and a graphic artist, was hired by Braziller to do the layout of *The Paris Diary*. He wanted the printed phrases not to be flush with the margins, but to ramble like handwriting. This was vetoed by everyone, and nothing remains of those early plans except his pretty good photo on the cover. For rea-sons of naturalism (or was it expense?) we all agreed not to have an index. Leonard Bernstein said, when *The Paris Diary* appeared, that it needed a list of names, with a plus or minus sign beside each one. Any-way, the device continued through *The Final Diary* (now titled *The Later Diaries*) and everyone, including me, finds it inconvenient. Or, as you say, maddening.

J. D. McCLATCHY

Music itself is a kind of diary—reflecting the moods and impulses of the days. I know the differences between the two activities—the one private, the other commissioned; the one read, the other performed; et cetera—but what would you say about the similarities?

ROREM

If the arts could express each other, we'd only need one art. As one of the few Americans (as distinct from Europeans who are—or used to be—all general practitioners) who practices two distinct arts professionally, I realize ever more clearly (though I didn't forty years ago) the evidence of the previous sentence. When my first book, *The Paris Diary*, was published, and I realized that strangers would be reading about presumably private thoughts, I immediately acquired a new sense of responsibility. Perhaps music is also about private thoughts, but who can prove it? It's not that music's too vague for words—it's too *precise* for words. Nor does it have the same audience as prose or pictures or verse. Observe painters: how unembarrassedly they admit to knowing nothing, and caring less, about classical music. Ditto writers. Not all. But most. It's inconceivable that a composer would admit to knowing nothing about, say, novels, or Matisse. Music is the most abstract of the arts, painting the most concrete. Which is why painters always label a picture *Abstraction Number 7*—because they know that, as with clouds, we'll always find a program there somewhere, while musicians are quick to call their pieces "La Mer" or "Alice in Wonderland," lest the listener lose his way. Anyhow, after that diary came out, my music (I like to think) became rougher, and my prose less scattered.

J. D. McCLATCHY

You've written several books of essays. Have your diaries served as a kind of seedbed or sounding board for ideas later expounded upon in essays?

ROREM

I began writing essays soon after the first diary appeared, and they have nothing of the diaristic about them—and seldom use the pronoun *I*.

When the University at Buffalo invited me in 1959 to present six lectures, each to be followed by a concert of my own devising, I asked myself: What do I know about music that nobody else knows in quite the same way—about the construction of a song, for example—and can this be put into words? Because there's nothing a composer can say, at least about his own music, that the music can't say better, except how it came to be made. These essays, like many reviews that followed, sought to be objective above all.

By today I've probably said, in words, everything I have to say, both about my navel and about other people's. (I hate, by the way, to write negatively about other people's music, and never do so, except for sociological purposes, as when writing of Elliott Carter.) Maybe I've also said everything I have to say, as well, in my musical voice. I'm seventy-five now, and if I died tonight I'd not be ashamed of much of a rather large catalogue. As for the diary, yes, I still keep it. But disparately. Once I wrote, "I won't have the courage to say in these pages what really matters until I'm of an age when that will seem obscene." Something like that. From where I now stand, nothing really counts anymore. Did it ever? The world has no overall meaning, and I have no crying urge to restate that truism in all sorts of luminous ways.

J. D. McCLATCHY

When you wrote both *The Paris Diary* and *The New York Diary*—do I have my dates right?—you were a famously heavy drinker. Did sobriety change your daily sense of things, or your writing habits?

ROREM

On first dipping my toe into AA in 1959 (it didn't take for another ten years, though) I realized I'd been subliminally alcoholic since childhood, and overtly since around age sixteen. Meaning that one drink was too many and twenty weren't enough. As for the reasons for alcoholism, like those for homosexuality, who knows? I never felt guilty about being gay so much as being passive, wanting to be adored, et cetera. When drunk, I had a good excuse. But beyond that? Anyway, my earliest unpublished diaries (I do quote from them some in *Knowing When to Stop*) do wallow a lot in booze, at least as a subject. But I never wrote either prose or music while drunk, always segregated good and bad, work and play. My drunk self is a schizoid other. Thus sobriety never changed my daily sense of things, or writing habits. But uttering these phrases today seems somehow trivial. I'm traversing the most melancholy valley of my life: Jim, my partner of thirty-one years, is dying. Nothing else seems important, not diaries or operas, or geophysics, nothing. And though it appears lofty to say that I've said all I have to say, it's nevertheless true. Don Bachardy did draw Christopher Isherwood during each last dying day. I approve. But what can I say that, for example, Joyce in "The Dead" hasn't said better in those hundred final words. An hour ago, anticipating your question, I opened the diary to July 7, 1967, *comme si par hasard:* "Is a diary, by its nature, more 'honest' than a novel? Probably not. The undisciplined first-person involuntarily inclines more to disguise than a novelist does. As to whether I know less 'who I am' than, say, Alfred Chester or James Purdy, neither they nor I will ever know, any more than we can perceive the self-awareness of that farmer, that nurse, that dogcatcher." Ah, silly superfluous art. Art.

J. D. McCLATCHY

Tell me about the actual writing. Has it been a daily task? Do you write into a notebook, or type up pages? And do you ever look back over an entry and revise?

ROREM

The first diaries, from 1945 through 1970, were written in notebooks in ballpoint. More recently, typed, since I type everything now. And yes, revised, of course. Because everything is revised merely by being reexamined. Everything is lost instantly (these words here, Jocasta's first view of Oedipus) and can only be retrieved through revision. Yet more literally, I revise in transit. From sentence to sentence, note to note. I do strongly disapprove of authors who, decades later in their

collected works, "improve" upon the initial afflatus. Auden. Paul Goodman. They are always wrong, for the early work no longer belongs to
them.

All literature is a diary. So indeed is all art, and all organized communication, in the sense of its being a reaction to any aspect of the
universe. A diary, no matter how scrupulously revised and edited, is
by its nature looser than a fugue or a court report.

J. D. McCLATCHY

When Cocteau's diaries were published in English some years ago,
I remember your review of them. You recorded your surprise when
discovering that Cocteau had written about an event you too had written up.

ROREM

That was only the second time I'd met Cocteau. The first time I went
to see him as a fan in October of 1950, and we got along fine. I didn't
know Marie-Laure then, but by the next summer I did, and Cocteau
told others—never me—"it's too bad that Rorem boy is shacked up
with Marie-Laure, because she can only destroy him." Of course she
didn't—nor were we shacking up. I was very anxious to be what I was—
namely, her intimate friend without having to put out. She much admired industry, and I worked hard, drunk or sober. What impressed
her is that I wasn't a silly gadabout. I worked several hours a day, every
day, in her house, both up in Paris and down south. She worked hard
too.

The first time I went down to visit her in the south of France, we
decided that we would go visit her spouse and mother, who both lived
in the town of Grasse in separate, very comfortable houses. Hyères is
a couple of hours away. She invited Cocteau over. So we all had lunch
at Charles's, her husband the Vicomte, the last great Proustian gentleman. I don't know what he thought of me. I do remember I stole a
little pair of cuticle scissors from his bathroom. Cocteau came in Mme.
Weissweiler's car. He wore a white leather jacket, which I thought

was terribly chic. He sat next to the chauffeur, but had a notebook on his lap. He was never not working. After lunch we took a car over to see Marie-Laure's mother. She had been married to Francis de Croisset, one of Reynaldo Hahn's librettists. Marie-Laure said Croisset used to make passes at her, and she wrote a novel called *La Chambre des écureuils,* about a man who made passes at his stepdaughter. Then *Bonjour Tristesse* came out, also about that sort of thing. She always felt Sagan had got there second but got more credit. Anyway, it was Marie-Laure's idea that I should play my ballet *Mélos* for Cocteau (she had done the scenario). So I played it for him, so they could all see if I had a *sens du théâtre.* We both wrote up the day.

J. D. McCLATCHY

I noticed in your kitchen that little photograph of you with Jean Marais.

ROREM

He just died, you know. Usually when you get to know really big movie stars, they turn out to be nice people. Jean was thoroughly modest. He wrote a not-bad autobiography called *Histoires de ma vie,* in which he's very frank about Cocteau. There was a question of *Dorian Gray* being made into a ballet. Henri Sauguet was asked but didn't want to do it and suggested my name instead. This was for the ballet company of the Opéra-Comique, and the chief dancer was an American named Georges Reich, a husky blond who was Marais's lover. He hardly spoke French and Marais didn't speak English. Reich was to dance Dorian, and Marais was to play the portrait. So Marais came to visit me. I lived in a teeny room on the fourth floor of the Hôtel des Saints-Pères. I still remember the doorman excitedly phoning to say *"M. Marais monte!"* Up came Jean to my humble room. On the sofa were some drawings by Cocteau, and he said, "Oh my God, I certainly feel at home here." It sounds naive to say, but he was just like anybody else. We went carefully through the ballet—this kind of music here, that kind of music there. As things worked out, I had of necessity to see

Marais quite often. By the way, the ballet was to be done in Barcelona, in May of 1952. And was. It flopped. After that, we exchanged letters every two or three years until he died, which came as a shock to me. I was pleased to see that he was given a sort of national funeral.

J. D. McCLATCHY

I've read that *The Paris Diary* is credited with helping the emergent gay-liberation movement along. Has that been your sense of things?

ROREM

When the book was reviewed in *The New York Times,* the word *homosexual* appeared in the headline and that gave me a jolt. I didn't think of myself as in any sense political or promotional. In the book, I was merely too lazy to pretend to be something I'm not. I refer in the book to a person named P, and did so grammatically in a way that it could be sexually either/or. Eventually I got tired of that. I was bemused to be taken as a guru, since I never thought of myself that way—as Allen Ginsberg did. But I had to take my name out of the phone directory. There'd been violent threats; and, just as bad, fans ringing the doorbell. I had mentioned in the diary that I'd introduced myself to Benjamin Britten by sending him a photograph of myself half-naked; now people began sending me nude photos of themselves, including women. On the other hand, I met Jim through the diary. He'd read *The New York Diary* and was told by a mutual friend to look me up. But it's not for me to talk here about the effect of my diary; that's for other people to say.

J. D. McCLATCHY

Do you read the diaries of others? I notice Dawn Powell's on your bookshelf.

ROREM

There are certain things I can't get the point of. Bagels, for instance. Why do people like them? I can't get the point of Berlioz. I can dislike a composer, while admitting what others see in him or her. But not Berlioz. Likewise Dawn Powell.

J. D. McCLATCHY

Well then, are there diarists whom you *do* read with admiration?

ROREM

Not today any longer. But I certainly read Gide, whom I still think is a marvelous diarist. And Isherwood. Julian Green's still means a great deal to me.

J. D. McCLATCHY

Did you learn how to write a diary by reading them? What to include? How to shape an anecdote?

ROREM

I could have. Nobody does anything without being impelled by something already existing. Every note composed, every brush stroke, everything we're saying here—nothing comes from nothing. Although I wouldn't have been attracted to Green's if I hadn't already been writing a diary myself since 1945.

J. D. McCLATCHY

Do you think the people who know your music know your diary, and the people who know your diary know your music?

ROREM

No. When the diary appeared I'd been a professional composer for about twenty years—meaning commissions, performances and so forth. But in six months I was far better known as a prose writer than as a musician. Nine out of ten people who played my music hadn't the faintest idea I wrote books, and certainly the people reading the diaries didn't know my music. I could tell from the letters I received. Even today, letters about music I get from strangers are all about a possible error, say, in measure thirty-four, whereas the letters about the diaries are invariably much more emotional. But then literary people — or most of them — know little about music. In America, we're getting more philistine by the minute. In France, things may be different.

J. D. McCLATCHY

Do you reread your own diaries?

ROREM

No, never. Well, in anticipation of your visit, I did glance over *The Paris Diary*. It's hard to read because I know it so well, even today. But sometimes I'll come upon sections in any of the diaries and think how good they are — I'd hit the nail of a given situation precisely on the head.

J. D. McCLATCHY

Does the Paris of the late fifties seem increasingly like a fictional world to you now, from the vantage of seedy New York on the brink of the millennium?

ROREM

Two or three years ago the French radio had Elliott Carter, me and a couple of others talk in French on a program about culture. Elliott, being God, did most of the talking. But when he said that after 1951 the musical world really started in France, I had to interrupt to say, "Oh, but that's about when it *stopped*." True, Poulenc still had *The Dialogues of the Carmelites* in him (I could see Elliott flinch), and true, Cocteau still had a play or two left in him, and Gide would die the following year, but the *great* France — and I'm right, of course — was over. The Proustian world still existed up until the mid-fifties — by which I mean literally that people who were friends of Proust or of that rarified milieu were still alive, with their tight-lipped upper-class accent, gleaned largely from their low-class English nannies. I wouldn't know whom to telephone now, if I went to Paris. Oh, James Lord, of course, but who else? Ed White's no longer there. But the older ones, the French writers

and musicians—no one's left. The young people in Paris nowadays I
don't find especially cute or especially smart, despite their high IQ. Performers are pretty good. Ballet dancers. But except for the movies, what
is going on creatively over there? No plays, no fiction. The other writing
is still all that bullshit about deconstruction. Paris has had its day.

1999

Lies: Notes on Craft

My work is my truth. Insofar as that work is also art it is also true for you. That that art may lie makes it no less true. A symbol posing as the real thing betrays itself, yet the betrayal can't disqualify the symbol's status as symbol.

That painting there's not true to life, it's scarcely true to paint. That tune's not natural, not birdsong, not wind's sough, it's false to outdoors. It sounds like nothing else. It lies.

According to who's listening we all are liars. Artists' fables are worth attending. Lies of art ring true.

Am I incapable of truth because I don't know what it is? Whatever truth may be, it's not the opposite of lie. In art it is that which can be cared about, that which we believe.

Those who say, "Look out, he'll quote you in that diary," are the very ones I never notice. The others, they're safe, they can't win, I don't quote, I misquote. Lurking behind the exquisite monster, I'm capable of guidance—that is, of guiding him. The matriarch's mother.

Who most loathe the diary are those depicted within. What they most loathe is not precious archness, not opinions stated as facts nor the

urbane reflections posing as pastorale *pensées*, but seeing their life reduced to anecdote, however crass or laudatory. "I was there," they say,
"I keep a diary too, I remember what happened, and you're wrong." Of
course there's no such thing as *the* truth, there is only *one's* truth, and
even that fluxes with each passing hour. Though I disown nothing, I've
come to value discretion, even to claim it among virtues broader than
mere truth. Mere truth. Yet in the old days it never occurred to me that
friends would feel hurt from my passing verities.

A book's a book, not real life. Yet when offered for real, as a diary,
the book must be arranged to seem real. The very arranging teaches an
author artifices of life itself, outgrowths which in the telling become
more natural than in their larval stage of mere being.

Was *Rashomon* three versions of a lie, or of a truth? Are diaries less
honest inherently than novels?

Diaries are a sideline, notebooks wherein a person records problems
of work and play. Nearly always, though, they are kept with the intention of being read; so like all art they dissimulate by becoming a code.
The diarist doesn't present himself, but an idea of himself, and only
that idea of himself which he chooses to publicize.

As a literary form the diary is hardly new (it's far older than the
novel) except as an indigenous American utterance, public confession
not having been our bent until recently. Yet confession risks adopting the features of the very mask novelists hide behind. Our century's
best-known diarist, André Gide, during the blitzes of World War Two,
blissfully notated adventures with Arab lads in his Biskra retreat. To
tell it like it is is no more a property of diaries than of fiction. Lives
are not facts, nor does the present moment exist; an author can necessarily record the present only after the fact. Of itself truth is not persuasive; even less is it art. And who, including the diarist himself, can
prove that the character represented is, in this guise, finally, the *real*
author? Does Baudelaire's journal disclose more to us of Baudelaire
than Genet's novels do of Genet? Could Philip Roth have composed
his complaint in another form without its becoming more rather than

less of a mask? To fictionalize the real makes it easier to be honest. The realist novel of the thirties became the unrealistic autobiography of the sixties. Still, all real works of art (be they geometric sculptures, children's poetry, or reports on Hanoi) speak to us, by definition, with their creator's voice.

A voice is a voice, unfakeable. We cannot lie, no matter what tone we pretend to—or in fact *do*—project, no matter how we try to shade or disguise that voice, no matter what master's words or songs we filch and, like reverse dybbuks, sing through our own lips. No one can lie, the body cannot lie, and the wiliest plagiarism is verifiable. What is not verifiable is why those fingerprints are more amusing than these, or why some standard stolen goods take on a wilder luster on a thief's back. Alas, most thefts are of trash and remain trash.

The difference between a journalist and a diarist is that one reports what happened, the other reports a reaction to what happened. Yet both are susceptible to cries of liar. Rightly. Less truthful than a painter, a photographer *is* bias: a camera selects the angle and snaps its subject unawares, especially if the subject is a tree. The tree is a lie, but not the picture of it. If truth is fact, then all art—which only represents fact, and one person's version of that—lies, but by extension speaks true.

JH confides he's been glancing through some of my notes, and hopes, should they ever be published, that I'll delete a reflection about his voice sounding sad on the phone. Now, I'm as responsive to the desires of JH as to those of any living person, but it is a diarist's nature to include precisely what others would have him exclude. There lies the danger. Estrangements don't come from what people find gossipy about other people, but from what they find incomplete—and thus untrue—about themselves, for truth means only the whole truth. Indeed, for me to read what's written about me is to see a life reduced to several lines—sometimes ecstatic, sometimes sarcastic—and to find myself miniaturized and existing for others who, because they see fractionally, find me peripheral to their own laws. In a diary no mention of a person can be, to that person, the *right* mention, since no mention of anything (even of E equals mc squared) is all-inclusive, and so can be only a lie. My own mention of others, even of myself, means to me only what it means during the moment of mention, since we change pores—natures, reality—with each fluid second.

What is comparatively stable is the sadness of JH's voice on the phone. If this were all that signified to me I would (at his request) omit mention of it, as wrongly I have omitted whimsies or eccentricities or passing "perversions," at their request, of others, thereby diluting the blood—the *truth, my* truth, however superficial—of the published diary in the past, because the diary became no longer a biased monologue but a fair exchange. If I mention the sadness of JH's voice it's because I am so vulnerable to the sound; in fact my susceptibility is such that, when we met a decade ago, I understood that for the remainder of my life another person would never fill his special shoes, and that I could (and largely did) renounce a certain sociability without feeling anything but richer. JH is everything, and to write that is to compromise us both far more than any mention of a sad voice. Should he choose that I also delete this paragraph, I shall. Though where then will be my documented verities, fragmented but contradictorily (if only through style), flowing, continual, and in a way necessary because inimitable?

Art moves us, propaganda changes us. Art takes us in a circle, propaganda in a straight line. Art collides with propaganda, producing a tantrum to attract the grownups who, being no less childlike than the artists, take it as a game, a game without rules that goes on forever, or at least—as in medieval oubliettes—until death.

Circling the square. Let the music flutter like leaves, be passive to the wind, assume a "natural" shape (which throughout the universe is circular) rather than the forced angles of art. Circling the square: cruising outside the central marketplace.

Freudian slips of the tongue would hold more interest if they were less just that: casual slips, a foot's accidental excursion into a puddle, which is not really so foreign an environment for feet. Sound-alikes are too predictably the result of fatigue or embarrassment, or of man's penchant for rhyme, for building on a given: mercy for merry, sorrow queen for sour cream, sew me to a sheet for show me to a seat, maybe money for honey. To call your present lover by the name of a previous lover is not so rare. Give me someone who unexpectedly says butterfly for oatmeal, says ambergris for confidential, yes for when, peach for swan, or who, at twenty and for the first time ever, calls his father mother.

Full time and willy-nilly do I chase two careers never knowing quite if their mutual infringement is harmful or fruitful. To spill out verbs instead of notes should disquiet me. Yet this prose is a sieve: What oozes through is rarefied, becomes distilled and turns to "abstract" sound on staves. Is whatever clogs the meshes scraped out and smeared undiluted onto diary paper?

How can I know if my prose and music interfere with each other? Without the prose would the music be better or just thicker? Without the music would there be a subject for the prose?

Only as a composer am I qualified to soliloquize, since my life is no longer amorous, voluble, or drunk, and since I've no more friends—certainly no new ones (who would they be? and what could they bring that I couldn't find in their works?—except a taxi to the hospital in moments of need, moments, however, growing paradoxically fewer as one gets feebler). Killing time. Now that I am allowed to speak, have I more to say?

Yet what's useless? At fifty one's perspective demonstrates that time's logic is contrary to the logic of space. The future shrinks as we approach, while the past, receding, expands. The expanse changes meaning daily through the knowledge that our remaining number of heartbeats grows always fewer like a speedometer being rewound—that is, wound back, but never to be started again.

Apparently I state with some succinctness on the art of others, putting a steady finger on how the method provokes rise or fall. What of my own art? Have I principles by which to proceed? Often noted here are comments that I'm composing this or that, or that that or this was premiered here or there (comments quaintly satirized by Howard Moss). But what I preach, or even practice, is best shown verbally in what I say of others. To explain that music must speak for itself is a lame out, since every artist, whatever he may admit, has both a technical and moral angle about the language he chooses to utter.

A diary—a public diary—is no more spontaneously composed than a symphony. Yes, themes may come all of a piece from the impulsive and recalcitrant muse, but they are set in gold alone, or sewn together, and forever revised before they are printed. That the expressive (the artistic, if you will) process can be untampered with is fallacy. Abandon takes rehearsal. Sometimes a song, a paragraph (like this one) emerges effortlessly. However it springs forth, art must seem seamless.

The hero of my diary is a fictional man upon whom I've worked hard but who has little to do with me—including the me penning this sentence, who is also the hero of my diary.

Music's the grandest lie. Music's not reality but a representation of one aspect of fact which in turn is but one aspect of truth. Possibly truth has no needed tie to fact. In which case, yes, truth approaches music (or vice versa) but only in that generalized befuddled Polonius-Keats equation of truth and beauty.

Friends never complain that they have been misrepresented in my music. Have they, indeed, been represented? Even the composer cannot say.

Persuasiveness of harmony. Harmony fixes mood more than do tune or rhythm. Thus it's Chopin, or 1930s swing, with the rapid shifting of regular secondary sevenths, that most moves me. . . . To no poet am I drawn more than to Goodman, to no painter more than to Vuillard, to no human visages more than to Belmondo's or Vitti's. No pastry's more tempting than warm pear tarts, no sonic formula more satisfying than Bach's sequences, no ambience more conclusive than a verdant cloister, and no time of day more pregnant than twilight if I'm not alone. No danger thwarts more than the past, no fragrance exalts more than winter chestnuts (though I loathe any odor of body, perfumed or natural, even of youth, which once I praised).

Beauty outlasts youth. Beauty's tougher than. Sex increasingly repels—the smell of it. To grow old is to climb higher and higher through branches which become scarcer, brittler. Almost alone up there one does see clearly far and wide and behind and beneath. But the seeing contains no understanding, nor is there much to look at, nothing to compel the gaze.

The Diabelli Variations: a magic mountain from a molehill.

People need formulas. They ask, "When do you work?" hoping to learn that composers put pen to paper each morning at seven and go on till tea. Now, by the time composers put pen to paper the composing is done; this is the inscription of the act, not the act itself.

Never say "I'm working well"; it brings bad luck. The nightmare—or rather, nightmare's sibling—which composers know too well: insomnia forcing them through the wee hours to jot notes which next morning ring false.

The sorry postponement of writing it down, writing it down . . . because when written down it might not be good enough. Such intellectual trepidation is, if you will, uncreative—and I say "intellectual" advisedly: the intelligence of certain composers impedes them from simply making it up as it goes along. Rule of thumb: Compose first, worry later. Or: Speak before you think and write it down afterwards. Actually all composers think before they speak. The speaking is the writing down.

Which came first, the punishment or the crime? Was the Inquisition concocted to legitimize the pleasures of torture? Are cruel acts, committed in the name of the Lord or for the good of the people, ever honestly meant for the good of the people or in the name of the Lord? Which came first, lawbreaker or law? In music, of course, rules came after the fact, to substantiate (to justify, *excuse*) what composers made up as they went along. Let a piece flow out, then think up reasons for the flow. Yet what teacher could thus counsel a student? Though precisely the reverse is strait-jacketing: to fear the flow because of reasons coming before the flow.

Composers' secrets? Some love to tell secrets of how a piece is made. It shouldn't be how, but how well. Describe form, and form is all a hearer hears. Then observe that fugue of Bach, crystalline, with friendly head or heads intermittently popping forth from the tangles. Tangles? No, tails continually attached. Friends in tangled tails, crystalline, which need not be sliced like Medusa's curls or the Gordian knot, for at the end the tails grow heads again, codas, stretti, logical hoorays.

I am never *not* working, yet I never catch myself in the act. At the end of each year I've somehow produced around an hour of music, and that hour is not a few sheets of penciled whole notes, but hundreds of pages of inked orchestration. Work is the process of composing—making it up as it goes along, which is the only precise description since Homer. The action is at once so disparate and so compact that the actor is unaware, which is doubtless why I "never find myself" etc. I don't consider as work the post-compositional drudgery (often pleasant) of copying, instrumentation, rehearsal, letter-writing, or dealing with publishers, though all this is time-consuming. Nor do I consider as work the compiling of my books, which is the assembling of prewritten fragments. I do consider as work the answering of this question: "When do you work?"—since it concerns, like musical composition, the placement of notion into order. As to when, and is it daily, I notate when I have a commissioned deadline and don't when I don't: the goal is functional, and its approach makes me scribble ten hours a day. Between commissions months are eaten looking at soap operas.

It's been decades since I've worked with the youthful Need to Express Myself. What I *do* express today is finer wrought and aims higher than yesterday although it might not ring truer. Our gifts are not gifts, but paid for terribly. Work is not play. The crunching responsibility forces many to throw in the sponge at the height of glory. Would they have persisted so long without encouragement?

I am able to postpone indefinitely the notation of a composition on the senseless rationale that, once written, it can never *become* written. With equal reason, I cannot complete a composition without feeling, well, there's one more piece chalked up before I die.

When do I work? Continually. Anyone's ego brings all to himself, leaves nothing for others, like pollen for bees. The ultimate honey isn't consciously manufactured to delight. When work? Between the lines of the soap opera I forever sift for useful matter. But I do work also to reconstruct the alchemy which fired those early songs which were sometimes of real gold, and which paradoxically had no formula beyond the one given by a hand which as easily took it away.

Every piece is the first. Over the years we learn to put notes mechanically together, yet the blank page remains no less terrifying than for a blocked beginner.

Stage fright. Each time's the first. If over the years I'm geared to play better in public than in private, I'm no less anxious before going to the lions. Still, to be on stage is exhilarating as sex: I do the work, but *they* are making me do it — they are not passive at all.

Of course, I'm never on stage except as pianist for my own songs. If something goes wrong, who's responsible? To sit impotently in the audience while the songs are massacred up there is the ultimate torment; the composer is held responsible for the singer's unwitting sabotage. I'd rather make my own music than hear it, even played well.

My musical memory is visual. Should the muse approach incongruously — on the subway, in a steam bath — and find me without a notebook, I will quickly picture in my mind the five strands of a staff, snatch from the air the inspiring notes glittering like bats, glue them to the staff, take a snapshot with an imaginary camera and, reaching home, develop the film on actual paper. The result is usually worthwhile, more so than similar transactions in dreams which next morning turn out to be trash. The music of night is unworked-for, untrue; true music, transmittable music, true ease, is difficult.

Being a computer, I lack imagination and cannot guess at meanings, so I must *learn* languages. I have no intuition and cannot recognize music unless I already know it, so I must memorize each example of a repertory. I have no ear and cannot think up colors or tunes, so to compose music I mimic the great (like the voiceless Chaplin who sings beautifully only when imitating Caruso). I am literal-minded and thus without humor, so I must employ a programmed wisdom which shows me what is truly witty. I explain all this to Felicia, who takes it at face value and offers her condolence.

⸮

Barbarity of refinement, ugliness of dinner parties. Words issuing from, as food enters, wet mouths. (Barbarians, in fact, move apart to eat.) Heredity and environment are one.

Ponderous snow, ponderous sunshine, the world crumbles and everything seems to hurt—poor nations, rich Americans, the tomato in the lunch pail, even the rocks. To sympathize and be of no help, there is no help. I'm not the person JH invents for himself. But if not, do I then exist? Can others become those we construct from need, if that need changes daily? Do we invent ourselves as well? If so, do the molecules of our work—our "product"—remain more stationary, more intact, than we do? A Chopin nocturne is more real than Chopin, but its reality exists in as many versions as there are people to hear it, and each version alters with each performance.

Any lie contains some truth by the fact of being uttered.

No one asks, "Do you think your songs lack strength?" unless he feels those songs lack strength. To think it (though the thought may be in but one head) means that somewhere the songs do lack strength—

strength for whatever strength means (since strength is not all force and muscle). Strength means spine. *Placet futile* is stronger than all the sound and fury of *Harold in Italy*.

Would I stand up for what I believe? What do I believe? Not, certainly, generalities, homeland or God or one genre of music locking antlers with another. I do believe in my work (although faith in that work hangs by a thread), and, maybe, in my many loves. But manifestation, proselytization, a raised voice, I shy from, and it's not just Midwestern boyishness. The *en masse* shriek at Chicago football games was always meaningless. Overt enthusiasm or defiance—re art or Israel or ESP—strikes me as common. Yet I'm more "outward" far than JH.

JH is not garrulous, he speaks when there's something to say. I talk all the time, for if there's never much that needs saying, the exercise stimulates, and "communication" comes by restating what *is*. Art is redundant. JH is really more Quaker than I.

Can silence be an art? A fine art? Silence, of course, is the very yeast that makes music breathe, but silence by itself is just silence, not an art.

"Who hath wrote so much as the Quakers?" asked Francis Bugg. "He that doth not write whilst he is alive, can't speak when he is dead," answered John Bellers in the seventeenth century. Silence as craft, however, is cultivated by Quakers, not to mention Trappists.

Each new word an infant learns withdraws him further from what we call nature. The wiser our books become, the less knowledge (knowledge?) we control of sensual things; yet it's too late to learn from or even play with the deer and the antelope as though they were like us, and music—with its poor, crafty, dislocated imitations—is all there remains for humans.

What I avidly believe for years and then finally freeze into words (freezing this phrase here too) I can no longer believe avidly. Like composing a piece. Once it's composed I obviously no longer need to compose it—it's verity no longer craved. Such sloughing off of a truth leaves me hollow and scared of death until I fall upon another truth to fertilize and forsake. For there are many truths, but alas, no One Truth. Except maybe memory, a receding street, a solacing blank.

The summer stint, because ending, looks to have been good; while it lasted I've never been more anxious: continual nasal allergy aggravated continual shrieking of the kids next door, plus being trapped in heaven, growing old in both skin and travail. God knows I've never allowed that experience had much to do with what we call creativity, for artists don't need knowledge, they need artistry. (You don't have to know what makes babies to make babies.) But I've not left this small island in nineteen weeks, and all I can see is myself.

Once upon a time when a piece was finished it was finished, *assez!*, don't look back; and ah, the bored bemusement that they for whom the piece was wrought (was finished) should now be taken by it, since I was elsewhere launched! Tonight, three weeks before another birthday, I scan the summer's many pieces like the final shot in *Citizen Kane* panning over the packed-up crockery, and wonder at my inability to duplicate some of them, not because they're bad but because they're good. No thrilling costly architecture proposed by the dentist will I accept now, just let him scrape the gums some, stanch the blood. Not rest, not yet, please. But to escape from the body.

1974

Becoming a Composer

"How do you plan to make a living?" asked Father, on learning that I wanted to be a composer when I grew up. Apparently I replied, "What difference does it make, if I can't be a composer?" That answer was so un-American as to impress Father, who, although a breadwinner, took seriously his not-so-sublimated baritone. To his eternal credit he agreed then and there to be supportive of the family freak. He has never been a Stage Mother, but Father nonetheless believed in work. It was time for a real teacher.

The former Julius Rosenwald mansion, located on Ellis and Fifty-first, was now the site of the Julius Rosenwald Fund. It had a richly antique ambiance, with its arched entrance for automobiles and a garden with more arches in granite and brick. I remember seeing, maybe even meeting, old man Rosenwald once or twice: he seemed mummified, like John D. Rockefeller, rather than handsome and easy-going like rich people in the movies. The Fund was not only the backbone of the Committee on the Cost of Medical Care, of which Father was co-ordinator, but sponsor for Negro fellowships in the Arts & Sciences. The comparative radicalism of this, coupled with our pacifist leanings, lent the Rorems a reputation for being benignly odd. We were no threat when we invited Negro guests to dine. Such guests invariably arrived late, or so it seemed, earning them the slogan CPT, or Colored People's Time. The lateness, Father explained, stemmed not from rudeness but from insecurity about the rare practice of interracial socializing. Among beneficiaries of the fellowships were Katherine Dunham, Marian Anderson, Howard Swanson, and Margaret Bonds.

The last-named at twenty-one was already a middle-western "personality," having played John Alden Carpenter's Concertino with the Chicago Symphony under the composer's direction, and being herself a composer of mainly spiritual arrangements and of original songs in collaboration with Langston Hughes. It was Margaret Bonds—*Miss* Bonds—who was to be my next piano teacher. Every Saturday morning I boarded the streetcar for her house in the ghetto of South Wabash. At our first lesson she played me some ear-openers: *The White Peacock* by Griffes, and Carpenter's *An American Tango*. Had I ever heard American music before, beyond "To a Wild Rose," which Mother used to thump out? Fired by my enthusiasm, she assigned these pieces on the spot, with no talk of scale-and-trill practice. In this day or any other it's scarcely revolutionary for a male pupil to have a woman tutor. But for a white child to have a black teacher was not standard practice in Chicago during the 1930s, and is there a reason not to be proud of it?

Margaret, ten years older than I, played with the authority of a professional, an authority I'd never heard in a living room, an authority stemming from the fact that she too was a composer and thus approached all music from the inside, an authority that was contagious. She dusted off the notion that music was solely for home use. She also showed me how to notate my ramblings—"Just look at how other composers put it down"—hoisting the ephemeral into the concrete: once his piece is on paper a composer is responsible for it, for it can now be reinterpreted by others, elating or shaming its maker.

My life as a composer remained unsupervised. Was there formal training for teenage composers in Chicago? Is there indeed such a beast today, other than through imitation? I continued writing pieces "in the style of," not knowing then, as I still don't know, that Art must be Original, though I'd already heard Rimbaud's much misused dictum, and thought it snazzy: "Il faut être absolument moderne."

Without ever having met another composer, something already told me that Originality is at best a minor virtue. Anyone can build a better mousetrap, but it still snares the same old mice. Poulenc, Britten, never set down an underivative measure, yet their every measure is stamped with their personality, involuntarily. In the thirties aesthetes shrieked their awe at Stravinsky's newness, while I, in my inadvertently proper education (that of learning my own century first and foremost), took Stravinsky as a *donnée,* not knowing, as I would years later, that all his devices were stolen goods.

Minor artists borrow, great ones steal. All art is clever theft. Conscious that he is stealing, the artist seeks to cover his traces. In so doing he expresses himself despite himself. The act of covering one's traces is the act of creation.

Art is a misquotation of something already heard. Thus, it becomes a quotation of something never heard.

So what I would be I already was, a practicing musician. The professionality (ability to notate) was there, though I'd never heard a note of mine played by someone else. The *sense* of music, of course, was absent, since music, as distinct from painting and poetry, has no sense. Despite my garrulous innocence, I inhabited an inviolable niche: my world versus *the* world—the physical drama of Then and Now. Despite future pleasures and wistful perils of sex and love and friendship, of travel and art and whisky, life and the universe seemed already veiled in a perpetual sadness without meaning.

1994

Jackson Park

Jackson Park in the thirties—maybe long before, maybe still today—was an irregular verdant expanse free of commerce, extending south from Fifty-sixth Street to around Sixty-seventh Street, bounded on the west by Stoney Island and on the east by Lake Michigan. Like an indelible squish of Prussian violet from Manet's tube, Chicago's noble lake has governed all mundane actions inviolably for centuries. The university's sages, the floating corpses, are all as one to the water, the water. At the top of the park looms the Museum of Science and Industry erected in 1929 by Julius Rosenwald. Memory hints that the structure is two storied, the top half held up by giant caryatids of granite, themselves four yards above ground level on a ledge a foot deep. Upon this ledge Jean Edwards and I, for no other reason than that it was there, once walked sideways for the entire mile-long circumference. Into the museum proper, a year or two later, I ventured with Norris Embry, who headed straight toward a phonographic display which allowed you to hear your own voice. Into a hand-held microphone Norris intoned:

Margaret, are you grieving
Over Goldengrove unleaving?
Leaves, like the things of man, you
With your fresh thoughts care for, can you?

with such simple eloquence that even before he pressed the playback
button, Hopkins's rhythm, new to me, was incised on my psyche and
would become the source of my first true song. Behind the museum
began the lagoon, wending its shallow path, wide and narrow, the
length of the park and emptying into the Great Lake. A quarter mile
from home, this area with its thousand crannies and thickets had been
familiar since perambulator days. It was there that I, age eleven, had
directed my steps in order to commit suicide, like Hedda Gabler, when
Father refused to let me buy a pair of cinnamon canaries from the pet
department of Marshall Field's ("We have enough birds in the house"),
and where Father secretly trailed me in the new blue Buick.

By night Jackson Park is a cruising ground. Same trees, same by-
ways, same oak and forsythia which in the afternoon seem real, even
banal, change meaning as shadows take over. The city's mouth exhales
over the vanished hubbub, emitting an incense of lust; children's cries
melt into silence, the ever-present odor of the lake intensifies with
menacing promise, a new provisional neighborhood vibrates on the
old soil; and the lovers' lanes, so lately quaint and precise, become a
blur of lewd possibility. In *The Grand Piano* Paul Goodman speaks of
the hours that grow into years while "looking for love where it can't be
found, waiting for love where it will not come," a refrain more familiar
to gay than to straight citizens, if only because promiscuity is—was—
a mode imposed from without. Might one argue that heterosexual
males, given the opportunity for unpunished promiscuity, would jump
at the chance? By extension they too might argue that sex with one
person doesn't necessarily "get better"; on the contrary, the first time
can be so great as to brook no repetition: anonymity releases inhibi-
tions (idiocy being the goal of good sex), and man-as-animal shows his

true nature. Gide even suggests (or makes his character Olivier suggest in *Les faux-monnayeurs*) that death is a lyrical reaction to the perfect screw—"He understood killing oneself, but only after having reached such heights of joy that anything afterward must be a descent." In any case, cruising in search of the chance encounter—an encounter more evaded than welcomed, since just around the corner something better, etcetera—is excellent exercise and geographically educational.

Such clever ruminations were far from my mind when Géorg Red-lich, knowing my limited sexual intercourse had hitherto been prac-ticed only among equally limited peers, led me into the park like a mother bear with her stupid cub, proposing to teach me the feints and ruses of the chase. I am not an aggressor (though I like to get my way), and my style, such as it was, would have to emerge solely through trial and error. So long as Géorg, or any other "peer" bent on mutual mis-chief, was with me in the park, I never did a thing.

One unseasonably mild March evening, when I was fourteen, I went alone into Jackson Park, veering now from the usual paths toward what was called The Wooded Island, a picturesque but remote area in the central lagoon, approached by bridges at either end that were closed off at midnight. Sporting a too-warm maroon crewneck sweater which I felt made an apt pedestal to offset my young head, and carrying Anatole France's *Le lys rouge*, partly because it was bound in matching ma-roon leather and partly for conversational purposes (yet who would converse?), I was perspiring at the gorgeous horror of the unknown. I had almost reached the second bridge without passing a soul and was about to turn back and call it a night when a form materialized from the gloom and planted itself before me. This was a man—that is, not a boy but a grown-up, a mystery, aged nineteen or maybe thirty, a novel category. He was bigger than I, virile and wiry, with black curly hair and a two-day stubble, smelling dimly but sexually of gasoline and whisky. He could have been a garage mechanic, a trigonometry major, or a shoe salesman. He sized me up with a charcoal gaze, then with-out a word steered me under the bridge where he pushed me, calmly but firmly, onto a heap of dry ferns which seemed to be there for just this purpose. I was tense, confused, thrilled, passive, not as a woman but as a little boy, as he bestrode me like a sheet of hot snow from lips to ankles. For several moments he lay thus, not moving; then quickly opened his pants, and mine, and for perhaps five minutes ground down on me interfemorally until he spewed a liquid paste across my thighs and belly. No word was spoken. Again he lay still until his panting subsided. Rising up he buttoned his clothes, and with a "So long, kid," disappeared forever through the dark elms.

At home in bed his sweat remained with me, the eternal fragrance of Lake Michigan was wafted through the window infusing the little room as it had infused the park an hour ago, and I felt dizzy with unreleased violence. Next night I looked for him in vain, finding only *Le lys rouge* forgotten among the leaves. The next week too I looked, and for the next few months.

If I describe this adventure so "finely" it's because I had fallen in love. The heart, when first taken out of its antiseptic box and exposed to air, aches more poignantly than it ever will again. I blush to note it here, but soon after this episode I sketched music for the famous verses: "By night on my bed I sought him whom my soul loveth: I sought him, but I found him not. I will rise now, and go about the city in the streets, and in the broad ways I will seek him whom my soul loveth." (Knowledge of this poetry came not from any Bible class but from my first Dietrich movie, *Song of Songs*.) In fact, I sought the man with the stubble more than "in the broad ways": I sought him in the gardens of Monet, the novels of Genet, the preludes of Ravel, the statues of Easter Island, the biographies of Jack the Ripper, and in a thousand beds and bars of Europe and the East. The *not finding* is, in a sense, art. Though art isn't, conversely, not finding. (Picasso: "Je trouve d'abord, je cherche après.") (Imagine being rich as Croesus and able to trace the past. Imagine being led to "his" hospital room today in, say, Urbana or Wichita, or rather, to his grave. The joke of it!) Those musical sketches for "Song of Songs" I showed to Leo Sowerby, but didn't tell him what had impelled me toward the text. I never told anyone.

The park became a habit. I would sit on a bench or not sit, wait or not wait, talk or not talk to strangers. Mostly I was a prick-tease, not knowing quite what was expected of me, or too shy to initiate, even to acknowledge, what I might ache to perform. Would I go home to cry or masturbate? Not always. Sometimes I'd go to "their place" and not put out. Most often what was done was done in the grass. Risks in retro-spect appear ghastly—weren't there muggings in the old days? Or was I too naive to sense danger in either anticipation or disappointment, and thus protected from evil? There is no god except for drunks, say the French.

Six conclusions:

1. Was he a child molester? (A mole-ster, as I used to misread the word, the way I misread goatherd as goath-erd.) The only trauma was a broken heart. I have never been molested by an adult, though as a minor I molested adults, in the sense of posing as inflammatory. The sense of myself as an erotic object, as it does with all children, came early. But I was never arrested for adult abuse.

2. The fact of being passive was something I took to like a duck to water, literally. That scene with the unshaven adult mirrors the im-printing of ducks which, hatched in a laboratory, think of humans as their mothers. Homosexuality is not a choice, but homosexual *roles* might be. The geography, the choreography, of our first gay experience, if we take to it (but we will take to it only if we're already queer), affects all ensuing experiences. Do I believe this? Or did my "role" already come naturally? (The business of role-playing may seem anathema to gays of the 1990s for whom turnabout seems always fair play.) My alcoholism, innate but revealed only years later, was at first an excuse to be passive without guilt. Yet to be passive—successfully so—is to be loved. Anyone can love, but to *be* loved requires qualities that are neither taught nor bought. *N'est pas aimé qui veut.*

3. Is the physically weaker person—the woman—always the subser-vient one? In choral music the basses are the bottoms, the sopranos the tops. But for every top there must be a bottom? Not so. An unac-companied soprano can be convincing. Yes, but a single line always has an implied harmony supporting it from below. (To the ancient Greeks

high and low in music meant the reverse of what they mean to us. Or so I once was told.)

4. Man is a preorganizer of his senses. That one sensual occasion, in all its solitudinous melancholy, did not make me what I was; I was what I was and thus sought and recognized that one sensual occasion, an occasion replicated ten thousand times, in fantasy and fact, with ten thousand stubble-chinned males. By the same token I later came to sigh with exasperation—won't they ever learn!—when reading yet again some biographical phrase like: "Rorem's long years in France were crucial in determining his musical style." My musical style was determined at birth, and was fully realized before I moved to France. (What are "long years" as distinct from "short" ones?)

5. Homosexuality in itself is not interesting, any more than heterosexuality. Only as a political issue—which it nearly always is today—does it become worth talking about. Except, of course, in autobiographies. So there's my dirty little secret. Not so dirty, really, and hardly a secret. Little? No, big as a cyclone enveloping my every behavioral viewpoint since infancy.

6. I don't much care for the "me" herein portrayed. But then, I am not my type.

1994

"P"

Well, the reason I'm learning Italian since three days ago is because last week in Cannes I met someone who works in a *magaz-
zino d'alimentazione* in the outskirts of Pavia (the Armenian works in
a *magasìn d'alimentation* in the outskirts of Marseilles), about whom I
brood incessantly with that pleasant nausea that comes at the beginnings of love; and though it is a sheer invention that may never be of
use, for the instant it's as precious as a beating blue heart in a crystal
box. A feeling that makes us wish to say: I love you, so leave the room
that I may suffer your absence agreeably, knowing you'll be back before the evening meal still with sea-salt to be licked from you; so leave
now, I'm impatient for you to leave (though I only met you yesterday)
that I may tell friends how happy I am; leave, so that expectancy for
your return may be stronger than your return; or leave forever so that I
may write you and suffer the only pleasant pangs that have any meaning, that make a difference; so that I may learn Italian and come maybe
next month with joy to visit you and be disappointed because love was
not designed for nourishment by the unfocusing imagination of absence, but meant for immediate consumption, and now it's too late;

because, even though you might be better, you're not the same as I remembered. . . . None of which keeps me now from hours of practice at learning to say in Italian such useful things as: "Where are the monks? Are they in the refectory?" I'm glad to know that nothing, nothing will ever ever kill the capacity for wanting to fall in love, even when the object seems ridiculous or impractical, or when work grows hollow during such meditations.

In Cannes again. It's six-thirty in the afternoon. I'm feeling low. This is a town invented for pleasure, where one has no right to depression, where one must bed with as many as possible in the shortest space, where I'm useless and forgotten, thinking on Pavia (I've had no letter) with that stifling empty choked screaming desperate ill sleepless sensation that comes to persons in love, no matter who. No matter who you are, a sick heart is a sick heart. The choice of lover is one's own business, but if you're Beethoven in love with a hat-check girl, or a hat-check girl in love with Beethoven, or Tristan, or Juliet, or Aschenbach, or the soldier on furlough, the suffering is equally intense and its expression just as banal. Helpful friends saying "It's not worth it!" are of no help; logic does not enter this domain of helplessness. So here I am dumbly in Cannes again where the remembered cobblestones of any alley appear yelling for help—all this for someone in Pavia who "isn't worth it." . . . These words are as commonplace as all others in love, but maybe they aid me a little. Each morning when I wake up I say today I'll think a little bit less about it, and if I eke out a bit of not-so-good work all goes well for awhile, *mais vient cet horrible cafard d'entre-chien-et-loup* and I'm reduced to the state of wasteful reflection that makes fools of greater than I.

Pavia (Albergo Moderno): A hangover can be transported from Marseille to Stockholm! You have only to get drunk and next day board a plane, getting off six hours later in a new country: a different language, but the same hangover. Loving hearts too can be carried about without harm, and, as Maggy used to say: "A good lay is worth going halfway around the world for" (to which Norris Embry used to add: "But I've *been* halfway around the world!"), which is exactly why I am in Pavia today and don't regret it. The tourist is truant here, and as I seem to be the only one I peer among the buzz of honest work feeling much as I did years ago when I'd ditched school, and having then nothing to do felt guilty at the sight of a bricklayer.

During the past three weeks in Hyères I spent two hours a day learning Italian alone in preparation for the magic Saturday when not three minutes after we'd met in the Milanese airport P. had slipped the gift of a gold medallion around my Quaker neck. Oh, the grown-up French and Swedes and Germans and English never were children, but Americans and Italians always stay so, and thank God I learned this language a little, for in Italy they go right to the point.

Today I will leave Pavia, go by motorcycle to Voghera which is cheaper, and nearer P.'s home-town of Dorno. Each tiny city in North Italy is sadder than the next, but this people has a different level of perception than the American and the poorest shepherd sports an enthusiastic heart. I've lost all sense of place, and being addressless, no "outside tie" could contact me. Am dominated by this impossible situation of love and no longer think of music. P., eyes all naïve, is excited by an article on me in the Milanese *Derby* which appeared coincidentally with my arrival in Italy Saturday. P. was born a twin and will live and die in poverty in that gloomy unheard-of village with a great heart, dear arms, animated ways, and preoccupation with what we ambitious ones name the "simple pleasures." Why are these worlds such oceans apart? Yet it is just the primary distances that make our chests bloom impossibly. I cannot live here forever as though I were like them, without those facilities which are myself. But then where *can* I live?

Voghera: Shorter days, a small town, a season is ending. After only twenty-four hours everybody knows me already as the stranger, and looks askance at my sloppy dress, the bleached streaks of my hair. The humblest Italian has more *chic* than the richest German.

It is six o'clock in the afternoon and hot. What a troubled summer it's been, the season speeding past like the wind of foul television seen here from my hotel window smothering the modern streets of this distant town. It is Thursday. Tomorrow P. will not come over from Dorno to see me because the day must be spent killing pigs. Maybe half my life is over. Saturday I leave alone for Venice, the city of death. I could kill myself from the tenderness that chokes even my impotence.

Yesterday we passed in the Chartreuse of Pavia, the land's most luxuriant sepulcher with its hot gardens. But would I have found it beautiful had I been alone? Afterwards we went to the church of San Michele where once more I was ready to die.

Garbo in this language means grace (*con garbo—avec grâce*).

When I am a hundred P. will be ninety-nine. Our centuries will always be different. Americans, Italians. . . . I was not ready to die.

The whole night long I cried, and again this morning. The strength of an Italian peasant family which I, as a rich creator, cannot combat. Even now that I have made this incredible *déplacement dans le bled* we're still able to meet for only two to three hours in the evening when P. should be sleeping, for the daily chores are far from here and P. gets up at 4 A.M. under the continual supervising eye of the ferocious *madre latina,* and the families of southern Europe are indissoluble or they would simply perish. These two or three hours then are pain to me and the other twenty-two or twenty-one I use up in crying. There is no piano here (I wouldn't play one if there were) and the city's without interest, dreary as any small town on earth (not unlike my childhood's South Dakota), where the foreigner can be only the intruder. This afternoon, with Gianni, P.'s sidekick who runs a haberdashery next to my hotel, to kill time (before my projected excursion into the wee weird town of Dorno tonight "to meet the family") I went swimming at the new glossy pool of which Voghera is proud. As I was moping at the water's edge reflecting in terms of tears and considering this scarily banal vicinity and how love can awe the vocal cords and cause a desire to die, as I moped, suddenly a loudspeaker, silent until now, beaming on our drops, without preliminary introduction began to emit the quieter piano music of Satie. Of all things! all times! places! All the music of my babyhood and I was overcome. What's more, the pianist turned out to be Poulenc, Poulenc's recorded fingers trickling out onto the ugly *piscina* of a town he's never heard of, while he himself lies delirious in Lausanne. Oh don't die friends, friends don't die. I want you always near, am in love, and miserable. We, we are in love. Don't, friends, die. . . . Perhaps I will never come back here again . . . it is easy to say. Now that my French is as good as English I don't want it anymore. I don't want music, I don't want the poems of Capetanakis (at moments like this the Bible, the solutions of poets don't hold up), don't care if Gold and Fizdale never play my pleasant piece with the voices they've not acknowledged, don't want good weather. I want you.

After a strenuous week in Venice where curiously the first people I saw (the sustenance of my stay) were Fizdale and Gold (with Jimmy Schuyler), I am now again, by contrast, in Pavia with much the same frame of mind as before except that meantime Derain has died, and I have not had a real bath since leaving Hyères eighteen days ago. This time my hotel, l'Albergo Corso, is across from the Monarchist head-quarters, though the Communist headquarters are in a classier neigh-borhood. I arrived here Saturday night.

Next day (the second of autumn). I'm writing this because I have nothing else to do. It's grown cold and tomorrow I go back into France, back to Hyères first and the comforting of Marie Laure and strange contrasts. Then up to Paris for three months of work (finish the Third Piano Sonata, orchestrate the Christmas Choruses and coloratura songs; write a piece for flute, and a Pindarian Hymn for Nadia's con-test). I'll be having another birthday too, oddly enough, and at the be-ginning of the year I'll *not* go to America but to Rome instead forever if I can find P. a job there and a way of living for myself, no matter how humble.

Of course all this is merely words and words, when really my one wish is to say I love you I love you and it wouldn't be the first diary filled with useless information, though really, like the changing weather the changes of the heart make about the sole subject worth discussing. It could never occur to me here now that a war or shift of fortune might arrive to disturb all this. I am in love and possessed and shorn of personality. Every time's the first time—thank God for that! and that I have no pride in such affairs. And every time I say where was I and how have I lived till now though when it's over nothing can be more over and the possibility of resumption is less adequate than rape after orgasm. Meanwhile I spend my afternoons watching Pavia's cinemascope where during the intermissions even here we can listen to Johnny Ray exercise his contagious neuroses at throat-ripping velocity. Then after *How to Marry a Millionaire* I come out again into the reality of Pavian light (which to me is not so real) and wait, and wait.

Hyères: There is nothing I need write to help recall the drama of parting yesterday at the Milan airport. The first thing to greet me when I arrived back tired and ill in France was a message (in what seemed to me perfectly literate Italian) from P.'s mother saying she'd discovered and read all my letters and that if I wrote once more she would notify the police. Her note was dated the nineteenth. I can't believe that her police could be interested in a correspondence between two adults, though those letters reveal sensual penchants more frankly than this diary. In any case, were I in Italy, this *virago* could probably be embarrassing, and meanwhile she's demoralized me to a point where I neither eat nor breathe nor sleep nor work. Oscar and Marie Laure are as comforting as is possible, but these useless ironies in a short life are impediments. Consolation is that God has presented a trial of love, so I shall cope with it, dangerous patience, though I don't know where the sickening business will end. Here, too, is where I wait. I think I see the first wrinkles about the eyes, and my flesh responds like ginger ale at the thought of those hands I love. I too have a mother and love her still and left her long ago in a country of the present. We are all so different. And I am so tired.

Under my plate this evening James Lord compassionately slipped this verse: ". . . and human nature is not conceived to conform to human needs."

Rome, via Angelo Masina, 5B. Haven't written this diary in over three months: 104 days, to be exact. Not because I've been particularly happy (and diaries are for the schmaltzy moments) or even occupied with music, but simply because I haven't had time, with P. abandoning family, at my encouragement, to look for a job in Paris, then leaving Paris to settle here a month ago, coping with the unrest and scandal all this gave rise to. For if I live three lives I mix them together (wrongly perhaps) and don't keep problems to myself. Similar to Cuenod who, when I once observed, "But you pass with no transition from the subject of rough trade to Monteverdi as though they were the same thing," answered, "To me they *are* the same thing."

P.'s gone now. An hour ago, for a long time to the North and a dying father. Another day of tears and tension unrelieved since August 8th. Back to that Pavian North for a death rattle in an *ambiance* of Catholic solidarity so foreign to me. (Are these the same Italians who astonish my tourist's eyes with their web of grafitti on holiest monuments? the same who produced the assassin Cannarozza—famous this week— who decapitated two ladies with a bomb in an Ancona cinema?) Yes, I am loved and in love and have never been so unhappy, with answerless questions, from a situation without solution. Is it worth it then to remain a month or four longer alone in Rome just to arrange a little concert at Mimi Pecci's or with Michel Chauveton to play my not-very-good fiddle sonata and not get paid, meanwhile not working and waiting and waiting for P.'s father to die, and then return to Rome where neither in spring will jobs be found, and always the money dwindles in spite of the three hundred dollars Miss Fleming mailed from New York? I'm getting to hate Rome, archeology where everywhere beauty smiles and smells of the dead, to hate Rome for all its warmth where even January roses vomit out among broken pillars in the Palatine, hate Rome (now all alone) in this good apartment at 35,000 lire with an out-of-tune piano on via Masina in the shadow of that institute of mediocrity, the American Academy—Rome, though in Paris with the animation there'd be the ice, and also Howard Swanson sitting dark on a *tabouret* in the Reine Blanche feeling sorry for himself. (Didn't I also look at Gina Lollobrigida two weeks ago sipping a soda at Greco's?) Though I do not drink I have bad dreams which I try to forget though they wish to be remembered.

But am I Job with this decision between love and ambition? Looking about, I perceive not only that indifference ubiquitous in each land, but personal plights as powerful and pathetic, and the sculpture of Mme. Ibert representing a mother who cannot help her child (we know her shock when her daughter lay dead for days in an elevator shaft); or the joyful Poulenc now with nerves and liver paralyzed, self-torturing in a Swiss hospital where he writes saying (because his circulation is bad and stigmata appear on his skin): *"Au moyen-âge on vous brûlait pour moins que ça!"* All this! Are we put on earth for such reactions? such wars? our miraculous brothers who slumber in the muddiest inertia too lazy to open their eyes? I've no more ideas, nor any desire to save our world. . . . On the walls in the crypt of the Convento dei Capucini, decorated like a wedding cake in human bones, are signs announcing that everything is vain save the humiliation of worship. I am more sympathetic to Rome's poet Penna who has given up versifying in favor of searching love in Trastevere's regions. But he is born of the Catholics. While I must continue writing music and remain alone.

You are my leather and my honey, my yellow roses (like those in the Spanish Place), my electric chair, my drum, drill, sweat, and my thistle. I love you. Floods in Paris, and weeks of twenty-below-zero in Chicago. Now a new war in Formosa. Is it really five years back that Korea made me mute, that I wrote another string quartet? I cannot read. My other starvation for books has all evaporated and I do not want to look again to see said better what it is all about. I prefer unable to sleep in the love rain and dying to ask what is it and receive my own less complicated more complex retort. How long could it all go on? Could we feel other-

wise than that this time you are leading me smack to destruction in
involition and whimpering? If I should die now here (I cry as I write it
and it must be known), all that I have, money and music and trinkets
and hair, is left for: P. F., via M——13, Dorno (Pavia), Italy.

Empty and depressed, depressed and empty, over and over again,
that's all, for the same reasons general and private, waiting for a foot-
step, sterile disinterest in work, lonesome for Paris whose any ash-can
is to me beautiful; lonesome most for you (for all words starting with
"P") whose any geography I'd disappear to always. Families, money, distances, these make me empty, depressed. Maschia Predit didn't work
out; empty things to do. This afternoon I'm off to see Petrassi again
with a musical briefcase under my arm; unless he's very encouraging
I'll return to Paris in two weeks, stopping in Milan to see *La Sonnambula* and try to put coherence into my love and my enemy Pavia. Tonight
I am to dine at Mimi Pecci's once more with Rieti (who tires me) and
Marcelle Meyer (about whom, like Germaine Lubin, they tell atrocities
from the Nazi period. But who am I to enter in? I was not here then).
. . . Iris Tree didn't say so, but she was disappointed by the songs to her
verse, yet I ask nothing better than to abandon subtlety and make a fortune. Meanwhile she is off to Marrakech with the affected and drunken
Diana C. who is Beauty become a urine-hued scarecrow. Well, let them
leave and leave me to my empty problem. This war will hang and settle
us all.

Tomorrow, as Ned Rorem, with Kubly and Bill Weaver I'll see Naples
for the first time, and die perhaps (getting *that* out of the way), and
this will pass time. Can I live only hopeless to cry sloppily again in the
smell of those caramel triceps. This page, that tree, and love, will soon
be long ago.

And I did die too perhaps. I'm back from the hot of the South of
Naples which I hated and its beautiful house of opera. There your chain
and gold medallion representing *La Madonna del Dito* with the engraved date of our meeting 9-8-54 were stolen by a trapezist (though

in my letter I didn't tell you it was a trapezist) and I am maybe punished — though as Bill Weaver said, the chain may one day catch in the trapeze and slit the thief's neck. Punished, I've said, for now returned, Naples, my hemorrhoids have recommenced so viciously that tomorrow I must enter the hospital. Thank you for your letters: how I love you; you are my glass and my key. I long for the fragrance of your arms far off which I see outstretched as we are crucified face to face watching each other die.

No relief. Love means being together; as I am, I grow daily weaker with my Naples illness rejoicing higher always so that I ache and cannot eat nor think of working, going to the dentist. This weekend I will come up to Milano to kiss your feet and beg you to leave and humiliate myself by classic banalities, and you too will turn humble and full of love, and we'll end at the beginning with the insoluble dilemmas. Far from you there's not one friend who doesn't bore me. As I perfect my Italian it becomes the language of my misery. Am sterile and bewitched. The dearest, tedious: Leo Coleman smiles in his Portuguese discs and Petrassi has lent me some rare Gabrieli, but I'm now deaf and blind, and scribbling here has no relief.

Yes, P. came and went and maybe now will come again, and I am going in a week. Back to Paris. After four months in Rome (during which I still haven't finished my *Poets' Requiem* but am covered with new acquaintances, also new wrinkles, paler and older, thinner and smarter, more streaks of peroxide making me red-haired: not really red of course: red hair actually is that usual baby orange of carrots or flame) Mimi Pecci will finally give me a concert next Wednesday in her castle where we'll try out (among other things) Frank O'Hara's *Four Dialogues for Two Voices and Two Pianos* which we'll record next day for the R.A.I. Then I am leaving (all of my new friends and those who've passed by). Back to Paris. By way of Florence and Milan, revisiting old friends and collecting souvenirs. They too'll've grown. Collect too many souvenirs and the basket breaks: that's death. But our baskets are stronger than we think! It's life. . . . I'm still in love with you and it will remain so; you, so far from me in every way, loving me, back in Dorno killing a hog each Friday. It won't be long again now. Charley Ford says love means wanting *to live with,* and applies not only to persons but pets and works of art. Back to Paris whose every ash-can is to me a diamond chalice. Our friend Rochas has died in these days, leaving a beautiful wife.

1954

New York Baths

A Turkish bath, like the Quaker service, is a place of silent meeting. The silence is shared solely by men, men who come uniquely together not to speak but to act. More even than the army, the bath is by definition a male, if not a masculine, domain. (Though in Paris, whimsically, it's a lady who presents you your *billet d'entrée*, robe and towel.) There are as many varieties of bath as of motel, from the scorpion-ridden hammams of Marrakech, where like Rimbaud in a boxcar you'll be systematically violated by a regiment, to the carpeted saunas of Frisco, where like a corpse in a glossy morgue you'll be a slab of flab on marble with Musak. There is no variety, however, in the purpose served: anonymous carnality. As in a whorehouse, you check interpersonal responsibility at the door; but unlike the whorehouse, here a *ménage* might accidentally meet in mutual infidelity. The ethical value too is like prostitution's: the consolation that no one can prove you are not more fulfilled by a stranger (precisely because there's no responsibility to deflect your fantasies—fantasies which now are real) than by the mate you dearly love, and the realization that Good Sex is not in performing as the other person wants but as you want. You will reconfirm this as you retreat into time through every bath of history.

For decades there has existed in central Manhattan one such establishment, notorious throughout the planet but never written about. Certainly this one seeks no publicity: word of mouth seems sufficient to promote its million-dollar business. Located in the heart of a wholesale floral district, there's small chance that an unsuspecting salesman might happen in for a simple rubdown, the nearest hotel being the Martha Washington—for women only. The customers do constitute as heterogeneous a cross section as you'll ever find. (There are only two uncategorizable phenomena: the care and feeding of so-called creative artists, and the nature of a Turkish bath's clientele.) Minors and majors, beatniks and bartenders, all ages and proclivities of the married and single, the famous and tough, so *many* from Jersey! but curiously few mad queens because it's hard to maintain a style stark naked. To run across your friends is less embarrassing than cumbersome: who wants gossip now?

You enter at any age, in any condition, any time of night or week, pay dearly for a fetid cubicle, and are given a torn gown and a pair of mismated slippers (insufficient against the grime that remains in your toes for days). You penetrate an obscure world, disrobe in private while reading graffiti, emerge rerobed into the public of gray wanderers so often compared to the lost souls of Dante, although this geography is not built of seven circles but of four square stories each capable of housing some eighty mortals. Once, you are told, this was a synagogue; today it's a brothel lit like *Guernica* by one nude bulb. The top floor is a suite of squalid rooms giving onto a corrodor from *The Blood of a Poet* with background music of a constant pitty-pat, whips and whispers, slurps and groans. The second floor, more of same, plus massive dormitory. On the ground floor are cubicles, a television room, a monastic refectory. The basement contains fringe benefits: a dryer, a massage room, a large dirty pool, and the famous steam-room wherein *partouzes* are not discouraged.

The personnel, working in shifts, comprises at any given time some ten people, including two masseurs and a uniformed policeman. Each of these appears dull-witted due to years of inhaling the gloomy disinfectant of locker room and hamburger grease.

There are feast and fast days, rough Spanish mornings and sneaky afternoons, even Embryo Night at the Baths. Eternal motion, never action (meaning production): despite a daily ocean of orgasm the ceaseless efforts at cross-breeding could hardly make a mule. Not from want of trying: at any time you may witness couplings of white with black, beauty with horror, aardvark with dinosaur, panda with pachyderm, skinny-old-slate-gray-potbelly-bald with chubby-old-slate-gray-potbelly-bald, heartbreakingly gentle with stimulatingly rugged—but always, paradoxically, like with like. Your pupils widen as a faun mounts that stevedore, or when a mountain descends on Mohammed. Some cluster forever together in a throbbing Medusa's head; others disentangle themselves to squat in foggy corners, immobile as carnivorous orchids, waiting to "go up" on whatever passes. There's one! on his knees, praying with tongue more active than a windmill in a hurricane, neck thrown back like Mata Hari's and smeared with tears nobody notices mingling with steam. All are centered on the spasm that in a fraction switches from sublime to ridiculous, the sickening spasm sought by poets and peasants, and which, like great love, makes the great seem silly. . . . Yet if at those suburban wife-swapping gangbangs there's risk of pregnancy, these mirthless matings stay sterile—not because the sexes aren't mixed but because the species *are*.

If you don't believe me, says Maldoror, go see for yourself. You won't believe it *of* yourself, the money and months you've passed, a cultured person lurking in shadows governed by groin! Did you *honestly* spend the night? Can you, with your splitting head, manage it down the hall to pee, through shafts of black sunlight and idiot eyes and churning mouths that never say die, and crunched on the floor those tropical roaches you hadn't noticed last evening? Don't slip in the sperm while retching at the fact that it's 8 A.M. and there's still a dull moan and a sound of belts (they've really no sense of proportion). So leave, descend while cackling still rends the ear, reclaim that responsibility checked with your wallet. Hate all those bad people; or, if you will, feel lightened and purged. Allow the sounds to dim—the anticlimactic puffing and shooting and slippery striving, the friendless hasty jerkings that could fertilize a universe in the dirty dark (*quel embarras de richesses!*). Quit the baths to go home and bathe, but make clear to yourself that such uncommitted hilarity doesn't necessarily preclude a throbbing heart. For three times there you found eternal love.

1967

Mescaline in the Poconos

The Mescaline House. Although tonight I'm exhausted from the weekend John G. arranged at his house in Crescoe, Pa., so that Paul Bowles and I (and he and a friend Anthony) could have an experiment in mescaline effects, I want nevertheless to note here the sequence of reactions while they're fresh.

Preliminarily let it be said that two exterior elements of preconditioning prejudiced—or at least tainted—my relish of the drug. First is a relation to Paul, who fascinated me from our first meeting in Taxco 1941 (I was sixteen) until our orgy of hashish on Rue de la Harpe in 1949 with Bill Flanagan and Shirley Gabis. I need him to know I exist, that I too am aware of evil (which however I am not in the sense he is). Second is the unheeded warning from Jane F., my A.A. sponsor, about whom I constantly thought.

As to a knowledge of mescaline itself, I'd read Huxley's first book, but felt already experienced in all that detail. But other fanatics, particularly Bill Miller, had so long sung its praises with such determined astonishment that I could no longer wait. They had explained mescaline as neither a soporific nor a stimulant, but a legal non-addictive device for showing how things are—not how they aren't (as do alcohol, heroin, or the self-imposed dullness of daily living). The pill is theoretically obtainable at any drugstore without prescription, but is now nearly obsolete, its medical function of inciting artificial schizophrenia never having been verified. By diverting us from the constant protective concerns of food and fear, by melting the censorial barriers of conditioning and removing us utterly from ourselves, by chemically lowering the armored instinct of self-preservation, mescaline heightens an awareness of what is about us always but to which we have blinded ourselves in order to live. It deflects from the business of our own death and permits full concentration on the slightest fact of surroundings. Under normal circumstances, perceiving the always present fact is no simple matter, even for the detailed maniac, or the genius who has occasional minutes of illumination which he strives to retain in memory and then preserve in marble. Today, on swallowing a tablet literally anyone can be exposed for hours to a "miracle" which hitherto only an artist or saint had known in scattered moments.

I had heard of this drug's ability to advance us a million years in evolution (or does it, rather, advance us backward to how we reacted in earlier states?), arousing an instant knowledge of true and false, an intuition of the speech of bees and unspoken thoughts, a recognition of color too bright for casual vision, a sense of electrons revolving in steel one trillion times per second, a sound of the live earth breathing into the feet—in short, a conscious observance of the never-still skeleton of our universe: no longer to see "through a glass darkly" but through the night rent by accurate lightning that continues its glare making a plausible world of every raindrop. And I had heard that all this was encountered without loss of control to body or mind, and no hangover! Who would not be tempted?

So I took mescaline, quite unprepared for what was to be thirteen hours of horror.

John drove Paul and me to his country mansion four hours from New York. (Anthony joined us later that night.) After some nourishing meals and a wonderful night's sleep we awoke into the fairest October Sunday one could hope for: acres of personal sky and miles of forest with blue and magenta leaves in total quiet. Europe may have the edge on us in many wonders, but nothing equals America's autumn of which this day was an ideal sample. The house itself was pleasant enough: Cape Cod cottage combined with heathen seraglio heaped to bursting with incongruous objects: stones, pods, Audubon prints, Persian editions, incense, velvet, chains, colors, stuffed animals, and a live female mongrel named Erix. This décor must have been established expressly for the use of mescaline novitiates.

We could have chewed John's dried peyote buttons, which are what the Indian discoverers use and cost seven cents, but as these cause nausea and hallucinations we swallowed instead, precisely at 2:15, the fifteen-dollar pills — although neither button nor pill was advisable for the weak liver of Paul, who was submitting to the experience as to a necessary operation.

For an hour, no effect. Paul and I strolled through the forest to a little river while the others weeded the garden. Then began an agreeable withdrawal as with an overdose of codeine. Things seemed the same (meaning beautiful as they should be right then) but lips grew icy, and face, and finally whole body, and as Paul was shivering we returned to the house. Neither of us had expected physical effects, but they grew worse. Our host and his friend now reappeared with prehistoric grins, and henceforth all came thick and fast.

We were invaded by violent lassitude in which the visual was super-clear. John took me to see a rose in the cool sun shuddering with luminous crimson pleasure: a puff of cigarette smoke and the flower recoiled. The cigarette was ludicrous, tasted false. We walked through a wood where trees murmured with reason: each seemed at once male and female embracing itself, arching toward the sky, to live, with ten thousand leaves twittering correctly. All was Life: the sky streaked with ivory veins, the hills breathing, nothing still, everything motion, inhaling, striving, fluttering, speaking delicate wounds. Whole outdoors a labyrinth of hypersensitivity: the sound of sap in the maple's arteries, the emerald chlorophyll throbbing through apples in the grass as I stepped compassionately among them. Nature in her force cares nothing for us except as we unite with her like a "thinking reed," more reed than thought. Mescaline banishes ambition along with vanity; cigarettes taste false because they have no part of living. And while on the verge of knowing the animals' language we have no desire to "write all this down for later." We are Now.

So the effects increased and were not all pleasant. Manmade insertions into this scene were outrageous: a slash of paint on bark, a bridge, strips of barbed wire seemed contradictory as death. Autos on the landscape were ridiculous, even indecent; all human indication was a blotch of blood. Blood everywhere: the wooden fence was a tree skinned alive, and a poplar whose low branches had been hacked off seemed really to gasp. Nature weeps, and though vegetation is not human we experience the lacerations of fruit or leaf as though they were ours. For all outdoors is flesh, even the wind.

My own physical state became at that point atrocious and I had no sense of touch, my body was glass and fear, and both Paul and I were taken with jitters, chills. Observing the faces of these friends, I saw only varicosed monsters of arteries and teeth. Teeth (and the marks of teeth in food) are the ugliest human possession and the real from the false are instantly perceived. Like cannibals we bite into a stalk of celery. Once back in the house ice became epileptic fire. The shocks continued.

Looking into a Goya reproduction the artist speaks out and you see through layers to canvas. The three-dimensional photos and advertisements in *Life* magazines scream with the mediocrity of all that's man, and men are vicious sheep, sad and scared. But my own hands were beautiful: a few days ago I had ripped open the cuticle of my thumb: now this small red hole was a great glowing pink marble entrance through which I could gaze into the mechanism of my inner body. I was afraid to turn around, felt menaced from all sides by my companions no longer human—or rather, more human than I, and so ugly. Knives. Everywhere knives and breathing veins. The presence of those kitchen choppers made me want to escape while too heavy on my feet to budge; not the familiar unsteadiness of alcohol for which I am prepared, but a new sluggish lucidity of dope from which there is no turning back. I felt out of control without knowing where to find the safety valve. No blur, it was freezingly clear, a total awareness of the state of unawareness, forced to examine, examine all in novel detail, like it or not, untrained, without order, not understanding pictures which spoke, moving objects, blood on the ceiling, knives, knives. I feared sharpness and being cut or cutting. Outdoors animals screeched, animal night noises all around, the dog looked at us and knew. (Or did she?) Matta's oils bled. My eyes bled. Paul, without feeling it, had a liver attack, his bony hands, luminous green and transparent, clutched at the organ and tore it out as he grinned, his face all molars. Each "normal" experience was now an involuntary experiment of perception. To satisfy this awful energy I drew twenty pictures in five minutes, all of them huge eyes. (John later declared them to be groins.)

Because of how the others looked, I was doubtful about seeing myself since I knew the reflection would be *a truth of flaws* to which I might even be indifferent; yet upstairs in the bathroom mirror I saw no change (except, of course, teeth, always yellow fangs, skeleton bursting out of our mouths, plus a few bemusing wrinkles I'd never admitted), and would have stayed riveted for hours if some flies with monstrous eyes buzzing about the bulb hadn't frightened me. I screamed for help and Paul came up and swatted them. (Poor precious dear sweet brother flies now stupidly dead there in the toilet bowl!)

They said my little speech defect had gone. Colors intensify greatly and take a new sense: synthetic dyes are immediately distinguishable from true vegetable tone. Blindfolded, one tells black from white by touch, and after the first frozen shakiness has worn off one finds a certain level of calm on which to examine. Authenticity can, to an extent, be distinguished from fakery, and the painting the artist made from his wife's menstrual blood looks just that. The stars, the whole mass of heaven, take on a bony form where the planets can be *seen* whirling through space at unthinkable speeds and all movement is related to all

other movement. The very globe of our world heaves and perspires beneath the feet. My own face seemed unmarked by the eternal qualities
of avarice and anguish, etc. John later said it was a *pure* face as opposed
to those other filigrees of rings and shadow. Since I am not basically
visual, everything I saw was a revelation, but my reaction to music and
literature, which normally mean most, were without interest: it was
difficult to concentrate on the printed word, and my discernment in
music seemed unchanged although the quality of performance is more
obvious. (I would like to have heard some of my own with the intention
of finding where I may have "conceded," but I doubt I'd have learned
much.) Appetite is decreased and meat—especially its odor—is out of
the question. For instance, when the dog was given her supper, the
smell infected the entire house like an *abattoir*. (Incidentally, I felt no
empathy for the dog because, as Michaux points out, dogs haven't any.)
If there is a craving it's for oranges, tomatoes, but it's cruel to eat even
them, they shriek.

Loss of balance. Sexual impulse reduced to nothing, though certain
affection came after fear of being attacked was overcome. I did not want
to be left alone with my razor which gleamed on the table like a gypsy
crystal—didn't wish to be left alone yet kept leaving the others to find
my own boredom of discovery out in the night which also scared me.

For night had fallen now. It was a green doped nightmare in part
quite vulgar. Ambition was plain silly. Paul sometimes reverted to
babyhood and I grew protective: qualities opposed to our natures. Of
the four, Paul appeared the validest human, especially after nightfall
(because sin is for darkness). Then Anthony brought me a welcome
cup of tea in what I think was the Holy Grail. Outside we examined
the heavens, their careless logic, felt Earth's revolving purpose rightly
placed and spinning about the neat framework. Then I peed for the first
time since morning.

All had been foreseen in that cat's face painted last month at the
Colony. There was nothing, nothing pleasant about it. Around nine the
effects wore off, thank God, little by little like petals drooping back
into place. During the long postmortem I was told my preadolescent

erections were inspired uniquely by sado-masochist images. John said my whole nonpleasurable tantrum was because I just couldn't face the truth mescaline offers. Is it the truth? After twenty years of drinking I am less a prophet for alcohol than he for this. At 3 A.M. after thirteen hours of unbroken tension I retired to a battered insomnia relieved only by an unusual nosebleed. I really learned little, though John's pose of sophisticated despair and nineteenth-century refinement was quite dismaying. (He's always struck me, at least in his writing, as the poor man's Paul Bowles—though of course much richer.) I'm already a selfish poet and since childhood have found flaming cities in the porous furrows of a common brick. Any poet has seen this, though perhaps not with such relentlessness, seen the stars fly and grasped their relation, felt the earth revolving, himself carried along through the galaxy like a well-built boat in the sea. I prefer to learn, to hide, in my own Ned way and never to meet them again.

The truth of beauty was evident, certainly, but had to be counterbalanced by the truth of ugliness. There is no shortcut for paradise, to coin a phrase. Today my eyes ache from having seen too much. Otherwise there is no hangover, the incident is finished. This morning (Monday) before returning to New York we inspected everything again, the trees and skies, the dog, the velvet. Everything looked exactly the same as under mescaline but also exactly different, without the vibrant hideous charm: all was, thank God, now quite banal. I recall the episode as "Dead of Night," a filmed country orgy far off, disagreeably weird, a fourth-dimensional fever, not forgotten but over, unnecessary surgery, a gash in consciousness and conscience, a slash in a vacuum, an acrid perfume which had always been around unsmelled. But I am a nearsighted Norwegian nun who still knows that vision is important only to the blind.

1967

Vocabulary

The phone intrudes like the person from Porlock, derailing my train of thought. A tenor, organizing a program around gay themes by gay composers, wonders if I will contribute. Certainly not. I'm a composer, not a gay composer. Sexuality may relate to an artist's becoming an artist, but not to his becoming a good artist. I want to be loved or hated, not for my nature, but for the quality of my nature. Anyone can be gay—it's no accomplishment—but only I can be me. (A concert of straight composers might be a novelty.)

I am not We, and am unable to verbalize collectively, much less identify with even such groups as composers or lovers. I can't say "we composers" or "my lover and me," but "lovers are," "composers are," "Americans are," "they are." Do I dread not being unique? With gays, I think Them, not Us. How can They, inherently more diverse than a Zulu tribe or even than an international bourgeoisie, merely magnify, with We, a sole thread of their complex web? I resent vouchsafing individuality even to such a category as Mankind (still, what can you do?), but classify myself as a homo-sapient musician who is sexual.

The sexual object is nobody's business, at least in public discussion. So diaries. If the goal of my drive becomes clear within their pages, such a "confession" is intended simply (simply?) as that of a human whose pangs of head and heart seem only too prevalent within the world's common groin.

Unlike negritude, homosexuality is not physically spottable, though gay clichés abound. A black when he's not Uncle Tomming is still black, and he's still black when he solves an algebraic equation. Is a queer queer when out of bed? When solving equations? Homosexuals have options: like heretics they can repent. A black cannot repent: he can only regret, or be proud.

Black Pride and Gay Pride are dangerous slogans, like White Pride or Straight Pride. Gay and black are not achievements but accidents of birth. One must not be ashamed, but that's not the same as being proud. Pride should lie only in what one does with one's blackness or gayness. Even so, has a straight or a white ever done anything to be proud of as a straight or a white?

Nor is the gay condition comparable to the female condition. A female remains so tomorrow. A lesbian (but who is not a lesbian?) may decide—consciously decide—not to be. Can change her mind. For a gay man to long to be treated like an unliberated woman is for him to have it both ways. A woman has no choice, but he can change his tune at any measure and never pay the piper.

How far must we discourage "isms" and promote tolerance? Is it antifeminist to be sexually unattracted to women? Or blondist to dislike blonds? Must gerontophiles in fairness also covet kids? By extension embryos and corpses become fair game. Can we believe James Baldwin when he claims to have reached a utopian state when once, years ago, he was unaware that a friend of his was indeed Algerian until a test moment brought the fact home? Must humanity be so ideally One that we don't (aren't allowed to) distinguish sexually between mentalities, colors, ages, sexes, or even species? We smile when Gore Vidal, to the question "Was your first experience with a man or a woman?" answers "I thought it would be rude to ask." Do I, less young than last year, require gerontophiles? Could my fantasies not instead be for an ancient father embodied in that brawny young farmer there? But if in fact fantasies nourish us to that extent, what prevents the makeshift coition with virtually anything—jars of mercury, cobras, dynamite sticks?

Though turnabout may be fair play, men who like to "do anything" are as a rule of average intelligence, generous, congenial, but without much artistic force. Those whom in America we call "achievers" are as a rule carnally self-restricted, play one role, and have a knack for extended concentration on things not sexual. *L'homme moyen sensuel* is by definition less human than the "achiever," if by human we define the logic which differentiates man from other mammals. Sex has nothing to do with logic, but achievers treat sex logically (hence their roles) while average men treat sex sensually.

Just as there is no real literature recounting exploits from the viewpoint of the passive male (the *enculé*) so there is no real literature, beyond the blues of Ma Rainey, describing lesbian carnality. Has any woman related—with the necessity and anxiety and joy of a Goodman or a Ginsberg—the strictly physical charge of lesbianism? Can she? Can, in fact, the "passive" man make art from the trials of Eros? Yes. Since he exists he can be subject as well as object. Forster tried.

"The world loves drunks, but it despises perverts," Jane Bowles once sadly wrote. And indeed, alcoholics can always find companions, in crime if not in love. But I drank to find companions in love—or rather, to be found by them. Crucial distinction. Note the passive mode, *to be found* (which makes me feel sexy because guilty), a mode of Anglo-Saxon parlance but rare to the unguilty French. The unguilty French seldom refer to getting screwed or getting laid, that is, *être baisé,* but place that so-called passive act into the active mode: to get yourself laid, that is, *se faire baiser.* Anyway, strong-willed though I was (I command you to rape me!) I passed myself off as a vulnerable bit of lavender fluff longing to be—*comment dirai-je?*—to be, well, soiled.

The French have no word for straight, as counterpart (I almost wrote opposite) of gay. Nor have they an adjective like gay, preferring a noun or verb like *tante* or *en être*. And they have no words for crooked, shallow, vicarious, urge, or gentile. Crooked, as distinct from straight in its upright meaning, they must call *courbé* (curved), *sinueux*, or *tortueux*. Shallow becomes *peu profond*. Vicarious stems from our Protestant "vicar"—not a Catholic concern (they would say *vicieux*), which also is why gentiles are conveniently *chrétiens*. The closest thing to our verb "to urge" is their *exhorter*. From this paragraph draw no conclusions about the French; draw conclusions only about my conclusions about the French.

The French, however *vicieux,* are of all Europeans the most heterosexual.

Maldoror made love with a shark—a female shark, needless to say.

Women classically take their husband's name. Unmarried artists declare, "My work is my wife," and give their name to their creation. But the creation, no sooner spawned, goes off to live or die independently. Work is not spouse but offspring.

That paragraph reeks chauvinism. Artist implies male artist.

Does a female artist seek a mate? Could she conceivably think of her work as a husband? I, Ned Rorem, don't want a wife in any form (though at times I want a husband), and less and less do I want children—the desire to see my flesh on other bones. My music's not my wife, nor my husband, nor my child. My music is my music. Once composed it is no longer even mine.

You do grow weary of "courageous" announcements of Homosexual Studies—of scientists achieving breakthroughs on this "complex condition." Do the scientists have courses in Heterosexual Studies? Might they then conclude that homosexuality is in fact a simple condition? That problem solved, they could go on to something important, like a cure for asthma.

As for the daring chic of the "new" bisexuality, why not talk of sexu-

ality *tout court*? How about autosexuality for the Paul Newmans of this
world? The term is more reasonable than the masturbatory *narcissism*
for one who enjoys turning on all the sexes; such a person is not *attracted to*, such a person is *attracted to being attractive*, works well at it,
and deserves all that she-he can get. (Not the love of self, but the love
of being loved.)

Is there a homosexual sensibility? people still ask. Why yes, no doubt.
But one would be hard put to show that sensibility defined, say, by the
homosexual's musical composition or poetry or law practice or medical notions, as distinct from the sensibility of one who screws too seldom or too often or is redheaded or over fifty or is more interested in
microscopes than in love or is dumb.

The trouble here is that "homosexual sensibility" is a slogan masked
as an idea. Until semantics are settled, perpetrators will cram the work
of gays into pigeonholes by cutting off limbs. Meanwhile, if there *is*
such a sensibility, dare you include Whitman (said to be queer) with
his careless macho rhapsodies to the great outdoors? Dare you omit
Beardsley (rumored to be straight) with his quaint sonatinas to a vast
powder puff?

Is there a gay sensibility? Define it, then I'll tell you if there's one.
Does God exist? Define him, then I'll tell you if he exists.

Gay militants question my refusal to ally myself.

On the principle that I was among the first to come out of the closet
(thereby, one might add, paving the way for their casualness in asking
me to ally myself) they feel I'm now backtracking. In fact, it was never
homosexuality but sexuality that I was open about. That the sexuality
may have leaned in one direction is an unimportant assumption. The
unimportance is the only importance which they should take from me
for their propaganda.

I have never suffered from it. Perhaps I yet will, for who knows how the regime may end? But what I have become is not stamped with childhood trauma. I say this, of course, divorcing myself from stereotypes, with the safety of hindsight. Yet hindsight's all I've got.

Yes, I outwardly loathed macho sports, but did not—like textbook fairies—secretly wish to enjoy them; to kick a ball around a field was dumb, where did it get you? I loathed female sports too (what's the feminine of macho?), nor did I—again, like textbook cases—secretly wish to enjoy them; to sew fine seams seemed vain, how long would seams last? Oh, I did have fun making cakes and rather liked to swim, yet felt neither truly domestic nor competitive. Sure, I was a sissy (from where does the word derive? Assisi? sister?), but my manifestation of this sissyhood wasn't easily mocked. I was a composer.

"Passivity" was due less to shyness, a negative virtue, than to the built-in convictions of Quakerism, convictions buttressed by sensible and sensitive parents.

I did not suffer from the queerness of sex but from the queerness of being a composer. The suffering stemmed from being ignored. So unswervingly convinced was I of music, from the age of seven on, it never occurred to me that all other boys and girls didn't go home after school and write pieces too. My greatest astonishment came, and remains today, from learning that people don't care.

I am not a gay activist, I am a gay pacifist.

Gay is a term I shun. Unlike *fairy* or *faggot*, the term was always used by gays themselves, so perhaps it's nice that now it's settling into the lingua franca. Yet *gay* is a post-Freudian colloquialism which, though possibly useful even for, say, Dag Hammarskjöld, seems jarring for such pre-twentieth-century homophiles as Socrates or Tchaikovsky or even Forster. What have I against the term? Not, certainly, its implication of merry for something so "serious." I prefer *queer* because that's how I was raised. Terminology's regional. Just as I never tasted pastrami or sour cream before moving to New York, so I never heard *dyke* or *straight*: Chicago Wasps didn't eat Mediterranean dishes, and Chi-

cago queers referred to minty and jam. Individual jargon is to be cher-
ished. But if Paris is worth a mass, and if now I say *black* for *Negro,* I
stick to *queer,* and that's my right, since . . .

JH tells me to stop declaring that I've not suffered from the stigma—
that I've felt less discriminated against than for being a composer. He
feels the declaration is, first of all, untrue, and also that, like an un-
scathed graduate of Buchenwald who found it "not so bad," I cheapen
the very real agony of others.

Probably no heterosexual, no matter how well-meaning, can know
what homosexuality "is," any more than whites know black. What difference does it make, since love has nothing to do with understanding,
and understanding can even bring an end to bodily love? (Zeus and
Hera quarreled, each claiming the other's sex was more capable of grati-
fication. To prove the point they called in the hermaphrodite Teresias.
"Who has more fun in bed, Teresias, man or woman?" "Woman." In
fury Hera struck Teresias blind. In compensation Zeus bestowed foresight upon him.) The homosexual artist, in a sense, has the edge, since
he or she intuits nuance, thanks to a lifelong immersion in a straight
element. But again, vocabulary here misleads. Before Freud, or even
just one generation ago, people didn't talk of, say, the "homosexual"
plays of Shakespeare or Marlowe or Wilde or Wilder or Williams or
Inge. No one, including the homosexual, has yet come up with a definition; and not one of the thousand homosexuals I personally know
seems queer for the weary psychoanalytical reason of strong mother
and cold father. Nature lets her chips fall everywhere, but whereas
those chips fell upon precise terminology millenniums ago for women
and Jews, in Lysistrata and Moses, only yesterday was homosexuality
coined.

People are given to believing that an artist (or a homosexual, for that
matter) is what he is by choice. Well, choice may be there on some childish level insofar as the vocation is practiced, but insofar as the urge
persists there is little choice, and even less, alas, for the quality of re-

sults. Often I hear, "Why did you become a composer?" I *was* a composer. The question is, Why did I persevere? Perseverance comes from applause, for which the need *chez moi* is no stronger than with Casals or Schubert or the Curies who, despite loneliness and self-sacrifice, etc., were, after all, aiming at the target of their fellowmen. Without tangible appreciation—performance, publication, money, comparative fame—who would persevere? Nothing's madder or sadder than stacks of unplayed scores. And the unknown genius is anathema to our age of speed. Why am I a composer? To dazzle those virile paragons who bullied me in gym class. Have they noticed? But now the ball's rolling and it's too late to stop.

1976

Being Alone

No matter how tenacious or, indeed, victorious in the ring, the bull is never spared. Though he fell the torero to become champion, the bull is doomed. Why? His use is used up. At a second "go" the animal knows the tricks, and like the wiliest pacifist he'll turn and run off. Similarly, we spectators are irreparably conditioned by our first corrida. You are deflowered only once.

I've attended two bullfights. The ordeal in Arles in 1952, with six consecutive *mises à mort*, was so gorgeously stigmatizing that I hadn't yet healed when, sixteen years later in Acapulco, I saw my second. Still, the first steeled me for the next. Forced to witness death, over and over in twenty-minute segments of identical choreography, one turns self-protectively blasé, even in a concentration camp. Or does one? Perhaps no amount of experience will ever immunize us to certain things: bullfights, sunsets, starvation, love.

I note these paragraphs while reading *Christopher and His Kind* with a disapproval of Isherwood's assumption that readers not only know but have cared about knowing his whole previous catalogue. An anxious nostalgia threads this presumably "honest" reweaving of old themes. Nothing is riskier than for an artist to set the record straight years after. Late truth lacks the energy of early distortion. And who, one might well ask, will in forty years reshuffle these current facts of Christopher? Art always hits the nail on the head, but accuracy for its own sake cannot guarantee art.

Delving further, disapproval gives way to bafflement: How, in the company of the major minds of his time, Christopher's unabashed carnality remains his sole subject matter! (Auden writes usually on ideas, Christopher seldom.) How, lest his public for one instant forget it, he repeats his name constantly, thereby paradoxically, unlike Proust, lending a vague impersonality to his narrator! (I always hesitate to speak my own name, feeling somehow that I am dropping it.) How, in his tastes both cultural and tactile, he is German as opposed to French! Am I in my Frenchness so far from him? Now, when the chips are down, what I deplore in his writing is what I defend in my own: the unembellished given of the self as subject. But there remains the nagging question: Can one's own behavior, and even one's presumable objectivity toward that behavior, be fair game on the literary racetrack?

"Life," claims Eric Bentley, "is seldom simple; art never." I reply: Life is never simple, art always. With its curving paths through multiple layers art nonetheless follows the straightest line between two points. How an artwork works is the only way for that work, whereas living is nothing but alternatives. Art is economy and shape, life is waste and disorder.

Happily it is not for an artist to define what he does. An artist doesn't do art, he does work. If that work turns out to be art, that is proclaimed through the judgment of lesser lights.

People are always asking, "How do you remember all that stuff? Me, I forget things as soon as they happen." But why live if that which occurs makes no impression, can't be used, even the endless boredom? Why live if only to forget having lived? This said, my notorious total recall is abetted by date books and diaries, and by recalling the months, and divisions thereof, of returns to America, of an affair with a certain person, of the impulse for a certain piece. To live is to improvise variations on our own theme, yet those improvisations are not random but (unbeknownst to us at the moment) formal and collective. How does one manage *not* to have total recall? of this unique rhubarb tart, that red-hot torso, these November leaves, all the wars, those dying friends?

Other people are always saying, "How can you live in the past?" But the present *is* the past (as Marcel was hardly the first to show), and the older we grow the more past we have. Our shriveling future may be all that we make of it, but so is our past which changes perspective with each new dawn. Life is awfully nice, yes, and keeps getting nicer, but never nice enough, surely not enough to have been born for. And is life short? To die at seventy-five will mean that eight thousand nights stretch on ahead. How to fill them? By using them through what's been learned so far? Now, on the contrary, could it be that the past grows smaller, like a blood-flavored popsicle on which we gnaw self-cannibalistically, and when it's melted utterly, we. . . ? Owls and tigers commence their flights and prowls at dusk, and thus might symbolize Death were it not that they too, God's creatures, prey upon their own pasts, their shrinking pasts. Endless, the future? Certainly not, since by definition the future does not exist.

Did I still keep a diary 'twould not serve to reveal secret sex and cake recipes. The disease and dying of dear friends ever more preoccupy us all, and wonder at the cheerlessness we come to.

Is my entire *oeuvre* an *oeuvre*? In that case I do not repeat myself, since each piece is part of a continuing whole. (And although such stuff as dreams are made on generally turns out to be sheer twaddle in the morning, my sleeping hours, unlike Ruth Kligman's, feel no less urgent than the waking.)

Tonight while reworking a choral version of Hardy's *The Oxen* composed twenty-four years ago (around the time I was reading Wharton), I feel for the thousandth time how time freezes during focus on the act. Musically the inspirational shove seems identical: I may have more or less energy (more technique, less facility), but the expressive line's the same, and also the special piquant secondal harmonic clots that make me wince nicely while imagining that I and only I have ever thought up such combinations. But further still, in this icy today on America's Seventieth Street, I find my very body resurrounded by those vases of vastly odoriferous tuberoses which graced the Noailles salon where once I labored on that evening of June 21, 1954. It is enough to pore over the Métro map of Paris to be transported there, back through the ether and years, smells above all. That is one way to learn a city, through odors, as through cruising parks and pissotières, the hard-boiled egg stench, the rotten seaweed stench, the dimple on the ruddy chin of that policeman, the etc. Why must we move through time, since time, whatever it is, says the same thing perpetually?

I am still hoping to retrieve that person (the one with the iron-blue hair) I was too drunk to accept in Jackson Park thirty-eight summers ago when now I enter this uptown bar. Or to relocate this person (the one with the strident nape muscles) whom I shunned gratuitously in the Luxembourg Gardens twenty-four autumns ago when now I enter that downtown café. Or that other paragon. Or this certain-to-be-love. And do you know? They can be found. Their actual flesh and blood can be found, but as overwhelmed by the passing ages as my own. Yet I still pursue the longed-for pursuers whom I'm certain could have given me that which is never given. I am still . . .

Rushing to the bathroom I grabbed the first book that came to hand, which turned out to be *The Age of Innocence*. There I read again those masterful (hmmm . . . *mistressful* isn't quite the word either) last paragraphs where Archer withdraws from a longed-for reunion "lest that last shadow of reality should lose its edge"—remembering when I'd first read them a quarter-century ago. It would have been an autumn afternoon (like today in Nantucket, warm and russet) on a café terrace, Rue Galilée, and I closed the book, moved, and filled with a Paris evoked by Wharton some thirty years earlier, fictional even then, and so real.

We have the choice, the passing choice, of returning and ruining, or of refraining and keeping. If we keep too long the living person in our heart (imagining that person in a firelit room across the ocean), that person will die. Which is the case with my Paris now. I can go back and rekindle in that same café the rekindling that fired me twenty-five years ago as I evoked Archer rekindling his past. But I cannot close the book—that physically same book—and rise to keep my date with Marie Laure (who was tolerant of lateness only when the need of a book retained her date), because Marie Laure lies underground. Yet, maybe fortunately, for me the power of places has always been stronger than the power of persons.

The older I get the aloner I feel. (But one can grow only so old.) The solitude, classically divorced from company or place, is hinged to a knowledge, recognized even by children, that we rise to heaven un-aided. *"Car le joli printemps / C'est le temps d'une aiguille,"* sang Fom-beure through Poulenc's lips. Our springtime's but a point, a needle point, in time, but rich and poor can pass with equal ease, though for-ever single file, through the needle's eye. (I never knew whether that needle's eye was the same as Gide's *Porte étroite*—the "straight gate" to paradise?—mentioned by Saint Matthew.) Those hundreds who per-ished "simultaneously" at Guyana really died, as the clock ticks, sepa-rately.

Alone in Nantucket. When JH leaves the lights go quite literally out. Here, when winter dusk sets in at three o'clock, he places candles throughout the house and an old-fashioned lemon-peel glow, more leveling, more unifying than death, warms us as one. Then in the flick-ering we forget for a while the rending disputes and sit down to a night of television.

The past year's been one of emerging from my massive depression only to witness JH sink even more deeply into his own (what used to be called) nervous breakdown, as into a leftover soup, for melancholy is catching. (Though by being passed on it is sometimes eliminated.) At least he has the gift of tears and vomit. On schedule he can weep or puke, which I cannot. I can write music, which is a kind of vomit, though it brings no relief. Yes, it does.

Over and beyond a scientific interest, does an entomologist develop or inherently possess a sympathetic, a "human," rapport with insects similar to the sentiments of a zoologist with apes, or, indeed, to the affections of any pet owner?

Despite the ever cooler afternoons the hydrangea in the front yard blooms greener and greener, sheltering (among a million more microscopic invertebrates) a lost mantis all foamy white and sea-colored and shivering crippled on a leaf. Did it or did it not feel differently about me from the way it might about some other person, as I aided it, examined it at point-blank range, purred to it about its pair of dear eyes that turned from right to left? Insects do make choices.

Perfect weather, and yes, alone: you've gone to the city. After these good eleven years you are still never easy to speak with, yet you keep things stirred up, and thus one feels a continual need to talk. There seems to be a crisis, not once a month but each single day. If I've not felt it so much lately it's because I see you provoke it with K. Still, your knack for rocking the boat stems of course from steering away from an "inner sanctum." If only, if only.

If only writing could get rid of it. Instead, writing locks it in.

Bees. When we returned after a season's absence a swarm throbbed on the south eave of the house, at once motionless and speedy, like a flying saucer. A neighbor said it'd been there for days. One hour later the bees vanished. Two days later they came back—or ten thousand like them. I was alone in the kitchen as the faint all-encompassing whir began. Gradually the entire lawn grew inhabited, then the house was surrounded, encased in a transluscent nacreous tent of yellow aspic, while the drone persisted, meaningless and purposeful like an Ashbery verse with a life of its own . . . Suddenly they evaporated. Oh, a few— maybe two dozen—hovered around the north roof, but for all practical purposes they'd gone. (In the basement three stray fighters buzzed frantically as the sun set, but quieted with the dark; and when my eyes panned in so close as to perhaps momentarily join their frame of reference the dying beauties came together, rubbed antlers, then ceased breathing utterly.)

Illusion. Those sentinels at the north eaves have remained. Indeed, they work for the cluster now ensconced in the house's framework. By the time the exterminator arrived you could feel them beating like red hot snowflakes against the warming parlor wall. The exterminator sprayed some cursory droplets under the eaves, said he'd be back next week if we needed him.

But the bees have moved in. Their intelligence lives in this home with us like Hitchcock's birds. It's midnight, I've taken a Valium. Are they in conference? Their pale angry roar continues, although the encyclopedia says they sleep quietly at night.

Next day, silence. The wall is cool. The bees have disappeared without a trace.

JH after a year makes scant progress. To understand that one cannot understand is as near as one can get: a glass fence rises between. In my maddest hangovers I always retained a sense of the future, even in suicide, but JH views the world quite literally as through a glass darkly. How cannot I bleed for his bleeding, impotent to help? Who will claim that they who only stand and wait are less battered than the actors in the fray?

Scant progress, but progress still . . . Alone and sour, and time passes so fast, so slowly. It's terribly late. Day after day of losing contact, of seeing our decade retreat like a galaxy, of the resultant gulf. Hopeless though it be, one part of it is not wholly disagreeable.

For months there's been a flutter in the wall, nocturnal, more irregular and forceful than the bees two years ago. Gnawing termites? Scurry of rat paws? If as t'is said a cat's mere presence discourages rodents, then we have no rodents, or Wallace (admittedly quite deaf now at thirteen) is not a cat. But yesterday morning on finding the stovetop strewn with what resembled caraway seeds, we finally decided, against our will, to set a trap (Against our will, for who are we to contrive the eradication of fellow mammals?) Last evening, not thirty minutes after placing the bait, there sounded the terrible snap. We paused long, fearful of what we'd find: sprayed blood? splayed bones yet still gasping? Together we went, and there sure enough was a mouse, limply dead. JH assured me it was killed before it knew what hit it—even before savoring the exquisite fatal Brie. The mouse was not of urban hue (not solid gray—indeed, like our mouse-colored Wallace, the royal Russian blue), but a clean golden fauve merging into sugary white on the belly, and with wide-open garnet eyes. We put it down the toilet but it wouldn't flush, kept belching back to haunt us like the corpse in *Purple Noon*. So we sealed it in plastic and flung it to the garbage, and wondered when its nest of starving offspring would start to rot and stink. The episode undid me, no less than the morning *Times*'s detailing tortures in far-off Persia, or the far-off boatloads of Vietnamese. I went to bed.

During the chaotic-seeming composites of dream after dream (which in fact are sanity-pure, including surely the dreams of the insane) there was a melding revivification of Vietnam and Persia, and of the mouse. If this morning I invoke the limitations of John Donne— since all men *are* islands who forever and vainly seek to play kneesies beneath the surface—I'd rather commit suicide than have it proved I'd ever been willfully physically cruel. I say physically, because all is fair in the "mental" game of broken hearts, nor is the will ever brought into play where love's concerned, love thriving as it does beyond the frontiers of time as in an ice-cold bubble where we breathe forever and don't grow old.

As far as anyone is ever cured, JH is. As far as any other can judge such things. The two-year stress, fanned by my own surrender to allergies (I've been taking shots just twenty-four months now and am doing better, thanks), has abated, due as much to illness running its course as to a fortieth birthday. He functions. What more can one note about any friend? It's feasible to resume the *égoïsme à deux*—the mutual solitude—as the French name marriage.

He functions too as translator of animals, being himself a thorough-bred, with psyche tuned to sea urchins no less than to bank clerks, exasperating bank clerks. My own loneliness has not in a decade been linked to the waiting for a silent phone to sound. Nor am I ever lonelier than when the phone is sounding. Question of priorities. The solitude of work, during which all priorities (happiness, death, taxes) are suspended, resembles like love that cold bubble.

On awakening in the night: That truth, *the* truth, such thick wet rightness, where flown? Can truth so rapidly like a shattered dram of scent have dissipated? Was it actually there?

The small sad need of wanting to be loved.

1978

Of Vanity

For months the tub faucet has leaked with a fragile steady flow finally forming an ineradicable brownish path through the porcelain. Sadness seeps from the spout, oozing there always, whether anyone's home or not. Yet I am unable to summon Manuel with his inexpert tools and recalcitrant Puerto Rican sass. The leak, like the poetic gladiator's slow and wasted hemorrhage, chides me for increasingly sloppy habits. Facts of life leak all over every day yet I'm no longer drawn to channel them quaintly, through prose or notes, so they streak down shapeless to the sea and are absorbed. Yet what's there to record? Brown leaves swirling in Central Park are now too much, while even Mozart and Ravel are now not enough. Nor do I in aging any longer *understand* our so-called finer stuff. I mean this literally. Hoping to model a new piece on "Sunday Morning" I've mulled the Stevens poem for hours, but can't begin to comprehend a single verse, a single image, while both Father and JH after one reading proffer their legitimate *comptes rendus*. Or Sondheim's simple "Send in the Clowns," so plaintive and evocative as a whole, in detail eludes me: what do those figures relate to? who are these people? why do average listeners nod knowingly while I stay in a cloud? All meaning and value and nuance of love and art and casual life escape uninterpreted through extravagant space, while one rude word from the checkout girl at the A&P can wreck my day.

People as they get older seem to ask themselves why they are alive. But more and more I know—feel—why I'm alive; the knowing is the feeling. Admittedly the life, by my own arranging, is ever more fenced in; I shy clear of the unpredictable adventure. No longer like young Narcissus do I contemplate the still pond, but like a castrated satyr catch the reflection in a rushing brook. That image stays fixed. Could the brook drag it rippling away? Oh, now I see: the brook's what the pond was: the ripples are wrinkles, the bottom's eroded, and yes, the face stays put, while all this flow is so fresh, so fresh. (The mirror becomes Narcissus's pool, so absorbed in reflection it stagnates in lovesickness and grows immune to medicine. Otherwise stated: message supplants catharsis, idea precedes style, and we live in a most Romantic Age.)

Visit from a youngish reporter planning a biography of Truman Capote. Disconcerting, the number of years and anecdotes surrounding my tangential acquaintance with that unsatisfactory author, from our first cool meeting with Jane and Paul Bowles in Tangier in 1949, through hectic Paris evenings that autumn, then in New York, then France again with Jack Dunphy in further seasons, and the ballet *Early Voyagers* with Valerie Bettis, to the last ugly contact in 1968. Today Truman's is a name uttered in hushed tones by the likes of Cher and Johnny Carson: he's the poor man's thinker, *le savant des pauvres* who are mostly quite rich. Not that the real intelligentsia is contemptuous, they just have nothing left to say. Truman sold his talent for a mess of pottage. (When later I tell JH how disconcerting it was to dredge up the past, he snorts, "The past? You have no past—you sold it for a mess of pottage.")

Question of ethics: Should a living subject of biography be paid? Should people being interviewed be paid? The biographer, after all, gets a fat advance and the publisher stands to make millions off the exploited subject. But we who were there did all the work.

(The first time I ever saw Marie Laure, months before actually meeting her, I was in the Pont Royale bar with Truman Capote who waved to her sitting across the room with a redhaired fellow who later turned out to be Tom Keogh. Recalling this today makes me feel warmly toward T.C.)

At X's party this afternoon a young Apollo comes up and declares: "I'm a poet." Is it wrong to smile? The announcement seems so somehow superfluous.

Thirty-two years ago, at one of Bu Faulkner's gin-soaked bashes in a featureless room of the Chelsea, I approached John Latouche with the words: "I'm Virgil's copyist, and I just made the parts for his Second String Quartet which is dedicated to you." "Really?" said John. "I didn't know people who looked like you ever did anything."

Frank O'Hara, telling about his first visit to Auden, described a sty with intimidated kids at the great man's feet. He whom Chester Kallman called Miss Master, smelling peculiar and four sheets to the wind, at one point quashed a brash quipster by saying: "You've got to be an Auden to get away with that remark." An Auden! thought Frank, gazing at the poet whose bourbon dribbled from an unshaved chin onto a maculate tie, from there into his lap, and thence down to his humid socks.

Sometimes when least aware of how we look we're told how well we look. The compliment's appreciated, one is grateful for the unexpected. We're at our most interesting when least conscious of appearance.

Beauty is never unaware of itself. Italians, so vain, are also so fair. Contradictorily, once they're dressed up and raring to go, knowing themselves fair, they concentrate on *you*. Young Americans today are unlovely moving as they do in collective anonymity, yet concentrating on just themselves.

The above re-emphasized: All young people are beautiful except those who think they are. That statement's probably false. Yes, beauty, like intelligence, is never unaware of itself; good features are good features, facts. But a beautiful expression is (sometimes) unconscious. Naturally some stupid people think they're intelligent, but nobody intelligent thinks he's stupid. Detectable are those, both stupid and unlovely, who sit around looking intelligent and lovely.

Any poor, ugly or stingy person can imagine himself as rich, pretty or generous; but it is impossible, claims Auden, to imagine oneself as either more or less imaginative than, in fact, one is. "A man whose every thought was commonplace could never know this to be the case." (*The Dyer's Hand*, p. 97.) Now, almost anyone who reads that will agree, and in agreeing will place himself among those who do not have commonplace thoughts.

I cannot concur. I have never had an uncommon thought. I state this with neither fake humility nor a wish to seem quaint. I know—as far as anyone can, according to Auden's claim—that my every thought is banal. Being intelligent (am I?), I suffer from this, and in swiping uncommonplace thoughts from others (such as Auden) I fool some people some of the time while knowing in my heart I'll go to the grave as a mediocre thinker, perhaps even with a mediocre heart.

But can a person's music—his talent, gift, "creative" genius—follow this pattern? Have there been great creators with so-so intellects? (Certain great interpreters, like chessplayers—Toscanini and Bobby Fischer, for example—would seem to be infants when off duty.) Art renders the obvious unique, and in turn renders the unique contagious. Art is a healthy disease.

My logical instincts as a composer sometimes clash with Auden's uncommonplace ideas about music. For instance, his notion (not all that uncommonplace) that film music "is bad film music if we become consciously aware of its existence" is refutable. Such music is not "bad," it's just not film music according to the function assigned it by Auden. No musician in the audience will ever be unaware of film music, no matter how "good" it is. Elsewhere Auden tumbles into the comparison trap, dangerous where the arts are concerned whether the comparison be of likenesses or distinctions. (There are seven arts precisely because they fill seven needs; if the arts could express each other we'd need only one.) Auden shows the difference between ear and eye by demonstrating the difference between motion in what he calls musical space and visual space. "An increase in the tension of the vocal cords is conceived in musical space as a going 'up,' a relaxation as a going 'down,'" says the poet, and continues: "But in visual space it is the bottom of the picture (which is also the foreground) which is felt as the region of greatest pressure and, as this rises up in the picture, it feels an increasing sense of lightness and freedom. The association of tension in hearing with up and seeing with down seems to correspond with the difference between our experience of the force of gravity in our own bodies and our experience of it in other bodies." Etcetera. No musician could have spun such words. The bass is as much a weighted foundation in music as in painting. The lowest-sounding strings on fiddle and guitar are the highest placed. Are sopranos, by virtue of being on top of the basses, performing the male's sexual role, or do they emerge from down under and rise toward heaven? In which case, doesn't their very lightness, their lack of tension, allow them to float upward? Meanwhile, in the visual, who agrees that the bottom is pressure? Is the acrobat hurled from above, or sucked from below?

Auden elsewhere and often is the canniest layman I've ever read on music, and then he becomes an Auden.

I never mean literally what I say, including this sentence.

Having met Elizabeth Hardwick at a party and very much felt a reciprocal rapport, I phoned to invite her over next Saturday. Without the slightest pause she said, "I couldn't possibly, I've much too much work." She proceeded genteelly to talk about the work, and filled out our conversation with this and that, but didn't mention a raincheck. Such a rebuff can set me back years, to when I wasn't accepted by "popular" classmates. But their rejection was in favor of their own sporty gorgeousness as against my eggheaded effeteness, while Hardwick and I are theoretically cut from the same cloth. That she should consider me a lesser cut cast an unredeeming shadow across the afternoon.

Obsequies as social: I'll go to your funeral if you go to mine.

The reason that good movies aren't often made from good books (or that, when both are good, they don't contain the same *kind* of goodness, and the author's first smell isn't brought to the film) is not that movies are condensed, condescending, unfaithful or vulgar. It's that books feed our personal imagination while movies do not. Thus the Absolute General (Josef K. or Everyman) can only disappoint when materialized since we've already envisaged him as ourself, and the Absolute Particular (Jesus C. or Charlus) can only shock, since we've already visualized him as himself.

Is there the phenomenon of pretending to live, as opposed to living? Who dares define it? An example: Robert de Montesquiou (model for Charlus) whose biographer, the canny (and now late) Philippe Jullian, wrote: "The anguish of being forgotten which haunted the poet's last years is that of a man who, instead of living, has given a good performance," and went on to equate living with participating (mainly in love and sex) rather than observing two-dimensionally. Now, who can prove that participator is more vital than spectator? and what indeed is participation? Is listener more passive than player? It takes two to tango. Everything alive *wants* to exist, even the iridescent orchid or amoeba, even the suicide in midair.

One does know what Jullian means. Life can seem over before it's over, when quips fall flat, flesh decays, and trends of the day pass you by. Still, can he show that life is less acute, less "real," in the idiot's focus on a birdsong than in Einstein's focus on . . . Life is no prelude, but a contrast, to death. Life is no defined activity. Life is life.

I'm now old enough, but perhaps you are not, to observe my own baby pictures as period pieces: those long nightgowns and bunting

caps and sepia-toned smiles all chubbily posed. Similarly, looking back
—*hearing* back—to my first French years with Marie Laure, there was
a certain tonality, a phraseology, in the uppercrust male voice (hetero
as well as homosexual) that was rarefied and raspish, fusing high-class
English R's with French lisps. Cocteau had it, and Charles de Noailles,
and they heard it from Proust and maybe from Montesquiou. Who talks
that way now? How the generations shift, substitute for each other, and
have no reference, beyond perhaps quality, for goodness or badness of
interpretation! The work itself (by Bach, say, or Tolstoy, or even Picasso)
may be fixed, impermeable, but our viewpoint ever fluxes. My God! if
I can't know what your green is, or your way of hearing ninth chords—
and you're right here beside me—how much less would I know how
Bach wants himself played. Not, surely, worshipfully. What stays? Does
greatness stay? If viewpoint swerves, how can that *about* which we have
viewpoint not also swerve? Who says Bach's so great?

How could a movie of Proust be anything but small? Pinter's screen-
play is in itself the finished work of art. But understatement is not an
American gift. Whether dealing with whales or the human heart our literature has always been outsize. Our pictures too, especially ones about
nature, incline to editorialize. It's hard for anyone to let a sunset speak
for itself. And Americans are literal: big things they make bigger, small
things smaller. But with the 1930s came the subtle shove of France. If
the inherently little, as given (through enlargement) new dimensions
of horror in the dolls of Balthus, has influenced the foodstuffs of a Roy
Lichtenstein, then the inherently huge, as given (through reduction) a
new sense of wonder in the townscapes of Jean Hugo, has influenced
the landscapes of a Wesley Wehr.

(I shan't pursue this unstable course, it's forced. Americans have
always made miniatures, while Europeans invented *the fact of size* with
all those cathedrals. True, certain Americans like Brion Gysin—he's
Canadian, actually—paint the whole Sahara on a six-by-nine-inch canvas, while Alfonso Ossorio—he's Filipino, originally—paints microbes
on a six-by-nine-*foot* canvas.)

How many angels dance on the head of a pin? Twelve, said Thaddeus. Twelve trillion, said Theobald. Thaddeus was wined, dined and sainted for his piety. Theobald was burned alive for his presumption.

If I grind axes as a composer in the world, as a composer composing I do not. In composition I've no method, have invented naught, have offered to the earth no *means* for producing; indeed, I allow myself to produce according to that most dangerous of all means: tailored impulse. Neither leader nor follower nor textbook maker, I am judged only as good or bad, not by whether through learned exegesis I conform to my own graphic system. Since critics don't know bad from good, they have difficulty assessing, much less (and this is the critic's chief chore) describing, me.

Ives, whom I despise, has in form if not in texture very much influenced me.

All writing, first and foremost, evokes. Some bad writing draws forth a "How true" while some good draws false conclusions. But the false and true are reactions to what the writing evokes of our own—not the writer's—experience. Scanning Susan Sontag's last photography essay, I read: "The primitive notion of the efficacy of images presumes that images possess the qualities of real things, but our inclination is to attribute to real things the qualities of an image."

Darius Milhaud in the late 1960s, although humorous and alert in his wheelchair, had long since given up on medicine. Milhaud's current consultant, a sort of diviner, was able by means of a scanning rod to examine a group photo in the day's paper and determine not only who among those featured had what disease, but even diagnose those (unseen at the extreme right or left) who had been cropped from the portrait. He did stress that the picture had not only to be recent (the image of a person now dead was useless) but reproduced by a small-circulation press (the more editions or replicas, the more evanescent the subject's "readable" specter).

Swing Band men of the thirties were famed through recordings. When hired for a hotel dance they felt obliged to recheck their own discs and to imitate by rote their recorded improvisations, so that the college kids would not feel cheated by living variations.

". . . our reluctance to tear up or throw away the photograph of a loved one, especially of someone dead or far away." Aren't we equally reluctant to throw out letters, or books, or quilts or locks of hair? Yet we do—and are instantly less bereft, more secure in what we call our memories.

One page of Susan elicits this page from me. If her evocations in themselves are not particularly sentimental, the reactions they call up, at least in me, are strong, and that is good for us both.

Cruelty in the name of truth, serpentine candor entwines the pillars of society. To tell someone (whether or not "for his own good") that someone else has slandered him, or that his nose is grotesque, or that his sister is a dyke (which maybe he never knew), is to relate facts (when in fact these are only facts), not truth. Fact is the odd side of fiction, while truth is the odd side of lie. A fact is not necessarily necessary; even truth need be called up only to set a fiction straight, when that fiction has been uselessly disruptive.

The contempt I can feel for even my closest friends.

Most of what we think about each other we don't say. Curiosity, hostility, lust, those suggestions "for his own good," or above all, boredom—these impulses, with the years, are kept more or less consciously quiescent, while amenities increasingly satisfy. The surface delight of regarding those bright persimmons on that deep blue plate, of regarding them with or without you, seems more urgent than falling in love again, or than working for justice in the world. Do I want to know you better? There is no better.

JH explains that suicide by throat-slashing results in an instinctive but vain attempt to rejoin the severed arteries gushing and then flowing and then dripping slowly, for months, like the bathtub faucet, eroding forever. The fact of Paris today: there's no point of reference (except the defunct past) in all these so-familiar lanes that yell for recognition.

On Dick Cavett's show Truman Capote, looking like that extraterrestrial embryo from the end of *Close Encounters,* posits the same defense of his upcoming nonbook as he posited last year and the year before: "Well, Marcel Proust did the very same thing." One might quickly reply: Yes, and so did Hedda Hopper. Every writer—or interpreter or conversationalist or archeologue (to avoid the word artist)—depicts reaction to milieu; there is literally no other material to work with, on or off the earth.

And what makes Earth turn?

Dream of an insomniac. Earth grinds to a halt. Peering now through his closed window as through a lens, he perceives that the world outside has stopped. Not stopped merely as in a photograph (in this case caught on the window's retina), for the immobile subject of a picture, while being scrutinized, still exists in time; but stopped utterly, the inanimate stopped, and the numberless molecules revolving at infinite speeds have also ceased to budge. The world's frozen in time. Except for him. He remains free to pace the interior of this fractured moment, to observe from his perch the gelatinized pedestrians, mouths half-opened on an unfinished verb, stopped, all stopped in this split second and caught forever in transparent lava.

He draws back from the window. With the hesitant élan of one who has made a distasteful choice and now must see it through, he lies flat as upon an auction block, fully clothed, and starts to onanize. From a swamp of thorns growing sadly desperate like the Leaning Tower of Pisa stuffed with the steaming custard of the sort they used to serve in kindergarten, friction begins slowly, mouth closing, opening, closing, descending along that female beach like a pear-colored peach, a hot Saint Bernard, a scorched leaf. Heated by his own blood, he does not increase, but as though caught on a fishhook moves his sweaty head from side to side, and tears gush.

Suddenly his fantasies are deflected by the breeze of an angel's wing, a memory of magic: here I am in my prime, with maybe just a few more months. The thought excites him so that a smoking liter of bloody mucus spurts all off-white toward the dark hairs of his belly like infected buttermilk. Silence.

Silence as in the subway. Stock still, mummified on the bed.

Now the fragile room quivers, so slightly. As in a swoon he turns his head again, only his fevered head softly, and gazes toward the open window more dejected than ever in his shortish life. From outside a spring wind brings sounds of forsythia blooming, the chirp of sparrows, the tingle of Good Humor wagons mingling with giggles of faraway children playing hopscotch on the wet pavement. Then softly he stirs his body through the sheets and closes his eyes, as the world gradually begins to move again.

Not intellect but sex, however paltry, in its thorough self-interest, makes the world go round.

Having now culled these presumably random but actually oh so alike posies from a diary of the last three years, I'd be tempted to beribbon the garland as "vanity" did that not apply finally to any collection, to any art, to indeed any effort by Caligula or Karl Marx, from childbirth to war, because, as the Preacher saith, all is. Not truly all perhaps, for beasts aren't vain—not in either sense of futile or conceited under the sun. Vanity is the paper-thin placenta of civilization that protects us awful humans, with a delicate transience, against the mad logic of the sky beyond the sun.

1978

INTERLUDE: ON MUSIC

What is music? Why, it's what musicians do! It's whatever a given listener feels it to be. It's any series of sounds and silences capable of moving at least one heart. It may move us, but won't change us. The experience of exposure to music may change us (though one may be exposed for years with immunity), but not the music itself; it can only awaken and make us more what we already are. Art has no ethical purpose and does not instruct. The same "message" can be reiterated by different artists but is most educational when least artistic (i.e., most literal).

I do not believe that music can be political—not, at least, in the sense that it can make us believe something we have not heretofore believed. Music has nothing to do with nobility or goodness, nor with evil or vanity. Music does not alter us, it confirms. Insofar as music does change us, it's not very good music.

What is *good* music? The music that is good for you, that disturbs involuntarily like an erection. Longevity is no prerequisite since "good" is not an artistic but a moral ingredient. . . . But *great* music doubtless does deal with Time, though not with decisions of the greatest number. The mass does not decide. If Michelangelo did create for a mass (debatable) his subject matter was the same as that of lesser artists. He was great not because of his material or mass appeal, but because he was Michelangelo. The masses don't know the difference. Ask them!

Until yesterday music's very nature was such that explanation was unimportant to appreciation (proof of the pudding was in the eating); today music's very nature is such that explanation is all-important to appreciation (like certain political polemicism which theorizes beyond proportion to reality). I say *appreciation* advisedly: *enjoyment* is now a niggardly, if not an obscene, consideration. That composition should need such verbal spokesmen indicates that, for the first time ever, the very essence of the art has changed. There's no more room for the *petit maître,* that "second-rater" (if you will) whose talent is to delight or, even sadly, to move his hearer to dance and sing. There is room for only masterpieces, for only masterpieces have the right to require the intellectual (as opposed to sensual) concentration and investigation needed for today's "in" music. Masterpieces are made by the few geniuses born each century. Yet hundreds now compose *in the genius style* while denigrating those who compose *what they hear.* Certain painting now is healthy if only because it's witty. Music, as always, trails humorlessly behind the other mediums.

The fact that music is scandalously received seems automatically to validate it for those afraid of ultimately being proved wrong.

Since we all must live in a cage (also the artist: without restraint he is not one), I prefer my own design. If I've not joined the avant-garde it's not that I don't approve of—or even agree with—them; it's because of a terror of losing my identity.

I don't know why I became obsessed with wanting to express myself through music. Any attempt to solve that mystery is never, to me, in the least bit cogent. People say, "How sad you must have been when you wrote this or that piece." When you're writing a sonata or a poem, you may have debts, an ache in your hip, or a souring love affair, yet in the act of creating, your worries are on hold. In other words, does a composer write sad music out of his own sadness, or what he knows of sadness? If you're writing a death scene in an opera, you can't have tears streaming down your face, because it takes perhaps a month to write the death scene. You write out of past experience — or rather an *imagined* past experience.

Music is a craft, it's not self-indulgence. What takes the most time is orchestration and copying, but that is not what causes the most agony. It's getting the ideas down, doing something with them, and then saying it's time to stop. Knowing when to stop is crucial, in life as in art.

PART 2

Music Matters

If a composer could state in words what being a composer
means, he would no longer need to be a composer.
I can't write music and write about music during the same
period; the two acts stimulate mutually repellent juices.

Pictures and Pieces

It is idle though not really odious to compare the arts, and people are always doing it. But they usually generalize on likeness, not disparity, lumping together all arts whose practitioners supposedly represent that portion of society which best enjoys "the gift of self-realization." No two expressions are more opposed than music and painting. Their function, the manner of their making, the characters of the workmen themselves are as dissimilar as the needs of their respective publics.

In childhood I believed that a given artist could have developed into any other kind—that he had only to choose between, say, prose or sculpture. Certainly all children are all things, close to natural truth and the origins of philosophy. Maturity's manners later stunt the imagination which had held a fantastic door ajar; to the more calloused this door closes forever. Composers and painters, in retaining initial fancies, stay children. That seems their sole point in common, as though mutual receptivity had been smothered in adolescence. A fair percentage of plastic artists appear all but tone-deaf and some fine musicians are not a bit visual.

Picasso, for example, typical of most people, is not very reactive to sound about him; his ears prefer the Iberian nostalgia of bullfight trumpets to more sophisticated music. But his eyes are black diamond bullets which never miss their mark yet never find repose.

Many a musician is oblivious to scenes before him. He too resembles most laymen in that years pass blindly, though he knows the pitch of an auto horn, a robin's cry, a faucet dripping blocks away.

Essentially music is abstract and painting is representational despite what we hear to the contrary. Music has no intellectual significance, no meaning outside itself. This is not less true of so-called programmatic than of absolute music wherein subjective connotations are not intended.

I believe that painting does have meaning outside itself. When abstract painters profess a striving to eliminate representation, their very effort implies camouflage. A musician feels no compunction to disguise "subject matter" and might even attempt to reveal it, safely assured that logicians will never decipher and expose his secret thoughts. No inquisition can intelligibly reproach a composer as it can a Goya for subversive or obscene notions.

Richard Strauss once declared himself capable of denoting a fork on a table through sound alone. Certainly his tone poems evoke realistic windmills, bleating sheep, human chatter and such. Any competent orchestrater can simulate worldly noises without much trouble, as a talented mimic can bark like a dog. (Charlie Chaplin, they say, once performed an aria, and beautifully, to everyone's amazement. "I can't really sing at all," he explained later. "I was just doing my Caruso number!") The closer these copies approach reality the farther they retreat from creation. Wilde's paradox: Nature imitates Art.

If we were not informed of Strauss's fork or sheep we'd either invent our own associations or listen as if to "pure" music. If told that these sounds meant knives or sea gulls we'd leave it at that. In music an image is no more than approximate.

Each century gives conventional symbols for general mood. In recent Western music minor means sad, though it had no such suggestion three hundred years ago; even today, who is saddened by the completely minor carol *God Rest You Merry Gentlemen?* The mode of C-major is supposed to be happy, but the Spartans considered it lascivious (which is not always the same thing). We don't disagree on what is termed joyous, tragic, or ecstatic, except when we read into the style of one musical period that which refers to another. In pictures, however, a wedding or funeral always mean just that, no matter when or where they were made.

Music is probably the least international of languages. During two years in Morocco I never encountered a native who could fathom our formal music any more than our Christian values. Only in the past century and to us of the West do Strauss's sheep or Ravel's sad birds, Respighi's trees or Honegger's engine, signify themselves in sound through habit and suggestion. And yet, when he knows what it represents, who, hearing Britten's *Sick Rose,* for instance, can restrain a spinal chill when that wormlike horn bores into the flower's heart? An Arab would not *see* this as we do—through the ears. We also, were we not told beforehand of the intended association, would miss our guess nine times out of ten even with such broad themes as love and war, festivity and madness. Scientific experiments have proved it. Gone are the days when Carl Maria von Weber's diminished-seventh tremolos will scare anyone.

Music's inherent abstraction is what renders it so malleable in collaborative fields. A choreographer may mold a narrative around absolute music, or effectively revise the story line of a programmatic work. Robbins' ballet on *The Afternoon of a Faun* is as plausible as Nijinsky's. And Nijinsky's version of *The Rite of Spring* was no more catastrophic than Disney's. Stravinsky's masterpiece, which suffocated both ballet and film, survives uniquely in concert halls. Music can make or break a ballet because sound is necessary to the dance. And although audiences will take a good deal more of the "unfamiliar" in spectacles which mix the arts than in music alone, when sound dominates the visual they revolt—as in the famous case of *The Rite of Spring*.

Music is less integral to the film medium, so even greater risks can be run. A musically untutored movie audience accepts without flinching a score whose audacity, if heard in concert, would send the elite yelling for mercy. The public is, and should be, mostly unconscious of movie music; a background fails when it distracts from central business. But such is music's strength that it may sugarcoat a tasteless film or poison one of quality. A recent drama of capital punishment, *I Want to Live,* excited extra tension through its sound-track of progressive jazz. *On the Beach,* whose subject was more timely still (terrestrial death through radioactivity), was devitalized by a score with old-fashioned associations.

Any music may persuasively accompany any image or story while inevitably dictating the *tone* of the joint effort. Music's power lies in an absence of human significance and this power dominates all mediums it contacts. When Auric composed the score for Jean Cocteau's film, *The Blood of a Poet,* he produced what is commonly known as love music for love scenes, game music for game scenes, funeral music for funeral scenes. Cocteau had the bright idea of replacing the love music with the funeral, game music with the love, funeral with game. And it worked—like prosciutto and melon. Nor did Cocteau commission a composer for his ballet of a modern young painter who hangs himself on stage; he used a passacaglia of Bach whose clash with the present ignited the eternal.

The sea reminds me of Debussy's *La Mer*—*La Mer* never reminds me of the sea. But if a picture recalls the sea, the sea conjures up no picture of anything beyond itself. In this sense water is as abstract as music, but a picture of water *represents* an abstraction. Whatever title Debussy may have chosen, his work is finally enjoyed as sheer music (though the earmarks of *La Mer* have so often been imitated for cinematic seascapes that the original now contains non-musical connotations). If a novice were told that the three movements of this piece illustrated three times of day, not on the sea but in a city, he wouldn't know the difference. Paintings also present different impressions to different people: as many interpretations exist as spectators. But I am speaking now of creative consciousness, not audience effect. At bottom a composer cannot work through visions. Painters, whether or not they're aware of it, always paint a picture of *something*. Some attempt to divorce nature and search for a plane as abstract as music's. While avoiding a title more committal than *Conception in Green* or *Study No. 2*, they are actually depicting tangibles which, like clouds, assume logical shape. Since a composer's auditor never has subject matter to cling to, hints may be dropped about some subjective idea as symbolic guide through an unknown formal region. To both artists the title is a forethought or afterthought extraneous to actual work. Human ideas are dissolved by music on its highest level, just as they are evolved by pictures. That is the reason it's easier to envisage an artist himself through his pictures than through his pieces.

The evocative title for other than vocal music has been alternately in and out of vogue since the fifteenth century. Debussy happened to be born to a period when descriptive music was stylish. Not only in *La Mer* but in his entire output he is linked with Impressionism, the only movement in which pictorial and sonic arts have tried meeting on common ground. Impressionism really has little to do with music. It names the desire of a group of nineteenth-century French painters to elicit an *impression* and avoid a clear-cut message. Since music never conveys (as painting can) a clear-cut message, it is always in a way impressionistic and hence need not be singled out as such. The painting's concern with illumination of a subject rather than the subject itself emphasized light rather than what was lighted. Now music has no color: at best the term "timbre" applies for varieties of sound combination. Musically "light" or "dark" tones are mere figures of speech.

The current Zen trend toward the Nowness of things relates to pictorial impressionism. Painters captured a momentary effect, a vague definition, a tree glimpsed through shifting fog at too close or far a distance for usual meaning. Monet's *Water Lilies* form a mental picture retreating as much as possible from physical resemblance while still retaining identity. Debussy stressed the same mood inversely by attempting to make sounds signify sights. Though their impressionistic aims appear synonymous, the devices of these men are not comparable because of a non-common language. Whether they succeeded in sharing their reactions with the public is unimportant so long as the result was complete in itself.

Rendition of things out of focus or as they exist for the fraction of a second is nevertheless rendition of *things*. Such things from new distances assume new meanings. A man is only visibly a man while in speaking range. A mile off he is a dot representing a man, an inch away he grows more than human. On this level the term "abstract" is not absurd for pictures because they can represent an abstraction of the specific. (If music represents an abstraction of the specific it has never been demonstrated.) The phrase "non-representational" is nonetheless inappropriate and should perhaps be substituted by "non-literal."

Single fields of vision force the eye to focus on but one object at a time; surroundings of that object are blurred. Impressionist painters concentrated on the blur seeking atmosphere rather than fine clarification. Debussy sought to clarify the blur. He pulverized sound into a prismatic mist like the confettied pointillist close-ups that produce a haze of overall coherence. Indeed, he achieved formal freedom in a manner hard to analyze, and longed to eliminate beginnings and ends from his art and retain only middles. Music naturally exists in time, so must start and stop in time. Painting also starts and stops, but in space and with no climax in the accumulative mobile sense. Climaxes are indigenous to all the "time arts," including dance which, though manifest in space like sculpture, is basically a moving picture.

Painting's symbolic "climax" is the static focal point which is always immediate—music's real climax is always kept waiting. Painters emulate time by copying recollections of a split moment as the Impressionists did, or like the realist portrait painter whose subject sits immobile for days to be reconstructed from the composite of a million moments.

The portraitist's eye disintegrates his model into fragments which his hand reassembles on canvas. The subject *feels* his dismembered sections float across the studio, controlled by the painter's magnet vision; like flies in amber they come to rest in oil. If the artist steals of his model forever, the model takes also from the artist: such relationships are never one-sided. But the union's pictorial result is frozen.

Music exists—not on canvas nor yet on the staff—only in motion. The good listener will hear it as the present prolonged. The good spectator will see a picture also as a whole even when he examines at close range images recreated from a distance, or from a distance images made at close range. Since a finished picture does not rely on time, the individual has more *time* to inspect it, whereas music's meaning (if any) must be caught on the run.

An entire painting is absorbed at the speed of light. The time it takes our eye to reach the canvas is all that's required for an image to be stamped indelibly on the brain. We seem to look into it, yet its third dimension is imaginary; we cannot penetrate increasingly as into the universe. We come to know it in many ways, each of which constitutes an indivisible moment of the present. . . . A whole piece of music is grasped only in retrospect. Were it feasible to condense a piece for performance at an infinite speed (say, a whole symphony lasting one second), time would still be the leading factor and the audience would still have to remain till the end without having *seen* the music as a static image. We can look away from pictures but we can't listen away from sounds. We accept in simile "the image of sound" yet we never speak of "the sound of image."

To convey through music a non-musical idea three formulas are available: the tone picture, the tone poem, and the incidental background for plays.

Tone pictures are puns which never need explanation to be enjoyed. The majority refer to aspects of nature, usually water or birds, or vistas including both, in specified attitudes at specified times of day. They may use the same title without necessarily sounding alike. How many pieces are called The Fountain! More rare are resemblant musics with diverse significance. The opening measures of Debussy's *Clouds*, of Mussorgsky's *Four Walls*, and of Stravinsky's *Nightingale* are too similar for coincidence, yet their literary intentions are unrelated. Different means are tried for the same subject and the same means for different subjects, but the musician won't name a work "Abstraction"—he doesn't have to. Nevertheless, he can't truly expect us to see sounds any more than we hear paint. A sonorous landscape by any other name would sound as sweet.

Tone poems tell stories. They involve direct emotions indirectly transported on wings of wordless song through fire, jealousy, and death. Like good tone pictures, they possess abstract coherence without a program.

The third division, the incidental background for plays, in turn serves three purposes, all very general. The first is for indicating weather conditions and originates from the tone picture; the second is for love scenes and derives from the tone poem; the last is for quieting the audience or getting actors on and off stage, and stems from the military fanfare. Music is never more explicit.

Actual paintings sometimes inspire music. The most famous example is *Pictures at an Exhibition*. And just this season new works by Diamond and Schuller used paintings of Paul Klee as "theme." Klee himself once said: "Art does not render the visible, but renders visible." He was speaking, I imagine, only of plastic art. It remains doubtful that his painting is rendered more visible as interpreted through an unrelated medium. Hindemith maintains that "the reactions music evokes are not feelings, but . . . memories of feelings." If a composer enjoins us to recall emotions about a picture, he distracts attention from his piece, since concentration is not wholly directed to more than one thing at a time.

Dallapiccola arranges notes on a staff to look like the Cross of Christ. Of course we don't hear a cross any more than we see tomorrow. If impatience leads us to conclude that certain music, like children, should be seen and not heard, Dallapiccola's device is not for that disqualified.

Do the typographical designs of Cummings' poetry disturb it when read aloud? or does the holy 3 of liturgical chant oblige us to feel the Trinity rather than a metrical pulse? Tricks are valid when used as cause and not effect. We judge by expressive results. . . . Virgil Thomson has posed people for musical portraits. This too is a means to an end like re-evaluating pictures by sound. The tonal image provides impetus to build an ultimate abstraction.

In like manner a painter on a dull day may get himself going by drawing geometric forms which eventually become representational. To Mondrian or Albers the geometric presents an end in itself. Dare I say this end is also representational? (Skeptics maintain such painting is merely unfinished while Freudians find in it God knows how many symbols.) Of course it is representational: nature abounds in geometry as she abounds in vibrations from which music is fashioned; yet psychoanalysts are shy of chords and scales. (It would be amusing to speculate about Ravel's fixation on the descending fourth whenever he sets the word *maman* to music!)

I too have written visual music, for I don't always practice what I preach. In a work called *Eagles for Orchestra* I followed a word picture of Whitman, but soon dispensed with all thought of birds and was impelled only by the flow of verse. Poetry, falling between the poles of sight and sound, supplies both image and movement. Still, I never see eagles when I hear my music, which could as easily represent a hurricane, or heavy traffic, or nothing at all. I used the title just because it's pretty.

Aesthetic difference in intention no doubt contributes to personality difference between makers of pictures and pieces. There are also practical reasons.

Painters don't need verbal articulation. Addressing the sense of sight through the sense of touch, they make by contact with canvas what will be seen. Doubly involved with the sensual, they are unconcerned with intellectual justification. Besides, they often have poets as spokesmen. Trends like Surrealism, which are considered the painters' pri-

vate property, are primarily literary movements which take up painters. None of these movements has ever dealt positively with music.

Composers as a race are more lucid. What we call a "primitive" in
painting (one without formal experience) is unimaginable in musical
composition, which is a craft whose elements are not implicit in the
growing-up process. Everyone from birth learns to speak and use his
hands, and literally anyone can write poems or draw pictures (drawing
is a kind of writing, and vice versa). But certain rudiments of composition must be encased before a minimal expression is plausible, because music requires an interpreter to whom the creator's intention
must be clear. Painting presupposes no interpretation other than by
the spectator; it needs no performing middleman.

On its lowest plane the pictorial is more accessible than the sonorous—the eye is a less complex instrument than the ear—so there are
more painters around than composers. In Paris alone forty thousand
are inscribed in the city census; not even a fifth that number of composers exists in the world. Quality, of course, smooths out the difference; each field claims the same small number of superior artists. . . .
Financially again the balance is unequal. A professional painter earns
directly through his work many times more than a composer of cor-
responding age and reputation. As a palpable commodity, painting is
a practical investment; music cannot be owned and hence lacks market value. The composer needs not only communication with his interpreter, but must develop extra-compositional articulation to earn a
living. The painter spends much of his time dealing directly with his
public, which the composer seldom does.

The formal aspects of painting and music contain noncomparable
dimensions, but their embellishments—color and orchestration—are
not dissimilar. Red cannot exist by itself (it cannot be conscious of
itself, so to speak) without being a red something; nor can a flute sound
be just that: it will always be a flute playing something. This is a relation, if not an infallible one, for color can indicate form in painting
while orchestration plays no formal part in music.

The element of professional *rapprochement* between these arts is happiest in the theater where the wedding is of mediums rather than of artists. Frequently the musician and set designer never meet. Their products are soldered together by a director upon whose talent the success of the marriage depends. It is rare that painter and composer collaborate freely as do poet and painter or composer and poet.

A given artist is usually well versed in one of the sister arts which he enjoys as a hobby. Musicians and painters, nonetheless, don't seem to need each other. Their chief similarity as private citizens is in mutual disregard. Creative Jacks-of-all-trades, from Leonardo to Noel Coward, have always been something of a rarity, and are becoming more so. This is not reprehensible: to a creator vast knowledge is unnecessary, sometimes even harmful.

Artists, like children, resist alienation from nature. None seek to copy so much as to join nature by opening a glass door to which they alone hold the key, but through which others can look. Painting's connection with nature (whether geometric or photographic) is more apparent than music's. The latter, like architecture, proceeds in indirect simulation by subduing inspiration to calculation. Its "unnatural" components are what render it the abstractest art, for one musical sound has meaning only in ordered relation to another, while in nature sound has unordered meaning in itself.

The truest relation between artists is not as thinkers but as doers obsessed with organized self-discovery. Composer and painter alike feel toward the tools of their expression as interpreters toward their instrument. The disheveled neatness atop the piano, the easel and chisel, pencil and paper, the assemblage of colors and staves and inks and rulers are as tenderly disinterested and aggravating as twins to these men. Both of them while working inhabit a strenuous cocoon removed from time and space, the better to deal objectively with space and time—for both share the immediate while in the act of making. The logic of hindsight alone demonstrates their dissimilar intentions.

To dispel a fallacy I have shown art as a fluid matter not to be judged by stagnant standards. My premise has been that music and painting

are less resemblant than generally supposed. Any theory which questions bromides is always partly valid. Sometime I'll try proving that
music is never abstract, painting always is. Such an approach merged
with the present one might allow that pictures and pieces are really the
same. A discouraging assumption. After all, if the arts could express
each other we wouldn't need more than one.

1960

Poetry of Music

Song is the reincarnation of a poem which was destroyed in order to live again in music. The composer, no matter how respectful, must treat poetry as a skeleton on which to bestow flesh, breaking a few bones in the process. He does not render a poem more *musical* (poetry isn't music, it's poetry); he weds it to sound, creating a third entity of different and sometimes greater magnitude than either parent. It too may ultimately stand alone, as those nineteenth-century songs now do despite being disowned at birth by their poetic fathers. *We* hear them as totalities without considering their growing pains.

Indeed, much past poetry is known to us exclusively through song settings, hence our unconscious assumption of such poetry's emanations of musical inevitability. Yet when it comes to his own work, today's poet has his own notion of inevitability. He is torn between a need to hear his words sung, yet for those words to retain their initial beat and echo, their identity proper. His "proper" must obligatorily be sacrificed; his notion of inevitability becomes the fly in the ointment. The only inevitable way to set poetry is the "right" way, and there is no one right way.

Song is the sole example of one preexisting art medium being juxtaposed intact upon another. The words of the poem are not *adapted*, like film scenarios from plays; they remain unaltered while being tampered with, and unlike other musical forms—fugue, for instance, or sonata—there exist no fixed rules for song.

There are as many "right" ways for tampering with a poem as there are poems and good composers, or different viewpoints of a single composer toward the same poem. A composer's viewpoint is right if it works, regardless of the poet's reaction. For the poet will never feel the song as he felt the poem which inspired the song. Debussy, Fauré, and Hahn all used the same verse of Verlaine, all convincingly, all more or less differently. More or less. *Clair de Lune* did suggest a similar built-in musical formula to French composers at the turn of the century.

On the principle that there is no one way to musicalize a poem I once composed a cycle by selecting eight works by as many Americans and setting each one to music twice, as contrastingly as possible. The performing sequence of the sixteen songs was pyramidal: one through eight, then back from eight to one. Although each poem is repeated, none of the music is; thus the poems supposedly take on new impact at second hearing not only by virtue of being sung at a later time, but also by being reinvested with another shape.

Good poetry won't always lend itself to music, i.e., won't of itself make good music even if the composer is good. Some poems more than others cry out to be sung (their authors' wishes, like Eliot's, notwithstanding), though different cries are heeded by different composers with different viewpoints on dealing with those cries—whether to clarify, dominate, obscure, or ride on them.

Still, better good poetry than bad. Music, being more immediately powerful, does tend to invisibilize all poems except bad ones. Despite popular notions to the contrary, it is a demonstrable fallacy that second-rate poems make the best songs.

Theodore Chanler may well have become America's greatest composer of the genre had not his small catalogue adhered to mainly one poetaster (Father Feeney) whose words sound even sillier framed by

lovely tunes which, through some inverted irony, end up being sub-
dued by those words. Duparc gained Parnassus on a lifetime output
of only thirteen songs; yet I wonder how they'd come off with other
verse than Baudelaire's. Chanler just may make it on his eight delicious
Epitaphs based on the solid words of Walter de la Mare.

How do you choose poems for setting to music?

Formerly by what's called inspiration, the yen for self-expression
that has nothing to do with talent. Today I choose them according to
pre-set requirements. My approach—fast or slow, soft or loud—to a
given poem varies according to whom I'm musicalizing it for, and to
whether it's to be one of a sequence or standing alone. Yes, I am drawn
to poetry which, as we Quakers say, speaks to my condition; and whatever my songs may be worth, I've never used a bad poem. But my *kind*
of good poem may not be your kind, sonically speaking—or singing.
I concede the greatness of much poetry that has no need to be put to
music, at least not by me.

Usable qualities are prescribed as much by sequence as by inspiration. (If we did not assume the true worth of an artist's inspiration
we wouldn't be concerned in the first place.) Otherwise stated: art is
the communicable ordering of your bright ideas. My essay, *Notes on
Death,* was originally narrational, glued together by characters speaking paragraphs. By cutting and reshifting, but by leaving unaltered all
that was salvaged, I fooled editor Nan Talese into accepting the new
version which she no longer recognized. Similarly, when I compose a
so-called cycle (has anyone ever defined that term?) the order of songs
is not necessarily determined until the writing is done. I may even add
a quick waltz here, a moody one there not because the verse decrees
the tempo, but because the theatricality of the whole requires contrast.
Poems work at any speed, or fail at any speed.

Do you set your own words to music?

As an author I'm a polemical diarist who wants to set matters
straight. But I can't set them straight to music, for I am not a poet. My
poetry is my music. If I could write the kind of poem that I like to set

to music, I wouldn't need to set it to music. Indeed, I would no longer be a composer but a poet.

Poetry isn't life, it's poetry, a distillation. Life has alternatives, dead ends. A poem is invariable, being the only possible arrangement of the words it contains. How insolent therefore that a composer should "enhance" those words with music. How much more insolent—since in any case he will break the metrical spine—that he should change the order of, or even repeat, certain words. Yet even Britten (why "even" Britten? is he God?) repeats words, and unimportant words at that. Britten does this no doubt in the tradition, and according to the ancient conceit, of Handel, who, however, repeated *important* words: *Alleluia, sing.* Britten is wrong. A composer who solves the problem of his song by altering the verse does not solve the problem of his song, insofar as song is the setting of a poem.

Despite whatever reputation I may hold in this area, I am not *just* a song composer in the sense that Duparc was. My three hundred plus songs written since childhood add up to as many hours labor and as many minutes hearing, nothing compared to the long labors of symphonic orchestrations and other works in the larger forms. Yet inasmuch as all real music is essentially a vocal utterance, be it *Danny Boy* or *Petruchka*, I *am* just a song composer.

If less is more, one great song is worth ten merely adroit symphonies. To say you can have it for a song, is to sell the form cheap.

I am fond of insisting that anyone can be taught to write a perfect song. It's a fact: for musical composition is a craft—as well as an art, whatever that means. Yes, anyone can be taught to write a perfect song, but no one, not even Schubert, knows how to lend that song a living pulse and inject it with flowing blood.

Art Song, our defensive reply to France's *mélodie* and Germany's *lied*, is so termed to distinguish the genre from Folk Song and Pop Song. Folk, anonymous and collective in composition, is unaccompanied, un-notated, ethnic, choral, and utters concerns of a group rather than of an individual. Pop, which ranges from Rag and Jazz to Rock and Broadway, generally concerns love or its lack, and can be sung by anyone of any sex at any speed in any key, with a steady-beat accompaniment. Art Song is built on a preexisting lyric for a trained voice to be performed with piano in concert. Not chameleonic like Pop, one can't imagine the setting of, say, James Agee by Samuel Barber in the mouth of Madonna, transposed down a fifth, beefed up with showbiz chords, and backed by a fifty-piece band.

Art Song in our United States has always been a specialty within a specialty. In the 1800s, except for Stephen Foster, song was peripheral to grander forms. For MacDowell, Griffes, Carpenter, and especially Ives, whose extravagant settings penned between 1893 and 1923 paved the way for all subsequent songsters, the medium was a side-interest. Between the wars song bloomed through Thomson, Blitzstein, Diamond, and a dozen sadly forgotten others like Citkowitz, Edmunds, Duke, Lockwood and Paul Bowles who used contemporaneously apt texts like Cummings, Stein, Wylie, Stevens and Tennessee Williams. In 1950 Aaron Copland's cycle *Twelve Poems of Emily Dickinson,* his sole excursion into the area, became as influential as Ives.

Indeed, 1950 can now be seen as our high point for Art Song. There was a bouquet of soloists—Phyllis Curtin, Donald Gramm, Jennie Tourel, Nell Tangeman, Adele Addison, Regina Sarfaty, Charles Bressler, Beverly Wolff—who did not blink at singing in their native tongue. They knew that diction is more urgent than interpretation, comprehending words more important than "feeling" words, and that all music, vocal or not, is molded on the spoken voice of its composer. Thus simultaneously there grew a new repertory of American song on American poetry by Daniel Pinkham, John Edmunds, Ben Weber, William Flanagan, Charles Jones, myself. Because the Second World War had shut us off from a century of European influence, American music, with crystalline simplicity, now came into its own.

But the good days soon ended.

Parallel with the McCarthy hearings came the infiltration of integral serialism by Pierre Boulez, who proclaimed: "Every musician who has not felt the necessity of the serial language is useless." (Omit the word "not," and I agree.) The defection from tonality was massive; Americans, arrogant in matters monetary and military, retained an inferiority complex vis-à-vis the arts, and regressed to the ways of prewar Europe. Music grew laughably, tragically, complicated. Composers like myself, too lazy to hoe the tone row, were ignored, but most capitulated, even Copland, even Stravinsky. Such American vocal music as was produced stressed a widening rather than a heightening of text (which now was often in a foreign tongue) by repeating phrases arbitrarily, and by protracting syllables to incomprehensible length, while the accompaniments were inevitably for chamber combos, in emulation of Boulez's *Marteau sans maître.* Song recital specialists died out.

The serial killings lasted a generation before relief came from an unexpected corner. In 1967 the dynamic advent of the Beatles provoked high-class endorsement from every side. Intellectuals, without guilt or censure, were suddenly free to listen to something they enjoyed. Many a closet tonalist slinked back to the sensual fold. Some even wrote Art Songs again. But who would sing them? In thirty years there has been not one American singer, not one, who makes a living primarily as a recitalist, let alone in home-grown repertory. Art Song has always had a tiny aristocratic audience and always will. Art Song writers have now become as rare among composers as composers are rare among tax collectors.

I compose what I need to hear because nobody else is doing it. Yet I feel guilty about what I do best—setting words to music. Because it comes easily, meaning naturally, I feel I'm cheating.

My songs are love letters. To whom? Like Vladimir Nabokov, I write "for myself in multiplicate," meaning for friends, those personal extremities. Are unheard melodies sweeter? Intelligence is silence, truth being invisible. But music does not (should not) appeal only to our intelligence, nor is it especially concerned with truth any more than poetry is.

Yet we're all afraid of being misrepresented, as though we didn't misrepresent ourselves every minute. A song is but a single facet of ourself, which the listener takes as the whole self.

Songs are my hobby. I believe only in hobbies. I have no profession — except piano playing. I abhor Major Statements, and so, in America, must perish.

The Beatles

I never go to classical concerts any more, and I don't know anyone who does. It's hard still to care whether some virtuoso tonight will perform the *Moonlight Sonata* a bit better or a bit worse than another virtuoso performed it last night.

I do often attend what used to be called avant-garde recitals, though seldom with delight, and inevitably I look around and wonder: What am I doing here? What am I learning? Where are the poets and painters and even composers who used to flock to these things? Well, perhaps what I'm doing here is a duty, keeping an ear on my profession so as to justify the joys of resentment, to steal an idea or two, or just to show charity toward some friend on the program. But I learn less and less. Meanwhile the absent artists are home playing records; they are *reacting* again, finally, to something they no longer find at concerts.

Reacting to what? To the Beatles, of course—the Beatles, whose arrival has proved one of the most healthy events in music since 1950. They and their offshoots represent—as any nonspecialized intellectual will tell you—the finest communicable music of our time.

This music was already sprouting a decade ago through such innocent male sex symbols as Presley in America and Johnny Halliday in France, both of whom were then caricatured by the English in a movie called *Expresso Bongo,* a precursor of *Privilege,* about a none-too-bright rock singer. These young soloists (still functioning and making lots of money) were the parents of more sophisticated, more *committed,* soloists like Dylan and Donovan, who in turn spawned a horde of masculine offspring including twins (Simon and Garfunkel, the most cultured), quintuplets (Country Joe & The Fish, the most exotic), sextuplets (The Association, the most nostalgic), even septuplets (Mothers of Invention, the most madly satirical). With much less frequency were born female descendants such as Janis Ian or Bobbie Gentry (each of whom has produced one, and only one, good song—and who may be forgotten or immortal by the time this is read) and the trio of Supremes. Unlike their "grandparents," all of these groups, plus some twenty other fairly good ones, write most of their own material, thus combining the traditions of 12th-century troubadours, 16th-century madrigalists, and 18th-century musical artisans who were always composer-performers—in short, combining all sung expression (except opera) as it was before the twentieth century.

Why are the Beatles superior? It is easy to say that most of their competition (like most everything everywhere) is junk; more important, their betterness is consistent: each of the songs from their last three albums is memorable. The best of these memorable tunes—and the best is a large percentage ("Here, There and Everywhere," "Good Day Sunshine," "Michelle," "Norwegian Wood" are already classics)—compare with those by composers from great eras of song: Monteverdi, Schumann, Poulenc.

Good melody—even perfect melody—can be both defined and taught, as indeed can the other three "dimensions" of music: rhythm, harmony, counterpoint (although rhythm is the only one that can exist alone). Melody may be described thus: a series of notes of varying pitch and length, which evolve into a recognizable musical shape. In the case of a melody (*tune* means the same thing) which is set to words, the musical line will flow in curves relating to the verse that propels it inevitably toward a "high" point, usually called climax, and thence to the moment of culmination. The *inevitable* element is what makes the melody good—or perfect. But perfection can be sterile, as witness the thousands of 32-bar models turned out yesterday in Tin Pan Alley, or today by, say, Jefferson Airplane. Can we really recall such tunes when divorced from their words?

Superior melody results from the same recipe, with the difference that certain of the ingredients are blessed with the Distortion of Genius. The Beatles' words often go against the music (the crushing poetry that opens "A Day in the Life" intoned to the blandest of tunes), even as Martha Graham's music often contradicts her dance (she gyrates hysterically to utter silence, or stands motionless while all hell breaks loose in the pit). Because the Beatles pervert with naturalness they usually build solid structures, whereas their rivals pervert with affectation, aping the gargoyles but not the cathedral.

The unexpected in itself, of course, is no virtue, though all great works seem to contain it. For instance, to cite as examples only the above four songs: "Here, There, and Everywhere" would seem at midhearing to be no more than a charming college show ballad, but once concluded it has grown immediately memorable. Why? Because of the minute harmonic shift on the words "wave of her hand," as surprising, yet as satisfyingly *right* as that in a Monteverdi madrigal like "A un giro sol." The notation of the hyper-exuberant rhythms in "Good Day Sunshine" was as aggravatingly elusive to me as some by Charles Ives, until I realized it was made by *triplets over the bar;* the "surprise" here was that the Beatles had made so simple a process *sound* so complex to a professional ear, and yet (by a third convolution) be instantly imitable by any amateur "with a beat." "Michelle" changes key on the very second measure (which is also the second word): in itself this is "allowed"— Poulenc often did it, and certainly he was the most derivative and correct composer who ever lived; the point is that he *chose* to do it on just the second measure, and that the choice worked. Genius doesn't lie in not being derivative, but in making right choices instead of wrong ones. As for "Norwegian Wood," again it is the arch of the tune—a movement growing increasingly disjunct, an inverted pyramid formed by a zigzag—which proves the song unique and memorable, rather than merely original.

Newness per se has never been the basis—or even especially an ingredient—of the Beatles' work. On the contrary, they have revitalized music's basics (harmony, counterpoint, rhythm, melody) by using them again in the simplest manner, a manner directed away from intellectualism and toward the heart. The Beatles' instrumentation may superficially sound far-out, but it apes the flashier element of electronic background no more advanced than the echo-chamber sound tracks of 1930s horror movies. Their "newest" thing is probably a kind of prosodic liberty; their rendition—their *realization*—often sounds contrary to the verses' predictable look on paper. Yet even at that, are they much different from our definitive songwriters of the past? From Purcell, say, or Debussy? It is not in their difference but in their betterness that their superiority lies.

But their betterness is not always apparent. Again, like Stravinsky, they are already classifiable with retrospective periods. Inasmuch as they try to surpass or even consciously to redefine themselves with each period, they fail, as they mostly have with their *Magical Mystery Tour*. This isn't surprising with persons so public and hence so vulnerable. But where, from this almost complacent "civilization," can they go from here?

Well, where does any artist go? Merely on. Still, it should now be clear that they are not the sum of their parts, but four distinct entities. Paul, I guess, is a genius with tunes; though what, finally, is genius without training? John, it seems, is no less clever than James Joyce; though where, ultimately, can that lead, when he is no *more* clever? George, they say, has brought East to West; but what, really, can that prove, when even Kipling realized it's not the twain of deeds but of concepts which never seem to meet? And Ringo, to at least one taste, is cute as a bug; though anyone, actually, can learn quick to play percussion, as our own George Plimpton now is demonstrating.

We've become so hung up on what they *mean,* we can no longer hear what they're performing. Nor was Beethoven ever so Freudianized.

Just as twenty years ago one found oneself reading more books about Kafka than reading Kafka himself, so today one gets embarrassed at being overheard in deep discussion of the Beatles. I love them. But I love them not as symbolic layers of "the scene" (or whatever it's called), and even less as caricatures of themselves (which, like Mae West, they're inclined to become). I love them as the hearty barbaric troubadours they essentially are. As such I hope they will continue to develop, together or apart, for they represent the most invigorating music of an era so civilized that it risks extinction less from fallout than from boredom.

1968

Edith Piaf and Billie Holiday

I arrived in Paris nineteen years ago, the day world champion Marcel Cerdan was killed in a plane crash. The same crash claimed violinist Ginette Neveu, and these two idols, different as night from day, were mourned together.

The French love their intellectual and popular heroes, and are loyal to both without distinguishing much between them. The humblest concierge, while he may identify more with the sagas of Fernandel, is proud to cite Debussy or Balzac; he may not know their works but he'll name a street for them. Culture was never a dirty word in Europe; in America the rare genuinely accepted culture heroes, as embodied in a Hemingway or an Orson Welles, were known for their *bon vivantisme* and not for what their art represented. In those good old 1940s, as in the days of Louis Quatorze, all France was aware of the privacy of her most public citizens. When Americans were not allowed then to consider their statesmen as having mistresses (or worse), the French followed with relish and approbation the anxieties and bedroom triumphs of the great. (Today, with de Gaulle and the Kennedys, the situation is somewhat reversed.)

So two masters, one of the boxing ring, the other of the concert stage, were conjointly lamented, as later Colette and Mistinguett would be, Gide and Louis Jouvet, Poulenc and Gérard Philipe. And on that awful October Friday of 1963 when Jean Cocteau and Edith Piaf fell dead, hand in hand so to speak, the rule was ironically reaffirmed. Cocteau, a jack-of-all-higher-trades, had been the esoteric darling of the elite. Piaf, a specialist of commoner emotions, had been the pathetic oracle of the workingman. Yet Cocteau had composed monologues for Piaf who, in turn, was Cerdan's mistress at the time of the boxer's death. Which brought the unhappy family about full circle.

At the time of my arrival Piaf was becoming her country's official widow. Humor, never her strong point, now utterly quit the repertory as her every private moan swelled into a public dirge, a culminating dirge of such importance that, despite the continuing New York heat of today, I'd like, before discussing other past and present French singers, to set their stage with this particular woman, my first and longest continental infatuation, *la môme*—as her countrymen called her—the little sparrow.

She was the greatest popular singer produced by France in this century. Of the genre she became an apex, and as such proved—while remaining utterly French—an exception to the French practice of nonspecialization.

The genre, of course, was the troubadour epic which ultimately evolved into the naturalistic *fin de siècle* café-concert narrations of Yvette Guilbert, a sort of contralto whose piquant physique was glorified by Lautrec as early as 1890, and whose bizarre vocality she herself engraved on wax as late as the mid-thirties. (But she died in only 1944, seven years after our Bessie Smith. Why, some of us could have known her!)

Piaf became an apex in that she stemmed directly from Guilbert, through Damia, and like those ladies used song successfully—at least for a time—as a weapon against life. Sharpening their best qualities into a perfect arrow, she pierced the hearts of literally all ensuing Parisian stylists, female and male, except maybe the late French rock crop who aren't really very French.

The utter Frenchness of Piaf came, negatively, through avoidance of Americanisms. If her accompaniments sometimes did insist on a Harlemesque "beat" plus an occasional saxophone (though let's not forget: the saxophone was invented in France a century ago), mostly her orchestrations emulated the oh-so-Latin accordions of the neighborhood *bal musette*. (Incidentally, France's "serious" composers, who always deemed Negro jazz the sole American product worth acknowledging, never managed, from Ravel to Milhaud, more than a translation of the outer trappings into their pristine counterfeits. But then in turn, we never found the key to their kitchen. Like cooking, music is not a universal language.) More positively, Edith Piaf's Frenchness came through the kind of tale she told. If Chevalier at eighty is still (understandably) his nation's official optimist, Piaf, during her forty-four brief years of consoling the urban underdog, represented the *grande pathétique*. Her verses spoke of love fermenting into murder, then of redemption and of love's return in heaven. They spoke of Sunday fairs in the squalid Vincennes park as reward for the barmaid's six-day week. They spoke of injustice in Pigalle's underworld—what Parisians call *le milieu*. They told also, like Jerome Kern's song *Bill*, of life sustained through fidelity to the unfaithful, but, unlike *Bill*, that life was prolonged more through words than music. More as *littérateuse* than as *musicienne* is the sparrow recalled today, as she was applauded in her prime.

As for evading the rule of nonspecialist, Piaf was indeed forever one-track-minded. The concentration made her unique. No *auteur compositeur*, she executed what others (mainly her friend Marguerite Monnot) created so accurately around her private experience of resigned—and not so resigned—distress. This she reexperienced publicly through the *chanson*, an art traditionally depicting city rather than rural problems through a form as valid as (and older than) the recital song as realized by Duparc, say, or Hugo Wolf. Of course, being famous, she was frequently called upon to reenact her number within trumped-up tales for theatre and screen, though she never brought it off. Whatever her number, it was not versatility.

This morning I played some early Ethel Merman records, alternating them with Piaf, and with another old and faithful love, Billie Holiday.

Merman belted solely as a technique: she was objective where Piaf was personal. Piaf could belt like Merman, but she melted Merman's brass into the pathos of Holiday.

In more ways than one Edith paralleled Billie. Professionally, though highly mannered vocally (manners, after all, are what make the great great, great being the quality of the inimitably imitable), neither had the least *mannerism* in stage comportment. They just stood there and sang, each in her invariable costume: for Billie the coiffed gardenia, for Edith the simple black dress. Oh, in moments of high emphasis Holiday might close her eyes, while Piaf would slightly raise an arm, as Lenya does, with the tragic simplicity that crumbles mountains; beyond that, nothing—nothing but the immutability of projection. They never "put over" a song other than through the song itself, a lesson our Tony Bennett or Johnny Mathis—to name but two—could nicely heed, inasmuch as they've learned more from women vocalists than from men.

Their personal lives intertwined as well, like Baudelaire's with Poe's, though they may never have heard of each other. Both emerged from the *bas fonds*, Piaf as blind adolescent crooning for pennies in suburban alleys, Holiday as pubescent Baltimore Oriole working the bars of Lenox Avenue. Both their repertories forever featured those youthful and apparently continuing hardships, though Billie became a millionaire and Edith's eventual bridesmaid was Marlene Dietrich. From first to last, though sometimes wealthy and all times beloved, both were victimized and exploited, as is ever the case with simple addicted geniuses whose hearts rule their heads. Both sank back into publicized poverty. Then both perished, early and accidentally, in the icy light of abject stardom.

Lotte Lenya

We Americans have no history of popular singers performing successfully in any language but their own. Nor, unlike the English, have
we any convincing bilingual actors. But the Weimar Republic did produce three chanteuses (only the French have a word for it) seemingly
as much at home in English as in their native tongue: Marlene Dietrich, Greta Keller, and Lotte Lenya. Since I don't know German, I'm no
final judge of these women as being actually stronger in their adopted
language, like Conrad and Dinesen and Nabokov who lent new dimensions to English. I do know that I thrill to them more in their guttural
Berlinese. Poulenc told me, after I proudly showed him a setting of
Ronsard, "Stick to American and leave French to us. You have too much
wonderful poetry to be dabbling in what we can do better." The advice sinks ever deeper as time flows by, and unlike Lenya, I was never
obliged to praise the Lord in a strange land.

Even among classical singers there is probably no genuine multi-
linguality. But if in stance and diction classical singers have much to
learn from pop singers (Bernac claimed to have gleaned more from
Maurice Chevalier than from any "concert artist"; and I myself, because

it was in the air, filched for my vocal writing the lilt and ebb of Billie Holiday's whine no less than the clean sweep of Schumann or Chabrier), God keep us from Grace Moore's hip descendants with a right to sing the blues—there is a difference *in kind*. And there is a difference in kind between overseas and home pop. When Lenya mouths the puns of Ira Gershwin, I cringe no less than when Balanchine stages the tunes of George Gershwin. To miss the point is not necessarily to be dumb, but Europeans don't swing.

During the 1950s I lived in what was maybe the most marvelous house in Paris, chez la Vicomtesse de Noailles, known to everyone as Marie-Laure. Exactly twenty-one years my senior (having been born on Halloween in 1902), Marie-Laure was a woman of fame, fortune, intelligence, power, and of eccentric handsomeness in the style of— well, look at the portrait by Balthus from whence she gazes at you with the candor of a naughty feline and whose startingly high forehead is framed by a Louis XIV coiffure. Herself a painter and poet of real gift, she was also no less an artist's patron than Misia, and much richer. With her spouse, Charles, Vicomte de Noailles, she was responsible during the late 1920s for, among other masterpieces, the movies of Dali and Buñuel. When, because of the young couple's sponsorship of *L'Age d'Or* the Vicomte was threatened with expulsion from not only the Holy Church but, far worse, from the Jockey Club, he decided to spend the rest of his days as a gentleman gardener, retaining Marie-Laure as fond friend and co-parent of two daughters but allowing her to lead her own—as he termed it—bohemian life.

Like so many visual and literary people Marie-Laure was not especially musical, but she loved, quite literally, musicians. How many major musical works would never have been heard but for Marie-Laure, works not only of the *petit cercle*—Poulenc, Auric, Markevitch, Sauguet—but of "foreigners," too! For instance, Kurt Weill.

In the spring of 1951, among the piles of inscribed scores by Britten, Rieti, Nabokov, et cetera, atop the white piano in Marie-Laure's ballroom, I found a dog-eared black-and-white piece called *Der Jasager* on the flyleaf of which appeared this phrase in india ink: *"Dem Grafen und der Gräfin de Noailles in Dankbarkeit für die ausgezeichnete aufführung 'Des Jasagers,'"* signed "Kurt Weill." I understood no word of this, nor of the text of the brief opera, which week after week I played on the white piano with love and awe. Few other pieces had struck me so fast and left me so long with their nourishing wounds—*Les Noces, L'Enfant, Socrate, Les Biches, La Mer,* what else? And *Jasager* alone among them was German. The music seemed sophisticated and savage, yes, but what was it *about*—children's games? Romantic love? War and hope? Indeed, is music, with or without words, "about" anything? I kept the score (coveted to this day), but it was not until 1953, when musicologist Marcel Schneider gave me a blow-by-blow translation into French, that I comprehended the hard-boiled parable, thus to admire further Weill's sly and touching setting.

Danny Kaye was, I suppose, my first connection, if not to Weill himself, at least to *Lady in the Dark,* with that crazy 78-rpm of "Jenny" and "Tchaikovsky" in 1940 when such canny upcoming composers as we in Chicago thought—how wrongly!—more about who performed than who wrote the music we were catching on to. Four years later when we had all relocated to the magic of Manhattan, it was still not so much to Weill as to Sono Osato dancing that I responded to *One Touch of Venus.* In 1944 Lys Bert (now Symonette), the first soprano ever to sing my songs in public, was working in *The Firebrand,* which she coaxed me to attend "because Lotte Lenya, who is married to the composer, is a wonderful singer and you have a lot to learn." But if the Black blues singers I'd been raised on had conditioned me to the straight vocal attacks that fan out into tearful vibratos, I was dismayed by Lenya's continual and suspiciously European glottal quiver. In high school we had accepted Marlene Dietrich's eerie baritone without flinching, but Lenya would take getting used to.

Lenya had more voice than Dietrich, less than Keller, but of course none of them had the "trained" voice improper to their repertory. She could carry a tune, she could "interpret," and like the grandest pop singers—Piaf, for example, or even Peggy Lee—she could put over a song through understatement, standing there in a little black dress, projecting the words, the *words,* eyes closed, hardly moving, the way Chinese actors hardly move except to lift a hand slowly as a mountain crumbles.

Chinese is just how her pinched soprano sounded on the disc Marie-Laure played of "Alabama Song," and the 1929 orchestra too had a rickshaw tilt. Mosquito-ish was the international timbre of all chanteuses (canaries, they were called) until the torch song of the 1930s lowered their range by an octave. For the 1960 *Mahagonny* recording Lenya becomes an alto, though retaining her role of Jenny, while Gisela Litz as Begbick slides off pitch on every note. Is this more "authentic," or less, than the old days? Hear now the gorgeous English vocalists in the 1975 DG recording. Their expertise shocks. Yet their understatement in its control has come to sound more necessary than the German singers' randomness, bringing tears to the eyes through an instrumental ensemble possessing both higher brute force and tenderer nuance.

Sure, tradition spawns tradition. But recordings can also show the gradual corrosion of tradition that the greatest music seems to withstand. (Never mind that modern gesellschaft renditions might sound like Greek to Bach himself.) Lenya sings from the horse's mouth, and oh, the fresh air she lets into a song! Yet is she, even in German, forever perfection? Observe her attack on the last word *blau*—sounding as two syllables—in the *Matrosen-Song,* as though overstruck with the amateur's last-ditch doubt that she might not have "sold" the tune. Consult then the lyrics in the Columbia booklet and see that (as a cover-up?) the word is printed *blau-au.* That reemphasis is absent from DG's booklet where the same lyrics are reprinted for Meriel Dickinson. Dickinson *is* perfect. Her perfection is based on Lenya's imperfection.

Indeed, Lenya is the model against whom all female pretenders will be appraised. Teresa Stratas' voice is ravishing and wise, to be sure, but has nothing to do with Weill. The well-focused genteel subtleties contradict Weill's admonishment to his wife: "Don't study it, it will spoil your musicality."

Lenya's career thrived for thirty years almost solely on interpretations of Weill's music. If it is idle to gauge what Weill's current status might be without the posthumous luck of a Lenya (Lenya, like Garbo or Misia, became a legend on a single proper name), one can safely conjecture that Weill's style, at least in the vocal music, will forever be colored by Lenya's style. If in America he had used her sparingly but regularly, as Fellini used Giullietta Masina, would his posthumous career have emerged otherwise? Well, Lenya the re-creator (unlike creators whose youth is "as good as") only grew into her myth with age, and her late timbre was more interesting than her early. Like Alice Toklas, Lenya needed widowhood to sanctify her love.

Marie-Laure died in 1970. The last time I was in Paris her marvelous house stood as it had for years, hollow and vast and dark in the Place des États-Unis, awaiting the wreckers. No wild Weillian strains wafted forth from the haunted casements, ah no! But Weill is heard ad nauseam all over Paris now, as he is heard around the world. I would like to believe that his popularity gained as much momentum from the early push of my dear friend as from Lenya, even though Weill is today in the position toward which all dead composers aspire, of being able to take care of himself.

1983

Opera Past, Present, and Future

A gift for song and a gift for opera are not interchangeable. How many songs do you know by Verdi or Puccini or Menotti, or even by Wagner? How many operas can you name by Wolf or Fauré or Chanler, or even by Schubert? True, some composers—think of Britten and Poulenc and maybe Virgil Thomson—are happy in both fields, but they are exceptions. A song is made in one sitting, in one breath; an opera is stitched together over many months. A song cannot have padding; an opera has almost nothing but. Opera, no matter how poetic, is mainly prose; Song, no matter how prosaic, is mainly poetry. Opera—at least what's come to be named Bel Canto—is more about singing than what's sung, while Song is an emanation of a text wherein the interpretor's ego vanishes. Because, like most song-makers, I am interested in raw music more than in its performance, I have never been comfortable with the opera medium, much less am I a buff. An opera is not a song-cycle; the chief concern for its composer is not sonic but dramatic: how will he (or she—for many of our leading composers today are women) get this or that character from point A to point Z without boring the audience.

Opera and Song are both bastards, insofar as they both mate two forms, words and music, which never asked to be mated. The process, by its very "illegitimacy," can produce healthy progeny as the inter-breeding of races always does, although Song is a child of economy and taste, while Opera is born of strength and silliness. A successful opera symbolizes for the song composer what hit plays do for poets: major acclaim by non-specialized theatergoers. But a failed opera carries a far more paralyzing after-effect than a failed song cycle. Outside invest-ments are too great. If at first you do not succeed at opera don't try again: the world will not permit you to be burned twice.

Confusion about American opera: outwardly we react as though it were European, inwardly we wish it to conform to our indigenous musical comedy.

European opera comes from experimental composers, Monteverdi and Purcell, Wagner and Mussorgsky, Berg and Henze. Diverted by visual tales their audience swallows without flinching that which, par-taken in concert, provokes nausea.

American opera comes from non-experimental composers. Our Bab-bitts and Cages and Carters never flirt with the form; our Floyds and Blitzsteins and Moores concentrate on the form exclusively, with a terseness of language that resembles the revue, yet with a scale of co-hesiveness that resembles grand opera.

Significantly, *The Rake's Progress*, Stravinsky's only opera composed during his United States residence, and his only extended work in En-glish, represents, in its diatonic pasticheries, the most accessible piece in his catalogue.

The sole difference today between American opera and musical comedy (which can be tragedy too, as *Show Boat* showed thirty years be-fore *West Side Story*) is that one uses conservatory-trained voices while the other uses microphone-trained voices.

The first American opera worthy of the name is Virgil Thomson's *Four Saints in Three Acts*, finished in 1928 on Gertrude Stein's text and Maurice Grosser's scenario, but not produced until 1933.

Why is *Four Saints* so American? Because Stein spent her life (as

Henry James did) perceiving herself as American, *being* American and exemplifying this on her terms with the clarity that only the distance of expatriatism could provide; because her word sequences, with their redundant nursery slang, possessed a colloquial diction that could only have sprung from the United States; because Virgil took this declamation and musicalized it intact with no Romantic elongations and no melisma; and because the tunes he used—his privately concocted folksong, if you wish—sprang from the plain unsensual churchly ditties of his Midwestern youth.

Is it subject matter alone, or treatment of subject matter, that makes an opera national? To hear *Don Giovanni* in Paris is to hear music by an Austrian about Spaniards composed in Italian but sung in French for Swedish tourists. Still, Mozart's national frontiers are apparent in the waltzes, slow and fast, teeming everywhere. (Did waltzes connote then what they did fifty years later?) Is it inapt to cite work from two centuries ago when composers from all countries used similar languages—or seemed to from our vantage, now that the radical edges are blurred? Well, Schoenberg too was Austrian, and his *Moses and Aaron* too teems with waltzes, yet it is hardly ballroom music, and was mostly composed in America. The text, of course, is nothing if not Jewish, and one cannot imagine a gentile being urged, as Schoenberg so desperately was, to use it. Still, generalities backfire. If Darius Milhaud, Schoenberg's sole Jewish contemporary in France, was also drawn to an Old Testament story, *David*, for a major opera, so was the anti-Semite Florent Schmitt with his *Salomé*, and the Huguenot Honegger—who was actually Swiss—with his *Judith*, a subject used again by the current gentile German, Siegfried Matthus. Mostly, though, the French stuck to Greek tragedy as updated by Cocteau, or kept safely within their borders, like Poulenc in all three of his operas, which are the best to come from modern France. Meanwhile, of the twenty-eight operas by Verdi, the ultimate Italian, only one is on an originally Italian text.

The game on our shores requires three considerations: the composer's style, his nationality, his subject. The subject of the "Indian" operas of yore was American with a vengeance as were the composers, but their language was European. The librettos to Copland's two operas are by and about Americans (Edward Denby wrote *The Second Hurricane*, dealing with high school kids lost on a picnic, and Eric Johns wrote *The Tender Land*, dealing with small-town romance), while of Thomson's three operas only one, *The Mother of Us All* (also on a Stein text), deals in Americana. *Four Saints* is Spanish, and the third opera, *Lord Byron*, libretto by Jack Larson of California, takes place in London. Raffaello de Banfield, the Triestine musician, also wrote, in English, a Lord Byron opera based on a Tennessee Williams playlet set in the New Orleans French Quarter around 1900; the tale is genteel-Southern but the soaring score is in the Cilea dialect. Will the real American please stand up!

My musical education, like everyone else's of my time, was equal parts classical and pop (or swing, as it was termed). My vocal writing was more influenced by Billie Holiday—not the tunes, but her way with the tunes—than by any famous diva. Did I *know* any divas? Opera, insofar as it was about singing per se, never interested me. Opera buffs, by and large, are not practicing musicians, or if they are, they are not composers. I was less drawn to singing than what was being sung, less drawn to what was being sung than to what the poetry imparted. Young composers in America today, like yesterday and the day before, aren't raised in standard opera, don't listen to it except as an extension of some 20th-century composer—Britten, Berg—or as a lesson in theatricality. Bel Canto is not despised, it is ignored.

As for *Miss Julie*, it is the only one of my five that's based on a foreign play. The others, all one-acters, are on words of Gertrude Stein, Kenneth Koch, Marianne Moore (after La Fontaine), Elliott Stein (after Hawthorne).

And in the 1980s? Philip Glass is something of a law unto himself. Music is not a universal language (play Mozart or Madonna for a Malayan or a moujik and see where you get), but Glass does aim for a sonic

Esperanto. His plots are hardly along the line of boy-meets-girl; rather, abetted by Robert Wilson, he has made himself into an Egyptian Virgil Thomson, with triadic *faux naif* ostinatos that echo Kansas while illustrating exotica. The only other operatic "minimalist" is John Adams whose *Nixon in China* is American to the teeth and financially successful. *The Death of Klinghoffer* would appear to be less of a contrast—a political gesture—than a sequel; and while one could have hoped for an about-face (a soaper like Fanny Hurst's *Imitation of Life,* perhaps), one awaits a U.S. hearing before drawing conclusions. The third official minimalist, Steve Reich, doesn't write operas, although his interminable vamping on 1930s pop harmonies might benefit from simultaneous visuals. David Del Tredici doesn't write operas either, but has spent his career transforming the oeuvre of the 19th-century Englishman Lewis Carroll into a twenty-hour tantrum which, despite an overlay of Mahler, is in its childishness deeply (or shallowly) American, and essentially operatic.

John Corigliano played his opera for me the other night—all four hours of it—and I was not bored for one second by its troubling, odd, sumptuous, skillful, contrasting, vast, and daring noises. The fast music, often *pasticheuse,* is inherently, kinetically, rewardingly fast, and the slow music heaves and surges with a knack that can't be faked or borrowed: true melody. No other composer today, except the ghost of Britten, possesses the gift of the *grande ligne* as naturally as John. In fact, ghosts are the stars of his very singable opera, which is based, as Milhaud's last opera in 1964 was based, on Beaumarchais's *La Mère Coupable.* Figaro, Marie Antoinette, and others are specters two centuries after the fact, observing how, for reasons of love, history might be rewritten. Or something—the story's overly complex and (to me) confused as realized by William Hoffman. Since Hoffman's play *As is* six years ago was a major statement, political and poetical, on the AIDS crisis, and since Corigliano's recent symphony is referred to by him as "an AIDS symphony," one wonders that the pair haven't written a more contemporaneous opera.

And one wonders why Tobias Picker, who has also written an expansive "AIDS symphony," should choose for his opera-in-the-works Judith (*Looking for Mr. Goodbar*) Rossner's *Emmeline,* a tale of nineteenth-century incest and the social cruelty that ensures. Will no one ever compose an unapologetic romance between two men? or two women? A setting of Genet perhaps, or of Forster's *Maurice,* or of Colette's *La Seconde?* Other than Britten's *Death in Venice,* and the role of Geshwitz in *Lulu,* are there any major references in opera to the love that dare not speak its name? Rarely by Americans, certainly, excepting Lou Harrison's incomplete puppet drama, *Young Caesar,* and Leonard Bernstein's *A Quiet Place.*

Young artists will justify anything they make by stating that art must reflect the times. They don't yet realize that any work of art, good or bad, reflects the times simply by virtue of inhabiting the times; that all times are chaotic; and that art *is* the times, by definition, which is why art, no matter how political its intent, cannot change the times. And which is why modernizing the past is mere desperation: it can't win.

I admire Peter Sellars's staging of *Nixon in China;* he and the composer breathe the same air. I sympathize, however, with those many who find his Mozart stagings *de trop.* What no one mentions in this dichotomy of motives is what most protrudes from the TV screen in *The Marriage of Figaro.* Mozart's plotting, with the set pieces and recitatives, runs according to leisurely and stylized 18th-century conventions—conventions which he himself established, moreover. Present-day comportment, on stage as in the street, moves faster and with less guile. To see well-off yuppies in the laundry of a skyscraper, forced by the music's pacing to stand still while intoning, in Italian, their formalized woes and joys, runs counter to both our and Mozart's metabolism. It's neither witty nor surrealist, it's dull.

But wait. Are Sellars's tamperings a betrayal (if that's the word) of Mozart? Are they not rather a betrayal of Da Ponte? Close your eyes and the music remains intact. Thus, the oft-heard analogy that what modernizing directors visit on a Mozart opera equates what conductors might visit on a Mozart symphony via a Moog synthesizer is a false analogy. Symphonies, if you will, are legitimate, while operas—like songs—are bastards. I have never set a poem to music without feeling like an interloper: who am I (or who is Schumann or Ravel, for that matter?) to take this poem of Sappho, of Emily Dickinson, of Elizabeth Bishop—perfect artworks quite capable of standing alone—and presume to lend it some new and needed dimension? Yet I do it anyway. If the poet is alive, he/she is usually both flattered and miffed by the resultant song which, no matter how workable from a singer's viewpoint (or earpoint), can never correspond to the poet's own inner music. A librettist, of course, unlike a poet, generally works in conjunction with a composer. Still, there are unlimited ways of staging a libretto while leaving the music intact. (So maybe we should ask Da Ponte how he feels.) But isn't there a point of no return, in staging, and hasn't Sellars—at least with classical operas—passed that point?

What kind of American opera *should* be composed now, assuming questions of morality are at stake (and they always are during droughts)? With assembly-line pop glutting the market on the one hand, inexpert avant-gardism-turned-commercial on the other, while in between the Bernstein *Mass* combines all elements of an essentially non-narrative ceremony, not advancing thereby, but reverting to pre-verismo musical theatrics, is there room for a just-plain opera?

The art of music is quiescent, like latent sanity. The reasons will never be clear, art has no reasons. But it is clear that since new languages won't rescue music, then all we need is a statement by a great man in whatever language he happens to speak. America has yet to come up with a conservative opera composer laureate like England's Britten. There have been contenders, from Deems Taylor to Douglas Moore, and recently a crop of hopefuls (Pasatieri, Hoiby, Coe). It is not the plainness of their music that seems dated, for pop is still plainer but utterly current; it is their soapy librettos that defeat them.

Art hurts. To select a predecessor as model is neither right nor wrong. But works by these hopefuls are identifiable only as Menotti's grandchildren. Though they are still young, their drama already creaks, while their melody winds its elegant way without a tragic flaw. If art is by nature beautiful, it must be ugly too. Any work of stature is battle-scarred. The main thing wrong with Menotti's grandchildren is that there is nothing wrong with them.

Future opera will be cultured Esperanto; not a new musical tongue but an amalgamation of tongues intoning literary works. Indeed, let a composer take some thirty-odd texts from Hawthorne and Dickinson to Ashbery and Purdy. Let him set them, in any order and for any combination of voices, forgetting his sense of consecutive urgency. Let him then trust these songs and choruses to a director who will superimpose a scenario dictated by tonal rises and falls. Let the composer allow visuals that enhance the sound rather than distract from it (a motionless trio singing Sidney Lanier on a distant platform, a quintet of baritones gliding in five slow directions as they chant Kenneth Koch). He will then have created a high-class version of the revue, and sooner or later he will give you, through these distillations, the great American opera.

Ravel

If my house were on fire and I could take only three records, they would all be *L'Enfant et les sortilèges*, the most beautiful music ever written. Yes, *Pelléas* and *Sacre* and *Wozzeck*, when I first heard them in adolescence, forever changed my state of mind. But Ravel's masterpiece changed my state of body. It became the one work which most overtly influenced my own, and which, in some far corner of my being, I have listened to every day of my life.

What we learn as children we question without question. That Ravel's music was standoffish, elegant, well made, and casual I took as fact, like the Oedipus complex or T. S. Eliot's genius, wondering uneasily why that special sound entered me like a heady draft of carnality throttling my Quaker frame to dwell on love and the pursuit of happiness.

It was in the summer of 1936 that I first heard him, on the antimacassared upright in Oberlin, Ohio. While kohlrabi fumes floated from the pantry, my cousin Kathleen performed the *Sonatine*, which awakened me forever. Thinking the composer's name was Reville, I could locate no more of his music.

By 1937 I knew the spelling plus every work on record. I'd even begun composing a bit of Ravel myself. On December 28 of that year, a Tuesday brimming with sunshine, Father (I still picture him there on the sofa) read aloud from the Chicago *Tribune:* FRENCH COMPOSER DIES. (His name didn't yet merit a headline.) Gershwin had gone that summer. Now this. Moved, I sat down and played the *Pavane.* "How obvious," snorted a fourteen-year-old pal when I told him later.

Ravel was born in 1875 of solvent and understanding parents in the village of Ciboure near the Spanish frontier. These few facts color all that he became. His art straddled the border as it straddled centuries, being in texture as opulent as a tourist's notion of Iberia, in shape as pristine as Rameau, in intent no less modern than ragas or group therapy, and in subject matter mostly antiromantic. Listen again to *Boléro.* ("It's my masterpiece," said the composer. "Unfortunately it contains no music.") French logic drenched in Basque mystery.

Like Minerva he emerged full blown. Like Chopin he did not "advance," have periods, grow more complex. He entered the world with the true artist's faculty for self-appraisal, and all his life wrote the same kind of music, consistently good. His sonorous stories never grazed grownup matters except in parody (licentious doings in *L'Heure espagnole*) or from a safe distance (slave revolt in *Chansons madécasses*). Otherwise he stayed close to home, which is to say, close to the nonsexual side of Colette (the librettist of *L'Enfant*). Nor did he ever, save for a brief minute in the early song *Sainte* on a poem by Mallarmé, musicalize even a quasi-religious verse: the gods forbid such breach of taste.

Influences we avow are, of course, the conscious ones—those we're sure don't show. Once assimilated, the property becomes ours. Magnanimously we admit the theft, safely knowing that no one detects the original beneath our paint. (Unconscious influence alone is damning.) Thus Ravel announces Saint-Saëns, Schubert, Mozart as his progenitors. Who would guess it?

His influence on others? On Poulenc it is obvious, though no one ever points out the harmonic progression of three chords in Ravel's

L'Indifférent (1905) pilfered intact fifty years later to form the motto of Poulenc's *Dialogues des Carmélites*. More interestingly no one ever points out the cadenza for two clarinets in Ravel's *Rapsodie espagnole* (1908), pilfered intact three years later to form the motto for Stravinsky's *Petrouchka* ballet. That bitonal *Petrouchka* sound outlined Stravinsky's harmony for the next decade, and by extension most Western music for the next half century, yet the sound demonstrably stems from a few casual bars in the French musician's pseudo-Spanish idiom.

He evolutionized keyboard virtuosity more than anyone since Liszt, yet his complete solo piano works fit comfortably into one evening's program.

In his sixty-two years Ravel, who worked constantly, didn't turn out more than eight hours' worth of music, as contrasted with Debussy's sixteen, Beethoven's thirty, Wagner's fifty, Bach's seventy, Ives's two thousand, or Webern's two. Of those eight hours none is slipshod or routine. Not that he was a miniaturist; he was a perfectionist. So was Bach a perfectionist—different times, different mores—but a page of Ravel's orchestration is twenty times busier than a page of Bach's. (Still, since Stravinsky was twice as busy as Ravel, yet twice as prolific, we draw no conclusions.)

He was a classicist, yes, sometimes, in those square-structured suites, concertos, and pastiches with their recapitulations and so-called symmetrical melodies. (Symmetrical is a poor word, since time cannot have symmetry.) But so many other pieces are truly impressionist— all of *Gaspard de la nuit,* most of *Miroirs,* many of the straight orchestra numbers (though none of the thirty-three songs, curiously, since songs, being based on words, are by definition musically free). Such pieces are not so much heard as overheard, come upon, already transpiring before they start, evanescent. Made solely of middles, without beginnings or ends, they emerge from nowhere, from a mist, trouble us for a dazzling while, then without notice vanish like Scarbo, fade like Ondine. Any of these sparklers could be convincing shorter or convincing longer, for they have been spinning always and will always continue, though within human earshot only for those fugitive minutes.

Ravel's signatures are harmony and tune. His melodies are based on and emerge from chords. His identity (like Puccini's) lies in long line. For me, the revelation of *L'Enfant* lay in spaciousness, in sovereign melody. The notion of Modern Music in the 1940s tended toward the spare; Stravinsky and Copland, out of Nadia Boulanger and Debussy, eschewed *la grande ligne* in favor of motives, figures, frugal staples. Behold Maurice Ravel's cornucopia of tunes, tunes, tunes — of song without guilt. No two measures of his hour-long piece are barren of purposeful melody. From the outset a pair of malignant oboes twines around a high-pitched double-bass as the mezzo whines: three different-colored threads braided firmly, only to loosen into the Mother's theme (that falling fourth!) which in turn swells into the Boy's sequence of shrieks — each shriek a tune, not an "effect." The shrieks then dissipate into the frightful yet protecting dream where inanimate objects like teacups and armchairs sing songs as sad and silly as those we ourselves made up in the cradle.

Such logical elisions are of a born tunesmith who is also a Theater Man. Listen again as the Shepherds with their blue dog peel themselves from the nursery wallpaper in a two-part canon as touching as a Gluck ballet. Listen as the coloratura Fire, almost quenched by rippling clarinets, flows through the harp to the golden-haired Princess, and how she with her moon-colored flute becalms the recalcitrant child who then utters ("in a half-voice," the composer marks it) the famous Air which is close, but not too close for comfort, to Puccini's "Un bel dì." Listen to the Dragonfly Interlude as both choirs of unison violins weave a seamless never ending, ever shifting rainbow over a still more gorgeous new-forming melody of Frogs. Listen to the notorious Cat Duet (and invite your own cats: mine react wildly) which, though formed of screeches, is screeching to the gentlest theme of *La Valse*. And listen to the final six-part madrigal as it graduates into a curving cantilena like a caterpillar edging along a silky rope toward that pair of oboes, benign now, which have returned to say good-bye. Alone this ending, like the ending of Britten's *War Requiem* which springs from it, will have carried Maurice Ravel through the gates of Paradise.

Poulenc

If musical greatness, as Rimbaud claimed, is exclusive of innovation, then Francis Poulenc was a genius. If real artists, as Radiguet claimed, have their own voice and so need only to copy to prove their individuality, then Poulenc dignified the crime of plagiarism. And no composer of the past century, the only century in which originality was ever equated—by peasant and poet alike—with quality, was less concerned than Poulenc with originality.

Originality is a hollow virtue; everything's new under the sun. If to be novel were to be fresh and inventive and dramatic, Spohr would grab prizes from Wagner, Rebikov would drown Debussy in ninths, Schoenberg would expose Berg as an amateur theatricalist.

Poulenc was more than merely influenced: he rifled intact the treasure of others. This was once common practice (Bach-Vivaldi), and Poulenc revived the practice, a risky one for those few minor musicians who used him as model only to discover he was no model at all. For his practice was an end, not a beginning; like all strong artists he did not open doors but closed them.

He was a converse dybbuk. Using no mask, he sang through his own lips with other men's voices. His very lack of originality became the unabashed signature of unique glories.

The premise of unoriginality, it seems to me, must smooth the ground for any "original" assessment of Poulenc's current value. That ground, fertilized by music's five variables—melody, harmony, counterpoint, rhythm (the only component to exist by itself), and instrumentation—was plowed by the composer in his way, the way of pastiche that bloomed into personality. In the purely Puccinian sense of soaring sweep, Poulenc was no melodist at all. Though his fame was largely vocal, and vocal supposedly means tuneful, offhand his only sweep that comes to mind is orchestral: the *2-Piano Concerto*'s second theme, the one that sounds like "Jeepers Creepers." And even those nine swooning notes, like Debussy's *fausses grandes lignes* (in contrast with the true long lines of, say, Ravel's *Daphnis*), dissolve before they evolve. His tunes—usually they are true tunes, not recitations—stem from speech; he never squeezed verse into prewritten musical phrases. His concern for correct stress made even his lushest songs talky. Since most of those songs are composed on strict rhymed meter, and since the composer's instinctive language is diatonic, a formal squareness results that extends even to his opera recitatives on free prose. By further extension his instrumental pieces become, at heart, word settings from which the words are removed.

Poulenc composed three operas. None were collaborations, their librettos being prewritten plays by French authors who were more or less his contemporaries.

The first, *Les Mamelles de Tirésias* (1944), was based on the two-act dadaist farce of Apollinaire, whom Poulenc never met, but who was the poet for his earliest song cycle, *Le Bestiaire* (1918). Concerning women's suffrage and featuring Denise Duval, it succeeded where many operas stumble—at filling the audience with true hilarity without compromising the music. Like French operetta of the nineteenth century, it was built of set numbers. Leonard Bernstein it was who on his Tenth Street

Baldwin first played me this highest piece of camp since *Così fan tutte*. Lenny had returned from Europe in the autumn of 1947 with a signed copy (a signed copy? had he actually met the master?) of *Mamelles* under his arm. "Just show me the divine parts," I requested, expecting the sort of Poulenciana I already knew—vaudevillian tongue twisters and lulling caramel plaints. So Lenny turned to the group number that begins *Comme il perdait au Zanzibar*. Well, if you think Ravel's "Toi le coeur" harks back to "One Fine Day," Poulenc's big chorale is a steal from Kern's "Fish Gotta Swim." (Ten years later we would hear the same corny sequences at the tragic peak of *Dialogues des Carmélites*.) Then and there I learned that although Poulenc never penned an original note, every note became pure Poulenc through some witty alchemy.

His third opera, *La Voix humaine* (1960), was based on the one-act realist monologue by Cocteau, who was Poulenc's dear friend and the poet for the composer's second song cycle, *Cocardes* (1918). Concerning a woman's suffering and again featuring the divine Duval, it worked where other operas collapse—at keeping recitative from flagging for forty-five minutes. Like no French lyric drama since *Pelléas*, it was built solely on speech patterns without set numbers.

Between *Les Mamelles* and *La Voix humaine*, both very profane, brief, and up to date, Poulenc commenced in 1953 composition on Georges Bernanos' very sacred, lengthy discourse about a tragedy of two centuries ago. Blanche de la Force was a fictional aristocrat who, through morose and partly imaginary terror at life's ugliness, entered the convent of Compiègne, only to die an uglier death along with her sisters (actual historical characters) during the early months of the French Revolution. The drama is less about the revolt than about fear, fear in the absolute: Blanche's introverted hysteria is endemic to all time and place, and except for the melodramatic finish, it runs a motionless course. Her conversations and those of her mothers and sisters are largely abstract, a bit pietistic, hardly touching on love (except for Christ), much less on the amorousness that ignites nearly every workable opera in history, including *Parsifal* and *Suor Angelica*. Not, one might suppose, a text for the bon vivant Poulenc.

With all the recitative (and he will use still more of it in *La Voix humaine*) one longs for—and suspects that Poulenc may have longed for—a bit more schmaltz and a lot more wit. The play, though touching and even grand, is smug. Poulenc's innate style—that creamy pop-aristocratic style—runs counter to the "fearsome" plot, and at one brief mention of Paris, when sub rosa he quotes his own so-sly *Mamelles* about that city, we swoon. Poulenc is a tragic humorist, and that isn't always clear here. The Latin sections of *Dialogues* are musically more French than the French sections. The score, after all, is modern, and the text is modern, too, even though about the past. But the overall tone is, if not exactly dated, really quite old-fashioned, and so would seem to require more old-fashioned tricks of the opera trade.

To recapitulate: while Poulenc in any one aspect of his art was not unusual—and was sometimes even crassly derivative—when two or more aspects fused, sparks flew and life emerged. The "why" is hard to focus on. But the "what" and the "how" are tangible. Although he is the most performed French vocal composer of his generation, the long-hewn spacious air is far less characteristic of Poulenc's melody than is the straightforward tune. Yet even his tunes, as the years rolled on, grew elliptical until, in *Dialogues des Carmélites* and all ensuing vocal works, the sung line became almost wholly recitative. Nevertheless this line, in whatever medium and however digested, seems to be the signature of Poulenc—the added ingredient that makes any robbed recipe his.

Thus stolen harmonies—lost chords—like objets trouvés become a personal brand by dint of the tune that binds them. Thus an assemblage of simple counterpoints conspires to form chords that vertically sound like someone else's but whose moving top voice chants pure Poulenc. Thus his rhythms (which like his tunes are quintessentially French in their foursquareness), although humdrum in themselves, present solid planks on which to build his special tunes.

Those tunes, like Ives's, all sprang from the town-band dance-hall memories of youth, seen through a glass darkly. If it could be argued that an artist is one who retrieves unbroken the fragility of his past, or that a child is "the musician beforehand," then Poulenc, as glimpsed through the bittersweet contagion of his vocal phrases, is the child-artist incarnate.

Pelléas et Mélisande

Every generation has its golden calf. Young composers in all countries, like young poets, are prone to admire, and so to being influenced by, a single recent work—though often these poets and composers (who never synchronize, so far as the texture of "trends" is concerned) are moved by opposing forces. Thus in the American fifties Ginsberg's rhapsodic *Howl,* which freed many a small Eliot from the previous decade, contrasted with Carter's formalistic quartets, which displaced the looser Coplandiana then in vogue. Thus in the Spanish twenties Falla's aristocratic Harpsichord Concerto stamped exotic classicism onto all Hispanic musicians for the next two decades, while Lorca's plebeian surrealism has yet to be superseded. And thus in France at the start of the twentieth century, when new writers and painters were dizzied by Valéry's brains and Braque's cubes, every composer in Paris staggered under the non-intellectual non-angular but leanly opulent and sensually clean impact of *Pelléas et Mélisande.*

It's my favorite opera. Yet it contains the two things I most abhor: the scrim, and the boy soprano. An audience, by the rules of the game, is plunged in darkness. To be thereupon for any length of time confronted with a stage plunged in darkness is to be cheated. Theater is make believe: real gloom cannot *represent* gloom, and scrims are the set designer's easy (I mean hard) way out. As to children who sing, I am in a class with those philistines who hooted Yniold off the stage during the dress rehearsal in 1902. Sung by a woman the part seems silly. Sung by a boy the insult of rasp is added to the injury of Yniold's music, which is second-rate and maddening.

Debussy is said to have said that he wanted to eliminate beginnings and ends, and to create a music consisting solely of middles. (Godard, asked to acknowledge the necessity for having a beginning, middle, and end in his films, replied: "Certainly, but not necessarily in that order.") But try switching scenes in *Pelléas*—and, of course, eliminating Yniold—and see how far you get. His music, all of it, was traditionally formal.

Virgil Thomson once wrote that Mélisande will do anything to avoid not being loved. "A lonely girl with a floating libido and no malice toward anyone can cause lots of trouble in a well-organized family. . . . The opera is her show, hers and the conductor's."

Thomson is right. It is no less right to claim that the opera is Golaud's show, his and the conductor's. (Within one artwork cannot two viewpoints paradoxically occupy the same space at the same time, like rain and landscape?) The drama's kernel lies in Golaud's jealousy which dictates—or rather, ignores—the comportment of his nearest and dearest. What others might say in their own defense goes unheard by Golaud, he is beyond the pale. He was a goner even before he met his bride, as he admits at the outset, likening the metaphoric loss during male menopause to the literal loss of Mélisande, who knows neither who nor where she is. Golaud's confusion, like Othello's, is a villainous weapon, razing those around him, finally himself.

No villain is all bad in opera. Iago, Claggart, Hérodiade, Sparafucile, because they sing, grow vulnerable, thus to some extent likable despite their absolute wickedness, for music is a great leveler. Of course, Golaud is not a villain—is, in fact, the play's most touching player, not merely acting but reacting, evolving and being allowed the only loud sounds. Do those reiterated anxious chords through which he pleads with a dying wife suspiciously echo Rodolfo's cry of "Mimi"? *Il Tabarro* may well have been cast up by *La Mer,* but *La Bohème* predated *Pelléas* by six years and would have been known to the Frenchman. (How wearisome to forever read of Debussy as Influence, especially to a background of Satie's *Sarabandes,* or even Rebikov's oozing ninths. Debussy was not cut from whole cloth, nor was he even so original. It's not that he was different than. He was better than.)

As for Debussy's opera being a conductor's show, great singers with a bad orchestra are unacceptable, whereas bona fide renditions with second-rate singers are feasible provided the orchestra excels. Witness the Boulez recording, a gargantuan symphonic canvas upon which pastel voices are permitted to limn inexpertly, though the net result comes over as faithful.

Similarly, *Pelléas* in translation is not a betrayal. My first hearing was in Philadelphian English, and a thrill, while all ensuing Parisian versions miscalculated perspective with histrionics and vibratos. When musical texts are so very French, perhaps they can be communicated only in English to Americans, whereas pieces in an "international" style (by Elgar, say, or Monteverdi, Massenet, Wagner) should be sung always in the original. The opposite could be posited: non-ornamental prosodic settings like Debussy's, or like Satie's *Socrate,* should never be translated, but nothing is lost when coloratura is Englished.

Maeterlinck's play is sophisticated, taken at face value rather than for symbolism. Mélisande becomes an Antonioni heroine, wealthy (as they all are) without explanation, who doesn't answer questions, and is herself not always given replies. Meanwhile the demented echoes, non sequiturs and shifting repetitions of speech sound as timeless as nursery rhymes or lovers' quarrels. Debussy responds to the text literally, even occasionally Mickey-Mousing (despite Satie's warning against letting the scenery make faces) when there is talk of fountains, sheep, death, creaking gates. Such effects are, of course, all instrumental.

Indeed, if Debussy demands the same requisites for finished performances as other opera composers—good singers, good orchestra, good blend of the two—he ideally demands more balanced proportions than, for instance, Donizetti, whose accompaniments can be so-so if the singers are sensational.

To psychoanalyze a composer according to subject matter is risky (but fun) even if the subject matter is literal—that is, extramusical— as with vocal settings, which reflect the poet's as well as the musician's preoccupations. Music's real subject, of course, is, as they say, abstract (motives, colors, dynamics, rhythms, shapes); and even if abstraction could be taken apart and psychologized, it would not be the composer's specific choice of abstraction (theme) so much as the composer's *way* with the choice which might "reveal" him or her. But if music is abstract, therapy is concrete; so if Debussy repeatedly deals in, say, water, what does that tell about Debussy, even after one discusses *how* he deals in water?

Unasked questions:

Is Pelléas gay? The sentiment and its realization were rife in the nineteenth as in every century, but the word and concept were not yet formulated by the mind doctors. Probably neither Maeterlinck nor Debussy, both bourgeois family men, were much concerned, even peripherally, with the love that dare not speak its name. Yet their unconscious slant on the hero seems . . . well, slanted. Who is the dying Marcellus for whom Pelléas would quit his own dying father? How could Pelléas help but resent everyone in the castle, most of all the new Mélisande, who keeps him from this friend, evoked anxiously, then never mentioned again? To worry the question may appear old-fashioned, yet if only one baritone could determine that, for himself, Pelléas was or was not homophilic (at least so far as Marcellus is involved), the rôle, and by extension the music for the rôle, would shed its habitual sappiness and don a carnal dimension, a fullness, a reasonableness that only Martial Singher has thus far lent to it.

Mélisande? Is she, as Mary Garden contended, Bluebeard's last spouse (". . . and I only am escaped to tell thee") wandering deranged, complete with crown, through this foreign forest? What ship brought her? the one with the *"grandes voiles"* now sailing off at full speed? Has she been weeping for a day, or a month? If for a month, what has she eaten? There is never talk of food, yet at one point we learn of famine in the land, of beggars dying in grottoes; but of this, as of Marcellus, there is no further mention, and the protagonists seem sufficiently healthy to languish only for love, nor do they trouble with government.

And where and when is Allemonde? (*Allemagne?*) In the fourth? the seventh? the eleventh century? Bluebeard, or Gilles de Raiz, was Joan of Arc's lover, but the traditional décor suggests a somberer era.

A dozen references to people's hands: by the men to Mélisande ("Donnez-moi la main"), Mélisande to herself ("On dirait que mes mains sont malades"), Golaud to Pelléas ("Donnez-moi—non, non, pas la main . . ."), but no tactile contact except with hair. Would that the audience followed suit. The final page is the most beautiful in history, yet I've never heard it live because, such hands as are not slipping on gloves while the heroine expires, are clapping as the curtain lowers.

Why do the characters say *vous* and *tu* to each other interchangeably?

One can detest opera yet love *Pelléas*. One can love opera yet detest *Pelléas*. And one can love both, so long as one does not search through Pelléas for mad airs and mob scenes. Yes, it is my favorite piece, but my wisest friends loathe it; wisdom does not reside in the ear, and I can only conclude that they are not hearing what I hear. For them the rôles come over as undifferentiated, monochrome. For me Debussy's vocality is not a series of soldered fragments but a concentrated melody (the "spun-out line" reduced to lowest terms, as opposed to Verdi's stretching of the line to highest terms, or to Webern's ultimate dismissal of such terms) which also often fulfills harmonic chores by replacing a "missing" instrument. If the score never blossoms in the usual sense, it does so in reverse, like a galaxy expanding under a microscope.

Hearing it in the inner ear as it *should* be done, how can I stand it as it *is* done? Alone at the keyboard I fabricate the greatest performances: in the flesh which I've added to the bones are embedded, like diamond shards, flecks of priceless melodic shape which have become mine alone. No living Arkel, perhaps not even Debussy himself in Heaven, will ever intone as capably as I do the inborn inevitability of certain phrases.

Such music exists only ideally, in the abstract. *Pelléas et Mélisande* is of that rare race of masterpiece which must never be performed.

1977

Carmen

Carmen, the most popular serious piece (or the most serious popular piece) ever penned, has entered the collective unconscious. As it happens, my young education converged perversely — and I believe correctly — around what used to be termed Modern Music. By the onset of puberty I had memorized *Petruschka, Pierrot* and *Daphnis,* not to mention Carpenter's *Skyscrapers* and Schelling's *Victory Ball,* yet I wouldn't have recognized a Brahms quartet, nor even a Bach gavotte. Contempt may breed contempt, but familiarity breeds only familiarity. Except for *Carmen,* I had to get used to "classics" as others get used to "moderns."

Wagner loved *Carmen.* Contrary to general thought, composers are more leery than indulgent of music which resembles their own. That Bizet was once deemed a Wagnerite seems now merely funny: *Carmen* is as wholeheartedly diatonic as *Tristan* is not. The Habañera? It is chromatic only melodically. Harmonically, with those 120 measures of seesawing over a pedal-D, it is more doggedly tonal than a Clementi sonata.

Nor was the lead-motive a Bizetian need; his airs once sung stay sung. True, strands dangling from certain early statements—Micaela's mainly—are sometimes tucked back into the formal fabric. But only the Death Tune, announced in the prelude, recurs and recurs and recurs, with that Cui-like augmented second which Frenchmen up to and through Ravel identify with sex, sex being always blamed on other countries and this interval deriving from Russia which used it to denote the wayward East.

Harmonically Bizet was not, as we say today, inventive: his chords are triadic, especially in set numbers, while diminished sevenths he employs forebodingly, according to the cliché of his day, to advance the plot. Chordal sequences, when at all tonally evasive, are so nearly always anchored to a drone that the device becomes a signature. Exceptional are the Séquedilla's precipitous modulations to the Neapolitan seventh, cribbed sixty years later by Prokofiev. And if the rare presence of secondary sevenths seems as pungent as, for example, the very cassia bloom José describes, the opening chords of the flower song could be by Fauré thirty years later, while the closing chords (as well as tune) were filched intact only fifteen years later for Tchaikovsky's *Pathétique*. So Bizet did shape the future somewhat, but through his harmonic quality, not originality.

Like a vat of sangria being brought to boil, the Gypsy Dance of Act II is as physical as the rumble from *West Side Story*. Rhythm alone explains the mounting wallop. Not rhythmic interest, however, but rhythmic *lack* of interest: hypnosis rather than psychedelia, monotony in place of variety. Bizet does step up the tempo thrice, building from a metronome 100 to 138; but the chief tactic, as with *Boléro*, lies in piling on of dynamics and weight rather than, as with *Sacre*, an increasing of metric intricacy. In song as in dance *Carmen* is straightforward; meters are never more eccentric than a square three or four, nor within the bar do there occur rhythmic enigmas, Chopinesque juxtapositions.

A steady beat makes the dance tick, but what makes it "good" is the strong line traced over the tambourines (though this line too is unchangingly reiterated). Indeed, melody, which makes all good opera good, is what makes *Carmen Carmen*. *Carmen* seethes with tune, apposite and first-rate, some of it stolen. If Prokofiev's Neapolitan mannerism stems from the Séquedilla, the Séquedilla itself stems from the orchestra of Mozart's Commendatore, while the Habañera grew from a nightclub song. And as in the orchestra of Mozart's Commendatore, certain of *Carmen*'s most ravishing curves unfurl without the distraction of a human voice: for instance, the thirty-eight measures of the second Entr'acte wherein single winds weave a nearly three-octave gamut like a silver snake through gold harp strings.

Bizet is less expert at *le mot juste* than at *la phrase juste*. Winton Dean calls him a "master of the paragraph," meaning that "the rise and fall of the melody produced whole numbers that seem to spring forth complete from the first bar to the last." But if Bizet did compose paragraphs, they were stanzaic, for he was no prosifier; and though music can't rhyme it can certainly echo. Perhaps he was more a master of the sentence, or rather, of the verse. Such verse swells not through development but through repetition.

Yet through all *Carmen* flows the technical inevitability one finds in a disco palace, a linking, an overlapping of numbers granting them both independence and interdependence, and sending them all finally to flight like some doomed Greek family, heroes and jesters alike, toward a horridly needed apotheosis.

Formally the opera bites off more than it can chew, then chews it.

She's a liberated woman, she makes the rules, and like great actresses she speaks of herself in the third person, especially as she nears the end. She's a merry and obsessive lover, but a sad and gluttonous one too, and death more than lust seems her dish. At the hour of her suicide —what else can you call it?—Carmen seems fed up. Why? Music explicates where psychoanalysis fumbles. But if Mérimée's tale continually instructs us (his limning of Spanish Romany is no less morosely veridical than his Corsican mafia in the masterpiece *Matteo Falcone*), who can deny that some pages of the opera sound silly? The males of the chorus, extrovert Latins though they be, are kidding when they ask Carmen when she'll love them (love them collectively?), whereas José, in taking her literally, shows himself crazy and provides his own doom. But Bizet was not kidding (and surely he, not his librettists, was responsible for the stretchings and ricochetings which veer toward farce) when he invites our sympathy during the G & S exchange between Micaela and the Garde Montante. Operetta conventions of yesterday are today unwilling suspensions of disbelief, and not only poor Micaela suffers in our eyes as she giddily parrots her would-be lover's remarks (*Sa mère, il la revoit* . . . etc.); Escamillo and Carmen too, glamorous public figures, go around saying they're in love—to just anyone.

There is little indication that Bizet and friends like Massenet or Saint-Saëns, at least in their musical speech, were out for a revolution. If things were different after *Carmen,* the difference lay in a (to us) minor French definition of what constitutes grand opera. So far as the ear is concerned, *Carmen,* while becoming the indisputably best lyric drama of its age in France, remains strictly in the tradition of *opéra comique,* unaltered by Delibes or Hahn, by Poulenc or Sauguet, or by Rosenthal or Damase a century later.

Half the opera is choral.

Do the choruses, in their inevitability at scene setting, their directness of melody, their lean virile languor and bull's-eye femininity, provide the most gorgeously inspired minutes?

Before deciding, listen again to *"La cloche a sonné"* as the unison tenors for only twelve bars intone a series of tetrachordal arches more perfectly symmetrical than those of the Pont du Gard (no, architecture is not frozen music), and which, though they speak but once, satisfy our memory over the context of the next two hours. How almost immoral that so telling a fragment be followed by another more elegant still: unison baritones, against sixteen measures of fluxing hues among undulating cellos and near-motionless reeds, chant but two notes, over and over, only sinking ecstatically to a third as they give way to the long-awaited girls. Hear these girls now, this time in pairs, curling their vowels around each other like the very smoke they evoke, and growing, growing ever higher in the air. Oh, one could go on. Yes, the choruses do form the most beautiful moments.

Paradoxically, it is possible to conceive a *Carmen* (as opposed to a *Meistersinger* or a *Dialogues des Carmélites*) without chorus. The drama is between the few, not the many, and requires no kibitzing. Carmen's choruses are marvelous clothes on a marvelous body.

Had I never heard the orchestration but only seen it, I'd say it couldn't work. I would be wrong. The chances we are taught to avoid when scoring for voice with instruments seem not to be chances to Bizet. Balances or areas that on the page look top-heavy or empty are to the ear always right: the scoring is unstintingly crystalline.

But the scoring is not unusual. Beyond a predilection for low flutes, for solo bassoon, and for crossed strings (listen to the sudden soft parentheses between which, after fifteen minutes of rattling fanfare, Escamillo emerges in the final act and, with string quartet, speaks his piece, ominously intimate and self-contained as a black opal centered in a crown of a thousand diamonds), Bizet doesn't really run risks.

Bizet is said to have said, "If they want trash I'll give them trash," and wrote the toreador song. Just who are "they," snug in their opera loges, crying "We want trash"? And just how is this song more trashy than another?

The world knows Faust through Gounod (not Goethe) and *taureau-machie* through Bizet (not Goya). Does the world know wrong? Toreador is a nonword, like glissando, good as any. We know love through Wagner.

Is *Carmen*, rather than *Fidelio* or *Lulu*, the perfect opera? Yes, because all the elements (beginning with the libretto—an improvement, at least in stageworthiness, on Mérimée's tale-*cum*-document) are first-rate: the traditional symmetries are perfect, the literal repeats are perfect, the exquisite banality is perfect. But perfection does not a chef d'oeuvre make. Many a masterpiece is flawed, for beauty limps, and grandeur, though spectacular, can turn top-heavy.

Then is *Carmen* a chef d'oeuvre? Yes, because the perfect elements all catch fire and gleam with life—they are, as we say, inspired, and together they jell: they have hardened into immortality.

1978

Bluebeard's Castle

Béla Bartók was pathologically private, even to keeping his marriage a secret. Nevertheless, although he declined an introduction to Saint-Saëns while in Paris in 1909, young Bartók yearned to meet Debussy. "But Debussy is crude and surly," he was told. "Do you want to be insulted by Debussy?" "Yes," he replied. These two facts — Bartók's conjugal circumspection, and his adoration of the French composer — provide as cogent a key (dare I say skeleton key?) as any with which to enter and catch a first look at Duke Bluebeard's ghastly and wondrous castle.

Like Anatole France's *Thaïs*, like Somerset Maugham's *Rain*, like Tennessee Williams's *Summer and Smoke,* each of which is a confrontation between saviour and sinner in which sinner is saved and saviour sins, *Bluebeard*'s tale is palindromic, shaped like an X, and so by extension is the music, more or less.

After an irrelevant and usually omitted Brechtian prologue spoken by the Bard ("This story, ladies and gentlemen, is about *you* . . ."), the curtain rises on a vast circular Gothic hall, the Bard drifts into the wings, and a sharp light finds Duke Bluebeard standing in an open doorway with his bride Judith. (Why Judith? This woman is the reverse of the biblical heroine who decapitated Holofernes; neither is she saved at the last minute by her brothers; nor does she flee, deranged, into the forests of Alemonde and take the name Mélisande who, as Mary Garden contended, was the wife that got away. She is passive, albeit willful, and in love. This Bluebeard, meanwhile, is remote from the first model, Gilles de Retz who, when jilted by Joan of Arc for God and country, became a child murderer. Rather he seems a nice old absolute monarch attempting one last May-December marriage.) He descends the stairs, asking: "Judith, do you follow? Do you miss your family? Why have you paused?" "It's just that my dress was caught on a nail." She proceeds, although he tells her there's still time to turn back. But with the ardor of a woman in love she longs for the secrets of her husband's past, hopes to discover them by opening the seven doors visible in the castle walls, and thus bring light into his dark heart and home. Reluctantly he cedes the keys to her. The first door swings open in a river of scarlet flashes to reveal a torture chamber. The second door conceals an armory with blood-stained weapons. The third shows a huge treasury whose every gorgeous ruby drips with blood. Judith grows increasingly nervous. She opens the fourth door to the aqua glare of a magic garden and cries out at the splendor, but here also she sees that the roses bleed. "Who watered this garden?" she asks, but Bluebeard now urges her toward the fifth portal. She discovers the duke's endless domain all bathed in shimmering sunlight warming green velvet orchards. "Ah!" gasps the mezzo on her unique high C. Now Judith perceives the very clouds seeping blood. Bluebeard implores her vainly to refrain from the remaining doors, but she will go on. Behind the sixth is an infinitely mournful opalescent lake. What is its source? "Könynyek, Judit, Könynyek"—Tears, Judith, tears—and the Magyar syllables resound, clipped yet sustained, with a sadness that English can only hint at. Hesitant, but knowing he cannot refuse permission to open the final door, he reassures her with a sense of destiny: "Open, look, there are my former wives. The first came at morning. The second at midday. The third at evening." Out step three beautiful ashen women. Judith breaks down, knowing she is doomed to their fate. Bluebeard throws a mantle over her, crowns her with gold, they gaze long into each other's eyes, she pleads to be spared, he declares, "Lovely vision, Beauty tends you," she staggers beneath the weight of her robes and her knowledge and her grief, heads slowly toward the seventh door through which the other wives have disappeared, then she herself disappears and the door swings shut. "Night," sings Duke Bluebeard. "Nothing but darkness is here, eternal darkness . . . ," *ejjel . . . ejjel,* like Mahler's *Ewig . . . ewig,* and blackness floods the stage, engulfing Bluebeard in the unresolved second inversion of the F-sharp minor tonality with which the tragedy began an hour earlier.

Moral: Curiosity killed the cat.

Duke Bluebeard's Castle is a parable on what today would be termed an antifeminist stance in marriage. Neither Bartók nor the librettist, Béla Balász, took a stand, allowing however that the inevitable is glum. This is a man's opera. The tragedy is Bluebeard's, not Judith's; she is the messenger who brought him the necessary night.

The palindrome is clear in the gradual switch between characters. Judith, at first passionate and protective, aches to free her husband from his past. Bluebeard, at first reticent and rational, nonetheless confides certain secrets, except for the last one, which would mean sacrificing his bride. But as the plot advances he grows increasingly dictatorial while she dwindles until she dissolves. The music mirrors this philosophical change—not perhaps as literally as Hindemith's *Hin and zurück* which is symmetrical as a butterfly, yet enough for any music lover to perceive. During the first half Judith is in the foreground with her continually enthusiastic cantilena queries, while Bluebeard replies in fits and starts, monosyllabically; as their relationship crisscrosses, his voice grows longer and louder, hers more sporadic and ever fainter.

Though Bartók and Stravinsky each rose out of Debussy, the two are as dissimilar as an Airedale and a leopard (Bartók being the Airedale) which both diverged a billion years ago from the same maternal amphibian. Still, they are the French musician's principal heirs.

Specifically in *Duke Bluebeard's Castle* Debussy's influence is pronounced, but more in morosely echoing empty halls of mood (in *Pelléas* as in *Bluebeard* the castle symbolizes the soul of its owner) than in harmony, more in oral device than in sonority. Debussy in his one opera is credited with creating the modern French recitative style, just as Bartók formed the Hungarian parlando-recitativo in *his* one opera. For me, *Pelléas et Mélisande* contains no recitative; rather, it posits a series of arias in miniature, or virtuoso turns in microcosm—to use the term Bartók made famous. The Pelleasian world contains countless examples of two-measure, three-measure, seven-measure sequences, restrained verbal outbursts complete in themselves yet part of the flow, and surely more tunefully infectious than Mozart recitatives. These outbursts, like tiny explosions in deep space, are patterns sewn on a huge instrumental fabric which is the core of the dramatic structure, which sometimes dominates with massive interludes, and which in the case of both composers claims the nonverbal last word. Bartók was proud of the affinity, emphasizing that his vocal style was in the "sharpest possible contrast to the Schoenbergian treatment of vocal parts." His melodies are more elastic than Debussy's, however, and stem tangibly from Hungarian peasant tunes. It's amusing that, as with Mussorgsky (another of his influences—and Debussy's too), peasant tunes dictate the swerves and curves when even the grandest of nobility is at song. As with *Pelléas*, *Bluebeard* has no ensemble singing, although the pair of voices eventually overlap a bit. But unlike *Pelléas,* which is sumptuously Spartan in that it boasts not one golden note too many and retains a dynamic level of mezzo-piano ninety percent of the time, *Bluebeard* is hyperthyroid, overly literal lest we miss the point, irritatingly climactic with lots of hysterical filler—what the French call *remplissage.*

Our judgment of a piece is always partly determined by the circumstances of our initial exposure to that piece. I first heard *Duke Bluebeard's Castle,* or some of it, on an autumn evening in the Poconos in 1958 (ten years before the dropping of acid, e.g., the use of LSD, was de rigueur for flower children) during a carefully supervised bout with mescaline, the hallucinogenic which supposedly opens the doors of perception onto our world as it really is, not as millenniums of human conditioning would have it be. Indeed, one does effortlessly see the universe in a grain of sand while being caressed by a snowy mass of clouds. But as the hours advanced I had a bad trip, the poplars seemed a fatal threat and bleeding veins streaked the sky. I didn't know it then, but my visions were similar to Judith's. At the height of the experiment my companion in crime, fellow composer Paul Bowles, knowing that under the drug "truth" speaks through art and that even a tone-deaf oaf can distinguish good music from bad, played a tape of the "Lake of Tears" from *Bluebeard*. I had never heard anything remotely like its melodic melancholy, its motionlessness (sound seemed suspended in time as well as space), and above all, its color. The highest compliment one composer can pay another is, "I don't know how you got that effect," and Bartók here had contrived an orchestration which it would take me thirty years to analyze; even today, with the full score on my knees, I'm not certain how the magic enters those twenty-nine swirls of demisemiquavers that surge, over and over, like blurred parentheses around the ceaseless plaint:

> *Waters, gray unmoving, mournful*
> *Waters, mournful silent waters,*
> *Waters still and dead: what brought them?*
> *Weeping brought them, Judith, weeping.*

Yes, I see on the staves that one flute and one clarinet repeatedly rise and fall at great speed in close harmony backed by three other flutes fluttertonguing, while one harp glissandos and another arpeggiates in close harmony with a celesta backed by muted strings divided into a thick A-minor triad—all of this pianississimo. But could I have guessed that the simultaneous hollow soughing stems from the sustained intoning of two low horns a fifth apart, doubled by a kettledrum chord and a large gong? Fifty separate human players produce this pale whisper. What if Haydn, not Bartók, had been played on that crucial night? Would I have been haunted with the same impression of break-through? In any case it is sonority chez Bartók—the hue of instrumentation in and for itself—that plays as strong a role in his opera as the two protagonists, and stronger than other of music's key components: melody, rhythm, harmony, counterpoint. The composer's orchestration is comparable to the scenery in an Antonioni movie; it determines the behavior and motives of the paltry mortals snared in its sonorous décor.

1988

Stravinsky

.

When I was twelve I heard *The Rite of Spring* and became sick—sick from the thrill of an instantaneous and permanent shift in metabolism. So this was music! A door had opened, the sun flowed in with its nourishing and mysterious gold. The occasion was a nationwide broadcast of the Philharmonic, Stravinsky conducting, which I caught in Chicago, and which (I later learned) was heard by every other twelve-year-old composer in America, with the same traumatic effect. Yes, he was our greatest composer, and his *Rite*, in turn, is so solid as to be The Absolute against which all other current art is judged. This said, do I adore Stravinsky as I adore others who are perhaps less overwhelming—Ravel, for example, or Poulenc? I am dazzled by his intelligence and scared by his force, but my heart is not melted.

Why call him great if I don't adore him?

Partly because I too am brainwashed. My nature prefers minor artists to the makers of Big Statements, which is why I'm drawn to French more than to German music. But there is a more objective reason. Stravinsky is what the French call a *monstre sacré*—one whose greatness depends on chronological place. The sacred monster is a personage who, through public exploitation of his personal accomplishment—an accomplishment always first-rate—grows so much larger than life as to seem no longer human. Generally he is a creative artist, though some performers and politicians fill the bill. He is, so to speak, a violent luxury which, because not really needed to make the world go round, concentrates no less on his product than on his persona, and peddles this persona no less to the discriminating aristocrat than to the philistine bourgeois.

Is his musical nature German or French (these constituting the sole pair of esthetics in the whole cosmos, all others—Dutch, Spanish, Siamese, etc.—being subdivisions thereof)?

His musical nature is French. Russia is French.

To be French is to stress a sense of proportion; to realize that humor and horror are not mutually exclusive; to be profound while retaining the spiritual levity required (at least in Paris) to get through life without collapsing, and to discover the profundity on the surface of things. To be French is to show three sides of a coin. French is witty, and wit, as exemplified by that most stylish of French composers, Franz Joseph Haydn, is ellipsis—knowing what to leave out. Wit depends on tonality and all French music true to the name is tonal.

Stravinsky, as Debussy's foremost heir, traced modernism along a diatonic course. Everyone knows that he abhorred Meaning in music, let alone deep meaning, but few stress his C-major frivolity, even silliness. Stravinsky was grandly aware of the importance of unimportance.

Is he harmonist or contrapuntist?

Harmonist, in the tradition of France. He wrote a fugue or two (so did Ravel), notably the one which forms the second movement of *Symphony of Psalms,* but we don't recall it as a fugue. Indeed, do we even recall it compared to that piece's celebrated opening sound—one of the composer's two most famous chords? This eight-voice E-minor triad is the essence of verticality, and while born for the orchestra was clearly concocted at the keyboard, so symmetrically does it fall beneath the two hands.

"Dance of the Adolescents" from *The Rite of Spring* contains Stravinsky's other famous chord, also in eight voices, a chord which more than any other represents The Sacre Sound. The Sacre Sound devolves not from the scoring of the chord (string double-stops eccentrically punctuated by horns), nor yet from its daring reiteration (280 times in the first seventy measures), but from the vertical clash between the four top and four bottom parts which we used to hear, at the very least, as bitonality. Today we hear it as an unresolved E-flat dominant seventh over a lowered submediant triad, both having the potent potential for resolving to an A-flat tonic.

Polyphony was Schoenberg's nature, as it must be for those who conceive by tone-row, but harmony was Stravinsky's, even when, late in life, he too composed according to a series. His music is always heard as tonal (of course, I hear everything as tonal, including Boulez and Babbitt—it's my conditioning—and I contend that everyone, including Babbitt and Boulez, hears everything as tonal), even when apparently sewn with independent threads. By extension, his music is heard harmonically: the entrances of voices on the first pages of *The Rite* to the eye may look like horizontal waves but to the ear they freeze into chunks.

What about his tunes, his rhythm, his color?

His melodic sense, even in vocal music, had an instrumental tang aimed like Beethoven's or Debussy's toward the reiterated slogan rather than, like Chopin's or Ravel's, toward the long arching line. Motives, not cantilena. The motives are contagious, being oft repeated. And they are repeated unaltered—that is Stravinsky's signature, a signature adapted to the various periods of his career. (Viz., the obstinate trumpet solos in "The Doll's Scene" of *Petrushka*, in *The Nightingale*, in *The Soldier's Story*, in *Agon*.) Though Stravinsky's melodies are not songlike, they are usually stated, as songs are, with simple support.

Ask anyone what single component most defines Stravinsky and he will answer rhythm. The rhythm in turn is characterized, like our jazz but unlike anything European, by metrical precision—by a persistent motoric beat that does not get faster or slower according to shades of dynamic, or according to non-symmetrical continually changing time signatures. Stravinsky's fast music is intrinsically fast, not slow music played fast.

His color comes through using the ordinary extrordinarily, like the aforementioned E-minor triad from *Symphony of Psalms*. His orchestration is recognizable as French by its avoidance of doublings, recognizable as Stravinsky by its assignment of the least obvious instruments to given phrases. (For an example of the no-doubling, see any tutti passage in *The Rite*. For an example of the least obvious instrument, see the renowned bassoon solo which opens the same work.) The economics of his orchestration altered with the world's economics, since no one after World War I could afford the mammoth Mahlerian agglomerations, but the principles of his orchestration remained fixed.

How was he as a word setter?

His editor confided that when the manuscript for *Three Songs from William Shakespeare* was submitted for engraving, it was necessary to tell Stravinsky that two verses were missing from the opening sonnet. The mortified master asked that the score be returned and that the affair remain secret. The restitution of the forgotten lines appears in the printed version of this song, a version which nevertheless contains what I deem a worse misdemeanor (though sanctioned by many): repeating words at whim.

That off my chest, let me say that Stravinsky was a marvelous composer for the voice. The marvel had nothing to do with proper wordsetting, i.e., concern for parsing, declamation, quantities, considerations aimed toward comprehensibility of a sung text. In a text sound more than sense absorbed him, which is why he was happiest and most convincing in Latin. Since no one knows how that language was spoken he is free to let accents fall where they may. From the start of *Oedipus Rex*, for instance, the hero's name is thrice intoned, each time with a new stress. In *The Wedding* the whining grace notes of the bride, the harrumphing swoops of the male guests, the ritual chanting and the moaning yelps, all these are novel sounds to vocal literature, apposite and exciting, indifferent to prosodic rules. By treating larynxes like woodwinds, even as he revolutionized orchestration by treating woodwinds like strings, Stravinsky deconventionalized common practice.

Most of Europe's masterworks have been for human voice. Exceptions are notably from the nineteenth century which, notwithstanding Wagner and Schubert and the Italians, was an instrumental age. Beethoven and Chopin are not primarily remembered for songs and choruses and operas, nor are Brahms, Schumann, Tchaikovsky. In our time Stravinsky too is an exception, in the light of Ravel and Schoenberg, Berg and Britten. He is the only great composer in history whose greatest works are for dancers.

The Rite is forever undanceable partly because the story is taken at face value, but mainly because the score smashes all contenders. True, Paul Taylor, avoiding the risky "pagan" tone of every version since 1912, did make a go of it; and he did ape Nijinsky's knock-kneed profiles. But Taylor's success owes much to the four-hand reduction: the black-and-white keyboard offsets the black-and-white comic-strip yarn in the black-and-white modernistic décor; and the Nijinsky stance is brash allusion, not sober homage. However, the music's glamour rests in orchestral color; were Taylor dumb enough to use the full score, his *Rite* would turn from comic-spooky to monotono-silly. (Disney's Technicolor version wasn't bad. He inclined, as they say out there, to Mickey-Mouse the music, but he, if anyone, had the right.)

Was he original?

By original, people really mean innovative, placing a high price on this Hollywoodian virtue. Yet the most remarkable innovators have never been the finest composers, because innovation and composition are separate professions and no one has time to excel in both. The big artist steals the raw novelties of the little artist, then cooks them with his own spices.

Stravinsky was always quick to promote his loves through pastiche (notably of Pergolesi and Tchaikovsky in *Pulcinella* and *The Fairy's Kiss*) while belittling the procedure in others (notably Poulenc, whom he credited with giving plagiarism a new meaning). Yet the road from pastiche to paraphrase is short, and no one ever points out Stravinsky's shameless borrowings:

Is not the extended strident solo piano clattering above nervous strings in the first movement of his *Symphony in Three Movements,* written in 1943, too close for comfort to Bartók's extended strident solo piano clattering above nervous strings in the second movement of his *Music for Strings, Percussion and Celesta,* composed six years earlier?

What of the famous *Petrushka* texture, recognizable in a split second? Would these close-harmony roulades for a pair of clarinets have been scored that way in 1910, had not Ravel in 1908 invented an identical scoring in *Rapsodie Espagnole?*

More disconcerting are the three samples of parallel octaves meandering over forty years from Mussorgsky's *Sans Soleil* through Debussy's *Nuages* to Stravinsky's *Rossignol* prelude, the last named making no pretense of camouflage.

Getting us before we get him, Stravinsky acknowledges his debt to Verdi during the making of *Oedipus Rex,* though despite his E-flat tenor air in Latin being frankly a variation on Verdi's E-flat tenor air in Latin from the *Requiem,* who would mistake the one author for the other?

But would the rhythm beneath Jocasta's harangue, also from *Oedipus Rex,* have come off quite as it does had Bartók not written his first quartet in 1908?

And did not Satie's simple but singular ostinato, of three longs and a short, in *Socrate,* anticipate Stravinsky's *Tango?*

Despite what even the man himself contended, Stravinskyan flavor relies on a core of constant tonality permitting a colossal scope. The scope nonetheless has frontiers—not defects, but self-imposed limitations. From the bittersweet violence of the big ballets to the luxuriant chutzpah of the two-piano pieces, Stravinsky is powerful and profound, sparse and playful, indeed everything we connect with great masters, except pessimistic. The music is simply never depressing like, say, Bartók's *Bluebeard*, Berg's *Lulu* or Schoenberg's almost anything. On the other hand are those composers, with all their might, ever witty? It could be argued that wit, like charm, must reside in all genius (why, even Beethoven had charm!), or conversely that all genius must house a certain morosity.

Stravinsky's glibness was grave. His varied career produced few weak works. He robbed many a nest along the way, but some Borgesian alchemy arranged for each egg to hatch out another Igor.

1981

Gershwin

I've just listened nonstop to fifty-three songs by George and Ira Gershwin, and the effect is no less exhilarating than if the songs had been by Robert Schumann or Charles Ives. George's tunes are as memorable, Ira's texts as apt as those of the truest songmakers of yore. Ella Fitzgerald, the wistful baritone (she's as content cooing below the staff as sopranos are fifteen steps higher), proves as ideal a match for this team as Lotte Lehmann and Donald Gramm and Maggie Teyte were for the others. How she tints the tones (never an irrelevant ornament, only an occasional tilde) one by one, like those gray roses blushing toward pink in early Technicolor movies, then blends them into a bouquet of melody that evokes, over and over and over, your own first love. For the songs are virtually always about love—lost, found, longed for, disposed of—never about death. Death will come only with *Porgy and Bess.*

Hearing the songs in one fell swoop, most of them familiar as family, I realized I'd been living with Gershwin since the age of reason. Actually each of us lives daily with this most famous of modern composers, whose art surges forth from Musak all over the globe. Weaned on him, like most kids of the swing era, I never differentiated between Gershwin's basic worth and Ravel's but took him for granted (as I did Ravel) without analyzing wherein lay his charm and craft. At ten, thrilled by Paul Whiteman's theme song, I bought *Rhapsody in Blue* at the store next to the Frolic moviehouse on Chicago's Fifty-fifth Street (sheet-music shops, now nearly extinct, grew all over town then), and it still reposes on the piano, with my name childishly scrawled upon that friendly blue-and-gray Harms edition. Two years later my parents, ever alert to the Urban League and other racial betterment groups, came home late one night, flushed and dazzled and forever changed by the local premiere of the Negro spectacle *Porgy and Bess.* I envied them. "Summertime" took its place on the piano next to *Rhapsody in Blue.* Over the next decade, while learning by schooling the concert repertory from Couperin to Copland, I was learning by osmosis the words and airs of every Gershwin song. In the mid-1940s, as pianist for Eva Gauthier, I was often regaled by tales about another pianist she once hired, the young George Gershwin, who, on a program that began with piano-vocal excerpts from Schoenberg's *Gurreleider,* accompanied Madame Gauthier in "Stairway to Paradise," "Innocent Ingenue Baby," "Swanee," and "Do It Again." They brought down the house—with nobody questioning the legitimacy of such odd bedfellows. In 1948 I won the George Gershwin Memorial Award for my *Overture in C* (the piece did not deserve the prize, but I did), the premiere of which, under Mishel Piastro and the New York Philharmonic, was my first brush with the big time. On the program were Alec Templeton playing *Concerto in F,* Avon Long scatting "It Ain't Necessarily So," and Oscar Hammerstein, who in front of the audience handed me the award money, which was spent on a ticket to France where I stayed ten years. By the early 1950s, now myself an American in Paris, I was catching on to the Gershwin songs by their local plumage ("Quelqu'un m'adore" for "Somebody Loves Me," "Journée brumeuse" for "A Foggy Day," which seemed as smooth in French as in Ira's spirited English).

Ira's spirited English concerns me here. If as the stuff of good songs his words (called lyrics in Tin Pan Alley) don't quite vie with Goethe's, they are less bathetic and a good deal tighter than some of the poetasting used by, say, Schubert and Fauré. Witty, too, and ingeniously contrived. In the whole catalog I find but one trite line ("Oh if we ever part/Then that might break my heart"), and but one strained inversion ("And so all else above/I'm waiting for the man I love"). It's fun to play games of comparison ("You've got what gets me/What gets me you've got," writes Ira Gershwin in *Girl Crazy;* "I adore what you burn; you burn what I adore," writes Henry James in *The Tragic Muse*), or ponder the implications of lines like "I want to bite my initials on a sailor's neck" or "All the sexes from Maine to Texas," which seem every bit as equivocal as the *Erlkönig.* Ira likes to drop names such as Schopenhauer as something de trop when Eros is near (who disagrees?), or to suggest that "any Russian play" will guarantee fewer clouds of gray than when Eros has gone. The antiliterary Ira scores literary points about love, even as the learned Prioress in Poulenc's *Dialogues des Carmélites* loses meditational points about death when she realizes in her agony that a lifetime of prayer comes to naught in the end.

Ira's points are set to music by George according to the conventions of his day. He doesn't stretch the vocal line beyond a major tenth; is not melismatic—that is, doesn't use more than one note to a syllable (neither does Poulenc, his exact contemporary); and the shapes of each song are pretty much the same: a casual prelude succeeded by the requisite thirty-two-bar refrain of *a-a-b-a.* Yet there is as much variety—rhythmic, chordal, speedwise—as in the vocal output of Ravel. If a mannerism appears common from song to song, it's the tendency toward pentatonicism—arches confected from black-key rambling. Take at random "The Lorelei," "They All Laughed," "Maybe," "The Half of It," "Looking for the Boy," and see how each is built from the same rising sequence. Also the so-called blue note, a lowered third or seventh that *was* jazz in the 1920s (Darius Milhaud, striving toward timeliness, used more blue notes in his *Création du monde* of 1923 than did Gershwin in his *Rhapsody* of the same year), might seem overused were it not that each impulse takes on its own identity, then soars with a virile energy evoking a world as vulnerable and vast as the current world seems cool and stunted. For one belonging to both worlds, I find that every song still sends shivers of excruciating nostalgia up my spine, something no other music, past or present, seems to do anymore.

Gershwin's songs, his show tunes, are pure pop, or—as he would have said, ignoring our myriad current subdivisions—jazz. They withstand all manipulation, from the fuzzy-tragic wail of Billie Holiday (who was not even a fact when Gershwin died), with her vague groups of jam sessioneers, to Ella Fitzgerald's cool-as-sherbet diction backed by Nelson Riddle's great big band dolling up the tunes to within an inch of their lives. His concert music, notably *An American in Paris* and *Concerto in F,* is classical in that it is not adapted by "stylists" but performed intact. (Alone, *Rhapsody in Blue* inhabits a halfway house, being ostensibly a konzertstück but reshuffled, like Chabrier's *España,* for every profit-making combination imaginable.)

Porgy and Bess is grand opera in the highest sense and belongs in the world's great theaters. As a show-tune composer Gershwin is pop, as author of *Porgy* he is classical, but he is never both at the same time. The only other musician to straddle this schizophrenic fence successfully is Leonard Bernstein. Can it be more than coincidence that both men are American Jews and that both have been obsessed with musical realizations of the dybbuk? The dybbuk is a split-personality-inducing soul that, according to *Webster's,* "enters the body of a man and controls his actions until exorcised . . ."

Gershwin's ever-thwarted wish to study privately with the Great led to the oft-quoted reactions of Ravel—"You would stop writing good Gershwin and start writing bad Ravel"—and of Stravinsky—"With your royalties it's I who should take lessons from you." Interestingly, although Gershwin did write a lot of *good* Ravel, his opera shows no influence whatsoever of Stravinsky, not even in the balletic picnic scene marked *Molto barbaro* where he could have nicely appropriated the eccentric "aboriginal" cross rhythms of *The Rite of Spring*. But jazz, finally a more magnetic lure for him than any classical composer could have been, derives not from an eccentric but a steady beat; indeed almost nowhere in the hotly danceable oeuvre of Gershwin does one find meters other than in a normal four. The brief 5/4 dance in that picnic scene, or the *trouvaille* of offbeat accents in early tunes like "Fascinatin' Rhythm," would seem as child's play to even a Tchaikovsky or a Brahms. In the long run Stravinsky, with his early *Tango* and later *Ebony Concerto*, took more from Gershwin than Gershwin ever took from him.

The texture of *Porgy and Bess*, like that of all jazz, derives (via its original Creole ambiance?) from French impressionism, rather than from German romanticism. Scarcely a chord is built on other than major or minor sevenths (or ninths or elevenths), *à la française*, rather than on the dominant or diminished triads and sevenths in use across the Rhine. Not that Gershwin's nest, like the magpie's, wasn't laced with a bit of everything around. *Porgy and Bess*, which was launched in Boston on September 30, 1935, owes a trick or two to *Wozzeck*, which had been performed seventeen seasons earlier in Philadelphia, not to mention to *Tosca* of 1900, as well as to (Gershwin had foresight) *Peter Grimes*, *West Side Story* and *Dialogues des Carmélites*. It was as influential as it was influenced.

In themselves the ingredients of *Porgy and Bess*—harmony, counterpoint, rhythm, melody, orchestral color, vocal concept for both solos and chorus, and the integrity of overall construction—are each first-rate in quality, professional in execution, and, despite the stolen threads common to most creators, utterly personal in impact. Like Mussorgsky, Gershwin was an elegant primitive; his own ways were ultimately more telling than those of his slick adapters. As to from where he learned, other than from Schillinger and from trial and error, not only the craft of instrumentation but the art of imbuing his music

—first in single songs, later in whole garlands of song called musical comedies, finally in a three-hour drama—with the salubrious sap that makes it blossom and cohere from top to bottom, I wouldn't know. Does an artist *learn* such things?

After 1923, which saw the advent of *Rhapsody in Blue,* his first so-called classical concert piece, Gershwin orchestrated all of his own music. And although we know more about Monteverdi's operas than we do about Gershwin's so far as *procedure* of orchestration is concerned (the lead sheets, abbreviations, makeshift rehearsal scores for *Porgy* having all vanished), the net result is crystalline, never over-laden or intrusive. Aware of the basics—that strings are the body of any orchestra, woodwinds the soul, brass the clothing, and percussion the jewelry (the less you wear, the more effective)—Gershwin did occasionally go against typecasting. By and large, though, he didn't take more chances than, say, Respighi, whose sonorities he emulated a bit too closely for comfort (on page 508 of the *Porgy* score you will not hear, as marked, "a Sleeping Negro" but "The Pines of Rome"). Yet somehow, indefinably, his scoring is identifiably his. Who but Gershwin would have chosen, as background for Serena's impassioned recitative "Oh, Doctor Jesus," a soft trill, not on a drum or a cello but on a *piano!*

Just as the neighborhood Catfish Row plays its musical part in *Porgy and Bess,* so does the Chorus announce its own intense identity in a role longer, timewise and pagewise, than that of both principals combined. As cast member the Chorus is more indispensable even than *Carmen*'s chorus, being composed of personalities. Yet so familiar are the seventeen arias that we forget they are almost incidental—some a mere ten measures long—as against the grand set numbers of the group that account for three-quarters of the opera. The opera, thanks in large part to the choruses that support it like marble pillars placed between moments of slapstick and joy and horror and death, is in any case adeptly structured, with slows and fasts and highs and lows and mobs and solos and sads and sillies, all satisfyingly intermixed, each exquisite in itself. George's innate sense of unity owes much to the dozen earlier collaborations with Ira. (The book for *Of Thee I Sing*, sans music, won the Pulitzer prize in 1933.) Yes, the third act flags, especially when Crown's meaningless "A Redheaded Woman" comes out of left field, and later when a resetting of the normal tone seems to drag on forever before the ghastly truth is sprung on the hero. But beyond this there's scarcely an uninspired or superfluous minute in all of *Porgy and Bess*. In effect the framework would seek to disavow (not with entire success) the set-piece format of Gluck or Weill, or indeed of Gershwin's own show-biz past, in favor of the unbroken line of Debussy and Wagner. *Porgy*, no more than *Pelléas* and *Parsifal*, needs applause.

If because he died young Gershwin now seems remote, so does the fact of *Porgy*. Mysteries remain within the text. When is the action? The published score, composed in 1934 (and, incidentally, dedicated simply "To My Parents"), bears the indication *Charleston, the recent past*. The novel, published in 1926, draws upon a news item of the teens (about a cripple, "Goat Sammy," who assaulted a woman) and supposedly draws also upon DuBose Heyward's own recollection of the 1911 hurricane. The "kindly" white man in the second act, Mr. Archdale, posts bail for Peter because "his folks used to belong to my family." But Gershwinophile Robert Kimball situates the action "in the 1930s," and no one then could have matter-of-factly had folks who were slaves. Also, what happens to Clara? If Crown survived, couldn't she and Jake have survived, or at least shouldn't their fates be explained?

Is *Porgy and Bess* a tragedy? Who is the hero? If Crown is the nominal villain, while Sportin' Life's merely a son of a bitch, virtually all the characters in the first act, except Porgy, turn their backs on Bess when she needs a friend. ("The God-fearing women and the God-damning men!") Meanwhile Porgy-as-murderer goes unpunished—is indeed condoned by his peers, although he played the coward at the police station—whereas Crown (also a murderer) is the sole character to display courage as he ventures out to save Clara in the eye of the storm.

"No other American composer had such a funeral service as that held last Thursday for Gershwin," wrote Olin Downes in 1937. "Not a Mac-Dowell, nor a Chadwick, not a Stephen Foster or John Philip Sousa received such parting honors." A few months later George Antheil wrote: "He has been recognized by everybody except those whose . . . understanding he most craved—the American Composer . . . [Even Virgil Thomson's words on Gershwin] were often as condescending as the others . . . America's 'recognized abroad' serious symphonic composers have remained strangely silent."

Serious. That was the aim of high art, an aim that in itself now seems less serious than solemn in our ever more agile age of Akhenatons and Alices. Arnold Schoenberg, a fellow portrait painter and tennis opponent during the mid-1930s, wrote this when his friend Gershwin died: "Many people do not consider [him] a serious composer. But they should understand that, serious or not, he is a composer—that is, a man who lives in music and expresses everything, serious or not, sound or superficial, by means of music, because it is his native language." Schoenberg does not add that *he* finds Gershwin's music, or even his own, serious, nor is the word defined.

Two years earlier Gershwin himself had said, "I chose the form I have used for *Porgy and Bess* because I believe that music lives only when it is in serious form. When I wrote the *Rhapsody in Blue* I took 'blues' and put them in a larger and more serious form. That was twelve years ago and the *Rhapsody in Blue* is still very much alive, whereas if I had taken the same themes and put them in songs they would have been gone long ago."

What the pop composer puts on paper (or whistles into a Dicta-phone, as with Noël Coward and Irving Berlin and others who can't read or write music) is less a composition than something to be re-composed, while what the classical composer puts on paper is final.

Performers of these two kinds of music, by virtue of their specialized training, do not overlap, although their careers, like church and state, have always run parallel. The only creators, as I wrote earlier, who've spanned the bridge are Gershwin and Bernstein. *Porgy* belongs more utterly to Gershwin than, say, *Sweeney Todd* belongs to Stephen Sondheim, because Gershwin is responsible for the sonority and placement of every note in the score. Of course, he was wrong about his songs—that since they weren't "serious" they wouldn't last. Were you forced to name the second greatest (anyone can name the first) melodist in our century, could you possibly place Puccini or Poulenc or Jerome Kern, Mahler or Ives or Harold Arlen, Messiaen or Chanler or Richard Rodgers ahead of the wondrous George?

1984

INTERLUDE: NOTES ON DEATH

In *Paul's Case* the boy committing suicide witnesses his own dying, until suddenly the witnessing mechanism snaps off, and in blackness all returns to natural order. In childhood I identified with Paul, the oversensitive parvenu who, like Lily Bart, could no longer bear it. At the same time I sensed that Lily and Paul were unfit subjects for grown-up books. To read Cather and Wharton was to indulge a guilty luxury (luxury of vicarious suicide) when my mind, like Paul's and Lily's, should have been on important items like gym class or useful contacts. Adults, one assumed, put away childish things, broken hearts.

One can live and die by literary reference, not so much because one cannot distinguish fact from fiction as because fiction imposes itself forever upon fact, gives fact fragrance and shape, never permits fact to function in the abstract. Unless the very abstraction of fact is itself a fiction.

Could I be dead (rather than dying), given the indifferent motion of shadows emitting perfumes of ginger and formaldehyde? Dead nostrils don't inhale. Nor does dead gray matter recall the skill of a Janet Frame whose nonhero, pronounced moribund, nevertheless arose from an unguarded coffin to walk home, where a distraught but aquiescent mate was unable to accept him as viable, and in the end, years later, the neighbors stoned him to death for real.

Misdiagnosed as dead. Misdiagnosed as living.

Awash in his own blood he wonders: Is a work of art that from which one is safe? Is the poem a bridge to danger? (Danger to the poet, that is. For the public a poem is ever a bridge to safety.)

Does art succeed when it fails? A suicide that fails—leaving the victim alive and therefore an observer of his own "demise"—succeeds. Here I lie in my life's blood grinning, and am I my art? Who takes thus this *coup de théâtre?*

If to suffer from unrequited love is a waste of time, why should the documentation of that love—rendering it as history, as art—be time wisely spent? (Such practical queries! When in reality the world is unreal.)

When Camus claimed that the primal philosophical premise—the question to be settled before further discussion—was that of suicide, of whether life were worth living at all, he skipped a point. If life were not worth living, who would bother to discuss even that question? And surely those successful suicides, of sound mind and body, should be consulted after the fact. The first premise should be whether the question of suicide merits discussion. If it does, discuss it only after consulting the dead.

Thus the initial concern is not whether life's worth living but whether death's worth dying. When it kills, suicide fails. True success is to come back, to have your cake and eat it. Mishima's cake took the form of an international press release, yet he couldn't eat it since he lost his head. Still, like Marilyn, he acted out a universal dream by bidding goodbye before too late, at the height of power and beauty.

Yes, the suicides that don't kill you are like keeping your cake. But an artist too has his cake and eats it. He suffers, but is appreciated for his suffering, and this very appreciation is an appeasement, a parole. Is the pain thus less intense, less aimless than an anonymous death in an internment camp? Does a rich person feel less ache, in the absolute, than a poor person with the same malady?

Art and unhappiness are unrelated. Because an artist sees the truth as a way out, and can do nothing, he is unhappy. Because he is seen seeing the way out, he is happy. And he often is willing to market his misery, sweep his madness onto a talk show and laugh at his own tears. Perhaps finally the greatest intelligence is an ability for joy. But joy in our land is equated with money. (It is a truth universally acknowledged that a single man in possession of a good fortune must be queer.)

Unhappy people are all alike; a happy person is happy in his own way. Every aphorism is reversible. Surely nothing's more monotone than misery, even the misery of philosophers and especially of lovers, whose individuality dissolves into uniform tears dampening their staunchest friendship. Unhappiness is a privilege of the young, the interresemblant young. But happy people are as unalike as snowflakes, though more . . . more elastic. Happiness, a prerogative of the wise, rejects nothing. Happiness cannot intrinsically lead to unhappiness any more than clarity comes of navel-gazing, but it can lead to ecstasy, even to death. Did not Olivier in *Les Faux Monnayeurs* declare that suicide alone was comprehensible after reaching such heights of joy that anything afterward must become a permanent letdown?

Is even suicide worth it? The small comfort of art. Art has even less "meaning" than life. Art does not outlast life. We've not the least notion of what Bach meant to Bach. Art salves loneliness perhaps, but is no cure for cancer.

Nausea at the news of a friend's death is balanced by guilty twinges of expectancy on turning to the obits: the disappointment when "nobody" today is commemorated. Yet for survivors each death brings the adventure of a new start. With one less acquaintance to distract them the road is cleared to fresh arrangements. The world's weight's changed. But soon these losses announce that they're just that, losses, potholes never to be filled, and those ever more numerous dead hail us with one moan that won't soften as it recedes, but grows more touching, ice clear, wished for, out of reach, adorable, tough.

Have I an *oeuvre*? If I die tonight what single piece do I leave? No *Maldoror* surely, no *Four Saints* nor even *Little Foxes*—none of those works, like Shostakovich's First Symphony, penned young and shining. It's not for me to say that my output, like Chopin's or Janet Flanner's, is an assemblage, letters and preludes, nourishing one-page meals. Second day of the blizzard, alone in Nantucket with thumping radiators and the slumping basement, humanoid moans from a crack in the wall all night and if that stricture in my chest flings me floorward how long do I lie?

Was that heart ever wrapped in *Serenade* which this morning I finished and mailed to Ohio? Must heart always distinguish output? Distinguished output should *appear* to have heart. Our best work is not always what we feel deepest but what we work hardest on. This is most true for long-term results like operas or "functioning" marriages. (The joke is when something we work on hard also flops.) Pieces dashed off, but dashed off with heart and that succeed, are generally short, like songs.

All is habit, and so is art. Death is the giving up of our last and hardest habit, life. Life is a rehearsal of death. But at the final curtain, the very pain of agony helps to mask the coming horror.

JH contends that whereas Virgil's prose is to instruct, mine is to punish.

Instruction and punishment are two sides of one coin (the third side is satire). What we call Life is the scattered attempt to get even with those who "misunderstood" us in childhood. What we call Art is the disciplined attempt to get even.

Auden says: Those who hate to go to bed fear death, those who hate to get up fear life.

Aren't these analogies identical? And isn't Auden anyway wrong? Children hate to go to bed, and they aren't conditioned to forebodings good or bad. It's rather a question of halting inertia, altering an aspect of life (for in life there is no death, not even dying is death). I, for one, enjoy waking up and enjoy going to sleep. Dreamland is not a void but a vital geography.

To be aware of your own death. Everyone else goes on to dumb festivities, while you stay home alone and die. To say this means in some way to care—that I'm not incapacitated. Yet I've said all I have to say. In which case, such a final saying seems . . . Long nights.

Most of the time I feel lousy. Unable to underplay, I recount my own misery. Why? It's not a pleasure to wonder how I'll kill myself; suicide's not child's play, nor can anyone accept, even for a moment, Freud's verses anymore. ("No man can believe in his own death. And when he tries to imagine it, he perceives that he really survives as a spectator.") Were it not for JH where would I be? The drift of a high-school lass's diary comes back to haunt us.

Back in New York to find Jay Harrison nailed in a coffin. Deaths which "don't come as a surprise" surprise us most. Being expected, we write them off before they occur. When they occur we're doubly grieved. No gulf is wider than between the almost dead and the dead.

Deaths today of Marcel Achard and of Harry Partch, the arrière-garde of France and the avant-garde of America. Why are we less attracted to a contemporary artist's work after he dies? When friends die the excruciation is that we'll never see them again. That "never" is what leaves me cold when artists pass away—artists, that is, who aren't particularly friends. That their catalogue is now complete lames rather than quickens interest.

Everything has ego. Not just cats and plants and that bowl of tortoise eggs, but a pile of pillows, a steel bed, radiators exist there, without moving, ominous, taking up your space. I am not nice. Pretend to be, even try to be. But I'm not. Also I'm dull, though having learned to feign sparkle, I get along.

Weary and without illusion, I persist in noting it. Why even write? Why even write "Why even write 'Why even write "Why even write"'"?

Place de la Madeleine. Given what finally emerged, could one claim that the potential was contained in the madeleine when first tasted? Can a man be potentially an artist (or a dreamer of the past) if he never realizes himself as an artist (or a dreamer)? If the future is contained, literally contained, in the present, supposing a man dies before the future (the eating of the second madeleine) arrives? What becomes of this nipped-in-the-bud future? The world existed in that madeleine not in fact but because Marcel said it did. (Interesting that in an earlier draft his madeleine was toast.)

Unrequited love, mystery of the common cold, hate for a person who's forgotten us, the women's vote, a crossword puzzle. Solutions often come from unexpected sources. Dazzled by the pearly gates we miss the trapdoor.

The life I lived was the life I lived; how could I have known it was history? History—who says? Could not the gardener—if not in name at least in shame or glory—have been fixed there too? If he *is* fixed there in my reverie, does he vanish with my death, though I remain fixed (fixed?) in notes and nouns?

Ten years ago the fatal premiere of *Miss Julie.* Could I do better tonight? Differently, surely, and time flies fast. Works of art, said Proust, are less disappointing than life, for they do not begin by giving us the best of themselves. Yet are not various great works for me now exhausted (some by Stravinsky, for example, which once drained us repeatedly while retaining their own vitality, movements of Mozart, or Rembrandt or of Proust himself), while "life"—indeed the very "affair" with JH—is in continual flowering with the "best" yet to come, or how go on? Nets were finally flung and for some months there's been proximity of death. I am his host for he inhabits me, and his guest since he's provisionally placed me in a transparent placenta sack which, rather sooner than later, he'll rip open to the world's air, like a gas chamber's. Meanwhile he parades me about, a corpse on parole, chuckling as I balk at meager deadlines, write tunes, but easily distracted by television's lure. Death's female to the French. West Chester Street. Is this a street or some ancient thoroughfare through cemeteries which now, with daylight saving rescinded, turn blue by 4 P.M.? Alone on this island where I know no one, own a house, plain but costly, for the first time ever like grown-ups, and each evening after supper of lentils and Jello, take a constitutional through the seasonal mist down Lily Street encountering not a soul, and return to the dubious welcome thirty minutes later of Wallace the cat. Like ghosts of Hammerfest or Thule, Nantucket is far from anywhere, from America, from even a memory of childhood, though not from plagues that could accompany us to Mars, not from masculine death who glides at any speed. Why Nantucket? Why, when I've never owned a thing, buy a house in this Huguenot anti-art cranberry bog rather than in beloved Provence?

Allergic not just to seed and perfume, but to the smell of dollar bills and newsprint, Kleenex, water and thoughts of horses wild. JH tries to cope with my inability myself to cope. I fall apart, suffocate, scream. It's easy to write this now—but just one hour ago I saw *him,* NR, in flames, and JH at sea.

Yet there are moments every few days in Nantucket—during a flash of light across the page, during an afternoon pause in the Quaker cemetery—moments filled with happiness so clean you'd think they sprang from paradise. But in retrospect, sometimes as soon as one hour after, these moments seem unbearably sad. Is it because such moments, experienced only when alone, are remorse from the comparative passivity of contentment, even the contentment of the intellect at work, in arguments with JH or of trying a new recipe? No, the shock of happiness is so positive it resembles an invasion, burning energy with such speed that the recipient is left flat or, sometimes, dead.

Anyone can close the eyes of the dead, but who can open the eyes of the living?

How much time is left? Will the end hurt?

Confession for the new year. My growing laziness (and this applies to general life as well as to this special paragraph—its style and content and dubious desire for being) stems from knowing I've uttered all that's in me in as many accents as can be counterfeited. In the half-million words published, and in the thirty-plus hours of music composed, I've probably said most of what I know. Does there remain only to say it all again differently? Were they to announce "You will stay known and loved, and need never express yourself again; you will be rich and admired, but will never more compose"—would I feel deprived or relieved?

Having writ this, having professed forever that I can't know how the quality of my nice music or mean prose would hold were they not interdependent, I now believe they wound each other. To write words is finally very bad for my music.

Why persist? When we were children, Mother's father, Granddaddy Miller in Yankton, taught us all to knit—everything except how to cast off. That scarf was luscious, longer day by day, every week, month upon month, a woolen snake of many colors, I couldn't stop. There it still is over there, ivory needles still caught in those forty feet of indecision, its option, and only Isadora could have put an end to it.

1976

PART 3

Portraits and Memorials

With each friend that dies some of me dies. I am bereft, not because that part of me which he embodied is lost, but because that part of him which I embodied is lost. He can no longer impart to others his version of myself.

Marc Blitzstein

Inside every composer lurks a singer longing to get out. What is called "the composer's voice"—that squeaky unpitched organ with which composers audition their vocal works to baffled sopranos or uninterested producers—may explain their becoming composers in the first place: the vengeance of frustration. The human voice is, after all, both the primal and the final expression, the instrument all others seek to emulate. We are what we sing; any music worthy of the name is inherently sung, whether it be written for tenor or tuba or tambourine.

When I was growing up I knew only two exceptions to the rule that the composer-as-singer sabotages his own work. One was Samuel Barber, whose still-available recording of his own *Dover Beach*, made sixty years ago, reveals a gently excellent baritone with the italianate *r*s still favored by the few Americans who sing in their own tongue. The other was Marc Blitzstein. True, Marc had a "composer's voice," but he composed specifically for such a voice, and could put over his own songs with a fearless conviction I've never heard anywhere else. Blitzstein, the pseudo-amateur, hypnotized the professionals about him. The whole spellbound cast of *The Threepenny Opera* sounds like him,

194 Portraits and Memorials

including Louis Armstrong and Lotte Lenya and Bobby Darin. Indeed, if you want to know the dancer from the dance, you need only hear a "real" voice intoning one of Marc's left-wing ditties to realize that both words and music are lessened by standard beauty.

Both Barber and Blitzstein were raised in well-off pre–World War I Philadelphia milieux, and veered thence in opposite directions—Sam toward the anxieties of mandarin individuals (Cleopatra, Prokosch, Kierkegaard, Vanessa), Marc toward the collective woes of Everyman. During the Second World War they did both serve in the military, which resulted in a jingoistic bomb from each one: Barber's Second Symphony (known as the *Night Flight*), which he finally withdrew, and Blitzstein's *Airborne Symphony*, which finally withdrew itself. Beyond this coincidence, the Paleface and the Redskin had nothing in common. That one was Episcopalian and the other Jewish, surely figured.

A more cogent comparison is between Pasolini and Blitzstein, both upper-crust Communists murdered by rough trade, the first in the outskirts of Rome by one of the very *ragazzi di vita* he had spent a lifetime nurturing, the second on the isle of Martinique by the very type of deprived seafaring gay-basher he had spent a lifetime defending. Though communism may have been a mere touristic escape in each man's life, it nonetheless formed the core of each man's art. "A scholar and a master of the Italian language, [Pasolini] picked up no grounding at all in the life of the proletariat," wrote Clive James recently. "He never did a day's manual labor then or later. This is a standard pattern for revolutionary intellectuals and can't usefully be called hypocrisy, since if there is such a thing as a proletarian consciousness then it is hard to see how any proletarian could escape from it without the help of the revolutionary intellectual—although just how the revolutionary intellectual manages to escape from bourgeois consciousness is a problem that better minds than Pasolini have never been able to solve without sleight of hand."

As for Marc, how might he have reacted to the "liberation" of Communists thirty years after his death? By seeing them as eager consumers, no better than they should be? (My father liked to refer to this or that achiever as "born of poor but dishonest parents.") Today we perceive a lopsided focus in certain visions of the golden past. Marc retained the focus to the end, though his friend Lillian Hellman wrote: "A younger generation . . . looks upon the 1930s radical and the 1930s red-baiter with equal amusement. I don't much enjoy their amusement, but they have some right to it."

In the mid-fifties, half my life ago, I was still young enough to be dazzled by my legendary seniors, and smug enough to feel a power when introducing, for the first time, one of these seniors to another. The great torch singer Libby Holman had become a friend. She had never met Marc, but would perhaps have enjoyed playing the role of Jenny in *The Threepenny Opera*, which at the time had made Marc (ironically, because he was only the translator, and because the late Kurt Weill, a homophobe, never cared for Marc's "cashing in") a rich star. One evening I brought them together in a bistro on West Twelfth Street. Libby, who years before had been tried for her husband's murder and acquitted, had inherited that husband's fortune but spent a goodly chunk of it on civil-rights groups, especially after her only son died while mountain climbing. There I sat, silent, as these two conversed intensely with their violent theatricality, their true unusualness. There I sat with her who had killed and would later kill herself, and with him who would be killed.

Libby never once mentioned the role of Jenny. Marc paid the bill.

Like most young composers in the 1940s, I knew Blitzstein's worth solely from hearsay. Textbooks were full of him as America's embodiment of Brecht's "art for society's sake"; he himself decreed that the creative artist must "transform himself from a parasite to a fighter." A parasite on whom? I wondered. A fighter for what? If I was not political, I *was* impressed by those who were: Lenny Bernstein and Aaron Copland constantly sang Marc's praises, making me feel guilty. Even Virgil Thomson, a sometime foe of Blitzstein and an aristocrat to the toenails, had declared years earlier: "*The Cradle Will Rock* is the gayest and most absorbing piece of musical theater that the American Left has inspired. . . . Long may it remind us that union cards can be as touchy a point of honor as marriage certificates." Beyond the force of these dynamos, Marc had the added glamour of *one who had been there*—of one now unavailably away in the wars. The music was no longer played but the spirit held firm.

Then suddenly he returned, a hero in uniform, and Lenny premiered, in April of 1946, the ambitious *Airborne Symphony*, with Orson Welles as narrator, eighty male members of Robert Shaw's Collegiate Chorale, and Leo Smit as pianist with the New York City Symphony. Who was I to express a purely artistic dissension in the face of these committed intellectuals? Yet I was appalled. What I intuited then I affirm today: the piece was patriotic smarm. Admittedly, I have an allergy to melodrama—to, that is, speechified music—unless the verbalism is tightly rhythmicized, as Walton so cannily rhythmicized Sitwell's *Façade*. (If the sung voice is the most musical of instruments, the spoken voice is the least.) Thus masterworks like Debussy's *Martyre*, Stravinsky's *Perséphone*, Honegger's *Jeanne* go against my grain even as I revel in their sonic superstructure and fairly classy texts. But Blitzstein's text for *Airborne* gives new meaning to the word *overstatement*. It's a *Reader's Digest* tribute to our air force—preachy, collegiate, unbuttressed (unlike Copland's corny *Lincoln Portrait*, which *is* buttressed) by a less than trite musical background. The few nonembarrassing moments in the score are too close for comfort to *L'Histoire du soldat*, and those in the libretto to Whitman's diary. Bernstein was to appropriate Blitzstein's sentimentality—the boyish belief in Man's Essential Good—and to use it better. (*Better* always means better tunes. Of music's five properties—harmony, counterpoint, rhythm, color, and melody—melody is sovereign; without a sense of contagious melody a composer is not a composer.)

A great work is one you can never get used to. I immediately got used to the *Airborne Symphony*, which went in one ear and out the other without leaving any trace of residue.

That July, after lying fallow during the war, Tanglewood splendidly reopened to a mass of talent unequaled since Paris in the twenties.

The student composers (I was one of them) were lodged at a vast girls' school in Barrington where we gave parties. To one of these Lenny brought his weekend guest, Marc Blitzstein, and we all played our little pieces, hoping to impress. Then Marc sat down and sang, one after another, his various hit ariettas—"Nickel under the Foot," "Penny Candy," "Zipperfly"—with such tough and telling charm that, yes, suddenly everything fell together, the pudding was in the eating, the components of his art meshed. Harmony churned, counterpoint spoke, the rhythm was catchy and the color luminous, the tunes came across— all precisely because they spewed from Marc's own body, then lingered like a necessary infection to love and not get used to, at least for one evening. Next morning, though the songs were gone, Marc's fragrance remained.

During the fall, as a student at Juilliard, where to qualify for a degree one had to take sociology, I phoned Marc to ask for an interview about his ideas on Art and Society. What do I recall of our talk that November afternoon in the one-room flat at 4 East Twelfth Street where he lived until his death, I who felt no relationship with—much less a need for diverting—the masses? I recall that Marc called Poulenc a sissy. That he called Cocteau a *true* artist, while claiming that anyone who could turn a fable of Love and Death into something as "chic" as *L'Eternel retour* (all the rage then in New York), especially by labeling the love potion "poison," was hardly a *great* artist. That all music to him was political. That he looked like Keenan Wynn. That he said, "Admit it, you didn't really come here to interview me for your class."

During the next sixteen years we were friends, even when far away —friends, that is, as much as quasi-mentor and reluctant pupil can platonically be. I sense that, while never saying so, Marc always misguidedly felt that I was too much the prey of the upper class to write important music. As for the lower class, I never saw that, except for sex, Marc was a mingler there. He liked good food and drink, and shunned the reality of deprivation.

Why, I recently asked someone who knew them both, was Lenny such a devoted admirer of Marc? Because, said the person, Marc was a failure. Well, Lenny worshipped Aaron too, and Aaron was a success.

Yes, but Aaron was that much older (he was born in 1900, five years before Marc), and a monolithic idol for us all. True, there are cases where two friends, one famous and one not, are switched overnight in the world's eye: so Lenny was switched in relation to the composer Paul Bowles, and later with Marc. Bowles went on to plow (successfully) other fields, while Marc persevered in Lenny's shade. But if Marc could ever have been deemed a failure, he is not that today. Since Marc's work is having a renaissance, and he is now a historical figure (he's been gone for nearly two generations), he can now be judged in perspective.

July 14, 1949. Dear Ned: Yes, you may use my name as reference for a Guggenheim. . . . I envy you Paris, and I remember that gone feeling. Me, I just sit chained to the desk, getting the orchestration of the new opera done in time for a deadline. . . . As ever, [signed] Marc Blitzstein

The new opera was *Regina,* his first in twelve years, which was premiered four months later.

November 8, 1957. Dear Ned: I was charmed and impressed with the tribute, and with the quality of the song. But when you go to the trouble of making a fine piece and dedicating it to me, why the hell don't you present it in person? My love. Marc

The "tribute" was a setting of Paul Goodman's "Such Beauty as Hurts to Behold," which I would have felt worthy of Marc. Earlier that year I had written a one-act opera, *The Robbers,* to my own text based on Chaucer's *The Pardoner's Tale.* Marc was dismayed—he said I'd got lost in "libretto land" with my arch and archaic locutions. He undertook to rewrite the entire text: without changing a note of the music he refashioned every verbal phrase so that it fell more trippingly on the tongue. This was a voluntary two-day job for which I thanked him with the little song.

Jan. 6, 1959. Dear Ned: Here is the piece, and a note to Bill Flanagan, which I beg you to deliver. I despair of reaching you by phone; my hours are a mess of disorganization. . . . Love, Marc

The "piece" was a five-hundred-word essay, "On Two Young Composers," contributed at my prodding to launch a program of songs by me and William Flanagan (whom he'd never met) which took place on February 24. The first general paragraph, beginning "Songs are a tricky business" (even more apt today than then), is wise, original, and bears reprinting. Of Bill he concludes: "A certain modesty dwells in his music; it should not be confused with smallness." Of me: "Ned Rorem makes thrusts, each of his songs is a kind of adventure. . . . It is a long time since anyone brought off the grand style, outsized sweeping line, thunder and all, that marks 'The Lordly Hudson.' He will one day write an impressive opera. . . ."

> August 6, 1959. Dear Ned: It was a glorious trip, from all points of view—including *amours* and the business aspect. And I want to thank you for your letters—although I never got to use the Auric or the Veyron-Lacroix; and Marie-Laure, after a series of *contretemps*, wired me to come see her in Hyères, which I couldn't. . . . I've tried to reach you by 'phone; now Golde tells me you are in Wis. I have decided to accept the song-cycle commission from Alice Esty (who tells me your Roethke songs are nearly finished, you dog); and it is in line with that that I write you now. . . . Did you make some kind of deal with Roethke regarding the commission? and if so, what? Do you mind telling me? I want to do the right thing; at the same time I am puzzled as to how to share the commission with the poet (of existing poems), if at all. So do write me here, outlining your own procedure in the matter. And love. Marc

Alice Esty, an adventuresome soprano, commissioned, between 1959 and 1966, three composers a year to write cycles for her, starting with Marc, me, and Virgil T. My cycle was on poems by Theodore Roethke, who sent me several lively letters, not at all about aesthetics, but setting forth in canny paragraphs exactly what he wanted in residuals, and asking for equal billing on the printed score. (We met only once, not at the concert where the songs were premiered, but at the party afterward, where he showed up, drunk.) I don't know what kind of a "deal" Marc finally made with *his* poet, E. E. Cummings, but his group of seven songs, *From Marian's Book,* is, for my metabolism, his very best work. Just as Tennessee Williams's best stories are better than his best plays, precisely because he realizes that those stories will never be known by the vast philistine matinee public and can thus with impunity be as convoluted and intimate as he feels, so Marc's concert songs do not, by definition, pander to the big audience. Not that such pandering is in itself wrong; it's wrong only when an intellectual aims at the hoi polloi. Marc was an intellectual; Lenny Bernstein was not (although he tried to be and was, in fact, smarter than many an intellectual). Lenny, like Poulenc, wrote the same *kind* of music for his sacred as for his profane works; Marc tempered his language according to whom he was addressing.

February 24, 1960. Dear Ned: A sweet wire, for which I thank you. I feel badly that our rehearsals didn't allow me to get to your concert. . . . I have just come from Carnegie Hall, where Poulenc stubbed his toe flatly in "La Voix humaine." A comic "camp" is bearable; a serious "camp" is utterly phony. Love. Marc.

June 29, 1960. Dear Ned: How good to hear from you. The name Yaddo awoke all sorts of fine memories. Do give my warmest to Elizabeth [Ames] and any others who remember me. . . . "Jasager" *is* a beautiful piece. As to copies of the piano-vocal score: I'm sure Lehman Engel must have at least one. He did it way back in the thirties, with the Henry Street Settlement chorus, I think; and I seem to remember it was in English. . . .

Incidentally, what about the Brecht estate? They'll raise a fit if it's known that an "unauthorized" translation has been made and used, even if non-commercially. Lenya, I have found to my sorrow, isn't enough when it's a Brecht-Weill work. . . .

I had Shirley Rhoads to my place for a swim yesterday. She is fine, still living (according to her) in a dump, this time in Lobsterville on the other end of this divine island. Maybe sometime in August you'd like to come visit me for a couple of days? Although I warn you I'll be lousy company; all work and swimming, that's me this summer. The opera is hard, hard. I do nearly twelve hours a day. I suppose I'll look back on this period of struggle with love and envy. All affection.

That would have been mailed to Yaddo. The opera he speaks of was the uncompleted *Sacco and Vanzetti*. References to Kurt Weill's *Der Jasager* concerned my project of producing it at the University of Buffalo. This I eventually did, with my own translation, and with nobody's permission.

Two years later it was Marc who was at Yaddo, I in New York. I planned to come to Yaddo in February, which would have meant my taking over Marc's room there, but I changed my mind, and instead remained in the city to rehearse for another of the American song concerts Bill Flanagan and I had made into an annual ritual. From Yaddo, then, came this postcard, the last written communication I had from Marc.

Feb. 22, 1962. Dear Ned: Thanks for the avìso. I shall probably stay on, as Elizabeth has asked me to. But I must come into town for some days: probably around March 18–19. Will you be seeable? Work goes fine, if slowly. . . . I wish I could come to your concert, no soap. I enjoyed the leaflet—but I wish you and Bill would stop those arty-farty *Harper's Bazaar* photos. Still, it's your face, and a beauty too. My love to Bill and you. Marc.

I have no copies of any letters I may have sent to Marc. But before he left for Martinique I made this entry in my diary:

3 October, 1963. Last night the Rémys came to dine, with Shirley and Marc Blitzstein. Marc gets pugnacious after two drinks, interpreting virtually any remark by anyone as either approbation of or a threat to some dream version of the Common Man who hasn't existed in thirty years. But the Rémys were bewitched, having

never encountered this particular breed of American, probably because Marc is a breed of one, who, like John Latouche in the old days, when on his best behavior, is the most irresistibly quick man in the world.

I never saw him again. Three weeks later he left for Fort-de-France in Martinique, and eleven weeks after that he was dead. On January 22, 1964, a shocked and respectful world received the news, on the front page of the *New York Times,* announced as an auto accident. Next day, the *Times* amended the story: he had been set upon by three Portuguese sailors who had lured him, with drunken promises of sex, into an alley. There they left him penniless, naked, and battered.

Beyond the horror and dejection, how did I react to Marc's death? With a sort of surprise? He had led, on his special terms, an organized and exemplary life, and was critical of those who hadn't. With me he was avuncular, and vaguely protective aesthetically and hygienically: Don't listen to too much Ravel; be sure to do this or that after sex with strangers. This grown-up, this model—how could he have . . . well, *allowed* himself to be murdered? And in midstream. His opera was definitely scheduled for the Met. (Rudolf Bing is said to have asked, Were Sacco and Vanzetti lovers, like Romeo and Juliet?)

27 January 1964. Except for Bill Flanagan, whom I see every day, Marc was the only composer I frequented *as a composer,* someone to compare notes with. When we'd finish a piece we'd show it to each other, as in student days, hoping for praise, getting practical suggestions. Our language, on the face of it, would seem to be the same (diatonic, lyric, simple). In fact, we barked up very different trees. Marc was nothing if not theatrical, and precisely for that he showed me how the element of theater was integral even to remote forms like recital songs.

Malamud is an author with whose subject matter (Jewish poverty in Brooklyn) I'd seem to have little in common, but with whose *Assistant* I identified wholly. It's discouraging to realize that Marc's best work was his last, *Idiots First,* which he played me just

weeks ago. Malamud would have continued to be his ideal collaborator.

My charm, if I have any, is economized for occasion. Marc's was
squandered freely. When as a Juilliard student I first knocked on
his door for an interview, Marc Blitzstein received me with a—
a sort of Catholic impatience, worn like a cloak, as he sat at his
piano criticizing Cocteau for being fashionable. Have been going
through my diary of that period, which talks of the slush in the
gutters, Marc's postwar indignations, etc. . . .

I've always felt it, of course, but more and more I've come actually to see that happiness not only precedes but accompanies ca-
lamity.

I have just listened, without intermission, to the new recording
of *Regina* (London 433 812–2, 2 CDS; Scottish Opera Orchestra and
Chorus, conducted by John Mauceri), all 153 minutes of it. Here are
some notes taken during that experience:

I am not a reviewer, I am a composer and a sometime critic; but I do
read reviews and see how they shouldn't be done. (Is the reviewer's description of a new work, for example, succinct enough to show whether
he or she likes it without saying "I like it"? Does the reviewer describe
the work, or the performance of the work?)

Much has been made about Lillian Hellman's continual interfer-
ence—how she forbade Blitzstein's numerous embellishments on her
play, *The Little Foxes*. Playwrights, if still alive, can be a thorn in a composer's side (so goes the received opinion); why don't they just shut up,
the play will survive on its own, and a composer's domain is a separate
dimension. During the lifetimes of Blitzstein and Hellman the opera
was never produced as the composer envisioned it. Am I a minority in
believing Hellman was right about the musicalizing of her play? The
present recording is the first complete version of *Regina,* and it proves
that more is less.

When Poulenc expands Bernanos's *Dialogues des Carmélites* from a

filmscript based on Gertrud von Le Fort's German novella, the Bernanos text stays intact, though Poulenc overlays it with settings of five
sections of the Latin liturgy. Four of these serve as prayers that close
scenes but do not advance the plot. The fifth, the final "Salve Regina,"
impels the action: with each crunch of the guillotine the music modu-
lates upward, thinning out bit by bit, until all sixteen nuns are dead.
These interpolations do not "open up" the story; they intensify a basically motionless drama by entering, as only music can, the mute interior of monastic life. The play is tightened into a necessary opera;
there is something to sing about.

When Blitzstein expands a densely plotted story about "the little
foxes that spoil the vines," he widely revises the Hellman text and adds
jazz bands, Negro spirituals, party music, and production numbers set
to his own doggerel. The play is loosened into an unnecessary extrava-
ganza, because otherwise there would be nothing to sing about. True,
certain non-Hellman parts of the piece—such as the "Rain Quartet"
and the terrific Dance Suite in act 2—make arguably the best music in
Regina, just as the Latin choral numbers are the most beautiful parts of
Dialogues; but where the former are extraneous the latter are integral.
Whatever else Hellman's play might be, it's economical: the power of
her craft lies in the claustrophobia of greed, and her principal characters are hopelessly naughty and unpoetic. Even without the composer's
accessories, it's questionable whether any opera can depict unalleviated
evil. Music, the most ambiguous of the seven arts, lends sympathy to
aberration. Are not Scarpia, Iago, and Claggart, as repainted by Puccini, Verdi, and Britten, raised from mere loathsomeness to a sort of
tragic pathos? To hear Regina Giddens and her relatives at song is to
defang them: our vines still have tender grapes, and gone is the hard
compulsory shell of Hellman.

Add to this that *Regina* is Blitzstein's only large work not designed
around his own singing voice—he used instead the tessituras of operatic professionals, as *Porgy and Bess* uses them—and you have a watery
version of the grandiose. Indeed, *Regina*'s tunes and texture are often

pure *Porgy,* but without the seductive guile of Gershwin's melody. Nor does Marc, with his frequent spoken interpolations, solve the unsolvable puzzle of how to set pedestrian matters to music. And I cannot seize the sense of some of Marc's text (what does the much-repeated "Naught's a naught" mean?); I cringe at the rhymes ("Greedy girl, what a greedy girl, / Got a greedy guiding star. / For a little girl, what a greedy girl you are") and at the anachronisms ("A bang-up party, and quaint withal, / To call the Hubbards the honored guests at their own ball").

This said, something in the sound grows occasionally touching, echoing a far past, as Monteverdi and Puccini did, except that this past of Marc's is mine, too. It is easy to dub him the poor man's Kurt Weill in his Common Man works; here lies no trace of Weill, but Copland rather, laced with Kern, insolently banal and gorgeously scored. Nor can I deny that I pillaged boldly Birdie's grand lament about the old homestead, Lionnet, for an aria in my own *Miss Julie.* The recurrent "dying fall" of a minor third, rising higher and higher, I owe utterly to Marc.

And I owe to Marc the recurrent motif (also a drooping minor third, this time fast and nasty) in my 1958 orchestral poem, *Eagles,* filched from *his* orchestral poem, *Lear,* written the year before. But in this case I borrowed a device (Strauss used it too, in *Salome*), not an aesthetic, for Marc did not even superficially influence me.

Leftover notes:

Although Lenny Bernstein would never have been quite what he was without the firm example of Marc Blitzstein, there's nothing Marc did that Lenny didn't do better. A like analogy may be drawn between what the giant developer, Aaron Copland, borrowed (and glorified) from the midget pioneer, Virgil Thomson — or between Britten and Holst, Debussy and Rebikov, Wagner and Spohr. The greatest masters are not the greatest innovators. (Picasso: *Je trouve d'abord, je cherche après.*) Marc Blitzstein, oddly, was not even an innovator, except geographically: what Weill stood for in Germany, Marc stood for in America — namely, the sophisticated soi-disant spokesman of the people. His biggest hit was the arrangement of Weill's "Mack the Knife," which infiltrated even *The Fantasticks.*

Marc, the populist, hung out with aristocrats; Poulenc, the aristocrat, hung out with bartenders.

Good reviews don't make me feel as good as bad reviews make me feel bad, but no reviews are worst of all. This sentiment, which all artists feel (don't they?), was rejected haughtily by Marc. Yet in 1955 when *Reuben Reuben* (on that hopeless subject, lack of communication) was so roundly loathed by the tryout audiences that they spat upon him, Marc was reduced to tears. Out of context I recall the songs, as he sang them to me, through my own tears. Indeed, so moved was I by the composer's wheezy intoning of "The Very Moment of Love," meant for a chorus in an insane asylum, that he copied it out for me in a little autograph album which lies before me now. That song, along with the songs in *Marian's Book,* the "Letter to Emily" in *Airborne,* and Birdie's aria—they stick in the mind.

Yet I am not a fan. I state this advisedly, knowing most of the music pretty well, and giving the man—because he was a friend—the benefit of the doubt (a benefit not accorded to, say, Philip Glass or Elliott Carter).

After having accepted the invitation to write this little essay I wished I'd refused, but it was too late. Of the fifty-odd articles I've written over the decades about twentieth-century matters musical, just one—about Virgil Thomson—has been a harsh reaction to the work of a friend.

We both lived to rue this. In 1972, after thirty years of mutely despising Thomson's music, and figuring that because he was a major critic who dished it out regularly, he wouldn't mind a taste of his own medicine, I presumed finally to voice my feelings in print. Virgil was not thrilled. When he deigned to speak to me five years later, I vowed never again to weaken a friendship by attacking the vital organs. (Contrary to some opinions, it is not pleasant to write unpleasant reviews.) In retrospect, probably it was better for my soul to have said my say and be remorseful than to have stayed mute and be regretful.

With Marc my ambivalence is by definition removed. I loved the man and hated much of the music, hated the man and loved much of the music. He can't defend himself today, but the music can. That music can shout me down. Still, I can live without it. For artistic if not for moral reasons I am unable to discuss it persuasively, so perhaps I should not have penned these pages. It's too soon to know if my soul is the better for it.

1993

Martha Graham

Everyone called her Martha, but no one was her confidant. She tore through society wearing blinders, looking neither to left nor right except to ferret out samples of what she would call "truth": children in the subway, a gazelle at the zoo, buildings, boulders. She had no urge for small talk or broken hearts, and thus, like most obsessives, lacked humor. (Actually, we all have humor, but yours may not be mine.) Yet her works, half of them, are about prefeminist strong-minded females, victims as well as predators, often embarrassingly horny; the other half are about transcendent saints or silly geese and can be genuinely funny. Being a genius, she fit no definition. The personal coldness, couched in a guise of extreme cordiality, was pure self-protection. Remoteness is the coin-of-involvement's flip side. She was Garbo's mirror — Graham acted, Garbo danced.

I had seen the Graham company years earlier, been impressed, found it agreeable with its seductive scores of Paul Nordoff, though not all that different from Chicago's own Ruth Page Company with its seductive scores of Jerome Moross. But in 1945 Martha, aged fifty-two, was at her peak (the redoubtable Sol Hurok had just signed her), and even I realized that there must be a discombobulation when one meets the original after one has already known the imitator.

So here I was, sitting across from the original, being interviewed for the position of classroom pianist—not, as I had hoped, of rehearsal pianist, which would have meant playing the new scores being choreographed for the coming season. She was all affability, now a flirting girl, now a grande dame, now a businesswoman, now a fellow musician. She did like me, or why put on such a show, yet I couldn't tell what was expected of me. "You know," she announced, "Leonard Bernstein once worked here. He really *was* 'On the Town' in those days. It didn't work out—he couldn't help playing 'real music' and mooning around at the keys, rather than playing rhythmic incitations."

Virgil Thomson once summed up the whole dance world in a phrase: "They are autoerotic and have no conversation." About Martha in particular, Agnes De Mille wrote: "No one can remember exactly what she says." Well, I can remember exactly two things: "The pay will be three dollars per class; and you will need a Social Security number." Thus Martha Graham became my first official employer.

The Graham studios were on lower Fifth Avenue, number 66, above the Cinema Playhouse, which showed a perennial double feature, *Blood of a Poet* and *Lot in Sodom*. Classes then, not unlike Yoga sessions now, built gradually from the floor to the ceiling systematically over ninety minutes, entirely on counts of eight, barefoot, stressing contraction and release. Six or seven girls, three or four boys, some of them students, most of them company members, began the session prone on the uncarpeted parquet. With lowered heads betwixt hunched shoulders, they exhaled to a beat of eight; then with head and shoulders thrown back they inhaled to another beat of eight. These sequences were replicated in different postures for half an hour, until, with a lovely sweep of arm and hip the assembly rose in unison to an upright stance, and the routine was repeated. For the final half hour, still on counts of eight, the class hopped about the room in various postures and at various speeds. Or so I recall. Current practitioners of the Graham Method (the method that rocked the world in one generation, it has been asserted, as opposed to the three centuries it took for ballet to evolve) would say I've got it wrong. Yes, probably. My fingertips are eidetic, but my torso is not kinetic; I never took a class, and improvised on the keyboard only according to what I thought (or vaguely felt) the class wanted. "Play any old notes," Martha advised, "as long as you keep the beat."

I performed for three classes a day, five days a week. The first was taught at 8:30 a.m. by Martha herself, whom we all agreed was "inspiring" ("we" being myself and the dancers, who had the souls of children and were easy to empathize with). She would talk a lot. Example: "Yesterday while wandering through the Museum of Oriental History I came across a Buddha of cobalt alabaster. His shaved pate was lowered in profound meditation and I felt a clash of East with West rush through me like slow lightning, a respect tinged with envy, an attitude it would be well for us all to emulate. It is such meditation—such *dynamic, fruitful* meditation—that I could hope each one of you might absorb." Then she would approach the thrilled and baffled youngsters and one by one stretch their limbs with her magic hands ("do as I do, not as I say"), while my improvised pianistic drumbeats, or sighs, orgasms, always to a throbbing count of eight, and sometimes using music of old masters—Prokofiev's *Visions fugitives,* for instance—tried to impel their movements.

The second class was led by Erick Hawkins, whom Martha loved (they would be married—briefly, catastrophically—shortly thereafter, during which this unique monster would legally become Martha Hawkins, a role from one of her hillbilly creations), and who was her company's romantic male dancer, with Merce Cunningham as comic or evil relief. Erick often joined the students as a warm-up in the earlier class, but everyone else was new—except me. He, too, would talk a lot. Example: "Recently I visited the Oriental Museum and came across a Buddha with a shaved head. This Buddha represented the rift between West and East, and I wish you could emulate him." Poor Erick, he longed to be taken for a thinker. But in appropriating Martha's non-anecdote (though he might well have been with her yesterday at the Oriental Museum—wherever that may be), he diminished himself in my eyes. Still, to watch him leap, or gyrate, or touch with such gentle formality a fellow moving body was to see Nijinsky converted to modern dance. Like most people, he resembled his name, with that aquiline nose, those chiseled cheeks, the Tom Cruise gaze, a craggy ramrod. He was less intimidating than Martha, easier to follow.

Easiest to follow was Margery Mazia, who conducted the third class. She didn't talk, at least not about "meaning," and never criticized my playing.

Quickly I came to worship with the entourage. As regular worker, Martha became a model of Spartan self-denial, sometimes scheduling classes for Sunday mornings when normal people should be abed, hungover. As exceptional artist, she showed us how to wander from the beaten track, but only *she* found her way back. Then as now she was America's first female, yet had to solicit subsidy despite the fame. The fame was such that all her girls wore their hair tight in abject adoration, their mouths slightly open, their thighs at odd angles—but only *she* brought it off. Then as now, or so I contended, Martha Graham was one of the four most significant influences of any sex, of any domain, of our century. (The others? Billie Holiday, Djuna Barnes, Mae West.) My dream was to compose for her.

But she fired me. Oh, quite nicely, because, as she rightly explained, improvisation was clumsy discipline for young composers. Her unspoken reason was my lack of the pianistic thrust needed to impel collective contractions and releases. Dance accompanists, to be good, must take classes themselves.

Early in 1946 we moved out of the studio and into the theater when she opened for the first time under the splashy sponsorship of Sol Hurok. This meant she now was on Broadway with a thirteen-piece orchestra and a three-week run. It meant too that certain students who had been drafted into the troupe would make their debuts, and that I would finally see the new Chávez score, whose sounds (fairly nondescript) had been filtering from one rehearsal room while I played classes in another. I'd already seen the costumes, such as they were— loincloths for the boys, red scarves for the girls—when they arrived two days earlier to the childlike glee of all. I'd already heard, too, Copland's *Appalachian Spring* in its full orchestra version, which had just won the Pulitzer Prize, and which Martha had premiered the previous year, along with Hindemith's *Hérodiade,* in Washington. These dance works, with the new *Dark Meadow,* were now before us in New York. The excitement resembled what a Diaghilev opening must have generated forty years earlier. I've never felt anything like it.

When the curtain rose on *Dark Meadow,* those daily faces—the lighthearted kids from dance class—were suddenly unfamiliar. Four boys squatting on their haunches clutched from behind, between their knees, four girls, also crouched, and like amoebas in slow motion they glided awkwardly about the stage in contradiction to Chávez's disappointingly precise but useful-enough score. Amid this octet Martha, as She Who Seeks, lay on the floor and rolled herself up in a rug, then unrolled herself, then rerolled herself, then reunrolled herself, while we, deep into Freud, were chilled to the core. (The next season Iva Kitchell, the comic mime, performed a hysterical parody of this behavior.) Though I must have seen it a dozen times, I recall no more of *Dark Meadow* than the close: a Noguchi tree suddenly sprouts tin leaves as the chorus moves obliquely to the front of the stage while Martha, back to audience, slants off to the wings, staggering slowly, arms raised and clutching a bright red menstrual rag.

Appalachian Spring, a ballet extolling family values with music by a man who never slept with a woman (Martha told me beforehand that the score was crystalline—her word—and apt to a tee, while Aaron explained to me afterward that it was composed "in the abstract," according to cues and lengths, and that he never knew the plot, much less the title, until the final rehearsal), is called a masterpiece, the right meeting of talents at the right time. Martha was perhaps a bit old for the role of Bride, and less enthralling than as another bride in *Hérodiade* where, with only Mae O'Donnell as lady-in-waiting, she prepares to marry Death while only a bassoon—Hindemith's bassoon—prods her magically.

At the peak of her fame (like Lenny Bernstein, she had always been famous, even before she was famous), Martha was nonetheless past her prime. What one now recalls is not her technical prowess — the swirled kicks or the hard heel resonantly crashing into the floor repeatedly like a flamenco — but the sheer presence, the morbid visage, the stillness. Immobile as a pillar, a liquid pillar, a pillar of brandy, she moved mountains.

Later that spring, at the old MacMillan Theater on the Columbia campus, she premiered yet another grand contraption to Samuel Barber's maybe best score, *The Serpent Heart*. Again Mae O'Donnell, in her cool blond beauty, provided the perfect foil as the chorus who graciously raises the curtain, again Martha with a snake in her mouth has a hair-raising solo on a boogie-woogie bass, and again Noguchi provides the ideal prop when Medea, as the curtains close, rides toward the audience madly in her shining chariot.

After the stint of working at her studio I did not meet Martha Graham for eight more years. Ah, the fact of her was forever around Manhattan — and much of musical life centered on that fact; composers were rated by some according to whether they had collaborated with her. By others, notably John Myers & Company, who felt Balanchine rightly ruled the roost, Graham was rated zero. But her myth advanced, aided by Hurok. I kept up, as young composers always do, if only to see what the competition consists of. But after moving to France in 1949, the fact of her dissipated.

In May of 1954 I wrote in my diary: "Martha Graham's company is here for the first time. The French who, if only on their deathbeds, do take their freewheeling birthright Catholicism for granted, do not therefore know how to take the implacable no-nonsense of Martha's pagan Jocastas or protestant Emilys. We had that with Kurth Jooss, they wrongly clarify (they, who ask with brave discovery if you know Brahms's quintets!). The French are still for toes and fairy tales, so they have put her down.

"Yesterday afternoon, emerging from the Eglise Saint-German into green sunlight, I spotted her at the Deux Magots terrace seated gauntly before a cold demitasse and a pile of dry brioches. For a moment we spoke—if indeed speaking is how one communicates with her, if one communicates—and I wandered off, caught again.

"Caught by the past when I was as young in New York as now I am in Paris, as enamoured there then of miraculous Frijshian ladies as I am here now of my Marie-Laure. And Martha again today, so out of context! How far, on this warm warm evening, were those nervous mornings during the war's end, of banging to a count of eight loudly, while in silence I worried that she choreographed *Dark Meadow* to Chávez's tunes, not mine. How far, those Grahamesque explications we all understood without understanding, that vague speech on mental landscapes of primeval ritual, which did somehow compel the dancers! For we were moved, it worked. . . .

"Tonight I took in again her *Night Journey,* dying. Afterward, alive in the wings, I asked Martha (hugely tiny among her winged Noguchis) how long she'd be in town, if we could have iced tea together, or could I show her Versailles. 'Yesterday would have been the time for that,' said she, 'when you passed by the Deux Magots. From now on I haven't a minute to myself.'"

Twelve years later. In the fall of 1966 her conductor, Eugene Lester, having read my recently published *Paris Diary,* felt he should bring me and Martha together again to discuss a collaboration.

I see her moving toward me across the immensely echoing floor of the rehearsal room, now up on East Sixty-third Street. Each step disintegrated the clock until her scarlet mouth was close, uttering the identical phrases of years ago, but which inevitably took new meanings according to occasion. We chatted only briefly. (She spoke disparagingly of Nureyev, whom she had just met, and who had flung his whisky glass across the room into the fireplace. "The arrogance!" said Martha, though it was a gesture she would have been capable of.) Then to business.

Stock still for twenty-seven minutes she listened to the tape of my *Eleven Studies for Eleven Instruments.* When it was over, she'd all but choreographed it in her head. We shook hands, kissed, it was a deal. Already she had a title, from Saint-Jean Perse, *The Terrible Frivolity of Hell,* and I recalled that, of course, Martha always spoke, ever so softly, in iambic pentameter.

Because I had to leave for several months in Utah, that was that. I knew she was working on "our" ballet for the winter season because she phoned occasionally—those inspired midnight calls with ice cubes tinkling through the wires across the land. (Her drinking, which was known, now seemed a crass contradiction of that earlier Spartan self-denial.) The ballet was evolving, but possibly because the music wasn't written for her, my feeling of high honor was coupled with disinterest. Also, the music had been used by others before her, though Martha didn't know it and I certainly didn't tell her. Valerie Bettis, Norman Walker, others . . . In her two hundred-plus creations, a mere handful were choreographed to already existing music. Just as American Song wouldn't be quite as it is without Janet Fairbank, so Martha Graham caused to exist a great bin of first-rate music. Would I have written something especially for her?

But in a sense, it *was* written for her, as I realized on returning to New York and, like Maldoror, seeing for myself. In the past, it's been shocking how dancers seem unaware of what composer they're dancing to. With Bettis and Walker and the others I'd been pleased but not dazzled: mostly they Mickey-Moused the music, doing what it so obviously told them to do. Not Martha's troupe: they demonstrated how I'd made *Eleven Studies in Search of an Author.* How unright that music was without this sight. How Helen McGehee's hops were inevitably correct against the amorphous trumpet! the group's immobility when my little orchestra goes wild! Robert Powell's rhythmic trance behind the screeching clarinet!

Because she was unliteral, and knew how to design *counter* to the yet indispensable music, Martha is my only collaborator (though she never once asked my advice) to have been right, all right, turning my disinterest to satisfaction.

1993

Paul Bowles

If all artists are the sum of their contradictions, then Paul Bowles is an extreme example of that definition. Throughout his nearly nine decades he practiced two parallel careers which seemingly never overlapped.

In 1949, with the publication of his very successful *Sheltering Sky* at the age of forty, Paul Bowles became the author-who-also-writes-music, after having long been the composer-who-also-writes-words. That success brought more than a reemphasis of reputation; from the musical community's standpoint it signaled the permanent divorce of a pair of professions. During the next two decades Paul Bowles produced fourteen books of various kinds, but little more than an hour's worth of music. Did he feel that one art, to survive, needed to swallow and forget the other? Surely he received more acclaim in a year for his novel than he had received in a lifetime for his music. This need not imply a superior literary talent; indeed, if history recalls him, it will be for his musical gifts. It's just that ten times more people read books than go to concerts.

Composer-authors generally compartmentalize their two vocations, allotting parts of each year, if not each day, to each career. But as authors their subject is invariably music (witness Berlioz, Schumann, Debussy, or Boulez, Sessions, Thomson), whereas Paul Bowles was a fiction-writing composer, the only significant one since Richard Wagner, and even Wagner's fiction was at the service of his operas. Except during the war years when he functioned as a music critic, Bowles's prose was antithetical to his music. Whatever resemblance exists between the working procedures for each craft, the difference between his results is like night and day.

His music is nostalgic and witty, evoking the times and places of its conception—Paris, New York, and Morocco during the twenties, thirties, and forties—through languorous triple meters, hot jazz, and Arabic sonorities. Like most nostalgic and witty music that works, Bowles's is all in short forms, vocal settings or instrumental suites. Even his two operas on Lorca texts are really garlands of songs tied together by spoken words. In 1936 Orson Welles's production of *Horse Eats Hat* became the first of some two dozen plays for which he provided the most distinguished incidental scores of the period. The theater accounts for a huge percentage of his music output, and for the milieu he frequented for a quarter-century, most latterly the milieu of Tennessee Williams, whose works would never have had quite the same tonality—the same fragrance—without Bowles's melodies emerging from them so pleasingly. Indeed, the intent of his music in all forms is to please, and to please through light colors and gentle textures and amusing rhythms, novel for the time, and quite lean, like their author.

Paul Bowles's fiction is dark and cruel, clearly meant to horrify in an impersonal sort of way. It often bizarrely details the humiliation and downfall of quite ordinary people, as though their very banality were deserving of punishment. Bowles develops such themes at length and with a far surer hand than in, say, his sonata structures. His formats in even the shorter stories are on a grander plan than in his music; at their weakest they persuasively elaborate their plots (albeit around ciphers, and in a style sometimes wilfully cheap); at their best they transport the reader through brand-new dimensions to nightmare geographies. Bowles communicates the incommunicable. But even at their most humane his tales steer clear of the "human," the romantic, while his music can be downright chummy. Indeed, so dissimilar are his two talents that it is hard to imagine him composing backgrounds to his own dramas.

Paul Bowles's real life was courageous and exotic. Whenever possible he spent it in what we like to call backward countries with hot climates, especially Ceylon and North Africa, like Prokosch before him, and Maugham. Yet no matter how far afield he wandered, he maintained active correspondence with the West, specifically American intellectuals who, since he seldom went to them, crossed oceans to meet him. Bowles, the social animal, traveled Everywhere, knew Everyone, and was much loved (though he never admitted to loving). His writings dealt extensively with the Everywhere, but never with the Everyone, until the autobiography, *Without Stopping,* which failed.

We met during the summer of 1941 in Mexico, where I was travelling with my father who felt I should get away from the corroding arty homophilia of our native Chicago. How little did he know! Paul was thirty, I sixteen, good-looking and with a roving eye. Paul later would pen a story, *Pages From Cold Point,* about an adolescent in Taxco who seduces many a local male including his own parent. Naughty gossips suggested that . . . etc.

Paul, meanwhile, was the first professional composer I'd ever encountered. He introduced me to the music of Copland and Thomson and, especially, himself. The main soprano aria from his zarzuela, *The Wind Remains,* with its recurring drop of a minor third—the so-called Mahlerian "dying fall"—so bewitched me that to this day it has been the single most telling influence in my several hundred hours of music.

For the next sixty years we saw each other fairly regularly, over there and over here, and otherwise we corresponded. The correspondence

Dear Paul, Dear Ned, was published a few years back, by Elysium Press, with an introduction by Gavin Lambert. How can I say how lucky I feel that this document remains of the most confusingly interesting, distantly lovable, gifted and reticent man who ever lived. The world weighs less with his departure.

1999

Francis Poulenc

Like his name he was both dapper and ungainly. His clothes came from Lanvin but were unpressed. His hands were scrubbed, but the fingernails were bitten to bone. His physiognomy showed a cross between weasel and trumpet, and featured a large nose through which he wittily spoke. His sun-swept apartment on the Luxembourg Gardens was grandly toned in orange plush, but the floors squeaked annoyingly. His social predilections were for duchesses and policemen, though he was born and lived as a wealthy bourgeois. His villa at Noizay was austere and immaculate, but surrounded by densely careless arbors. There he wrote the greatest vocal music of our century, all of it technically impeccable, and truly vulgar. He was deeply devout and uncontrollably sensual.

In short, his aspect and personality, taste and music each contained contrasts that were not alternating but simultaneous. In a single spoken paragraph he would express terror about a work in progress, hence his need for a pilgrimage to the Black Virgin's Shrine at Rocamadour; his next breath extolled the joys of cruising the Deauville boardwalk.

This was no non sequitur but the statement of a whole man always interlocking soul and flesh, sacred and profane; the double awareness of artists and of their emulators, the saints.

And, like artists, he was also a child; his self-absorption was stupefying. I recall once in Cannes his monologue to a baffled bartender about a series of triumphant modulations he had penned that afternoon. I remember also a river of tears as he listened to a record of his own *Stabat Mater*. "Robert Shaw," he wept, "is the greatest performer of our time: his tempi correspond to the very motion of my blood." And I remember a pair of elderly female instructors from the Tours lycée, each sporting a shirt and tie, who came for tea to his country home. While his big, liver-spotted hands popped tiny raspberry tarts into his mouth—washed down with *tilleul* (he seldom touched liquor)—he held forth on private Paris gossip, then talked for an hour about orchestration, all this to uncomprehending listeners, including the chauffeur, who was also at the party.

Yet he was not intellectual. Indeed, as a composer, he was never concerned with poetry's meaning beyond its musical possibilities. Which is why his songs surpass those of, say, Auric, who *knows* too much to release instinct. Songs are nonetheless a collaboration of both poet and musician. And though Poulenc is sung the world over, his chief bard, Paul Eluard, once told me that those songs obliterated the tunes he himself had heard while writing the verses. Which did not keep him from printing:

> *Francis, je ne m'écoutais pas*
> *Francis, je te dois de m'entendre.*

Because Francis was a friend, indiscriminately, generously! (He taught me more than anyone long before I dreamed of knowing him.) Both man and music were delicious—an adjective now suspect to the brainwashed public alerted to disrespect what it might understand or like. The very nature of Poulenc's art is to be liked and understood, which is therefore its momentary defeat.

So, although joyful by inclination, he nursed that special melancholy of the successful ones who are no longer admired by the young. Yet he did not attempt (as others may, if their powers wane) to seduce youth by adopting its mannerisms; his language remained constant. Self-centered though he was, he still remained one of the few composers I know who wasn't bored by the music of others. He regularly studied old scores while keeping his heart open to new trends.

Now that heart has killed him. Curiously, it was not his heart but his liver that plagued him during his later life (as it plagues all Frenchmen), in this case largely psychosomatic. When he was half finished with his *Dialogues* opera, there was a question of being denied the rights by the Bernanos estate. His organs grew paralyzed, he retired to a Swiss hospital where his circulation all but stopped and stigmata appeared on his wrists. He wrote farewell letters to everyone, exclaiming: "In the Middle Ages I'd have been burned alive for less than this!" When the rights were finally granted, he recovered overnight and completed the work which has since glorified our international stages. There again was the contradictory child.

That child said: "We put words to music; but we must also put to music what is found in the white margin." In translating that marginal whiteness Poulenc, like Ravel, became not different but better than anyone else. Nobody in Paris can do it now. Not since Ravel's death in 1937 (I was fourteen) can I recall being so disturbed as by the news of Poulenc last week. For Poulenc had inherited Ravel's mantle, and today in leaving us he has taken with him the best of what remained in musical France.

1963

Virgil Thomson

When I first beheld Virgil Thomson, in the early forties, he was on a stage for one of those benighted roundtables about Meaning in Music. His fellow panelists, straining for a definition of the art, were about to settle for the Bard's "concord of sweet sounds" when Thomson yelled: "Boy, was he wrong! You might as well call poetry a succession of lovely words, or painting a juxtaposition of pretty colors. Music's definition is: That which musicians do." Which settled the matter. If Shakespeare erred, albeit divinely, Congreve did too, with his "charms to soothe a savage breast." Thomson, like all composers, disdained metaphoric ascriptions to music as mere cushion for the emotions. His businesslike summation was the first professional remark I'd ever heard from a so-called creative artist, and I was soon to hear more, from the horse's mouth, when I quit school at age nineteen to work with the master.

I already knew of course that he was born in 1896 in Kansas City, excelled at Harvard, then moved to France in 1920. And that in the next two decades he sent back to America not only trunkloads of sonatas and songs, but quartets and symphonies, a ballet called *Filling Station,* scores for movies of Pare Lorentz, a best-selling book called *The State of Music,* and, above all, a collaboration with Gertrude Stein, *Four Saints in Three Acts,* which was then and perhaps remains the most viable opera by any American. Like all art it is rather mad and so beyond definition, yet like all madness it has a canny logic all its own. The music is neither particularly beautiful nor even interesting. Its chief originality lies in its willful diatonicism at a time when dissonance was the rage. Nor is the libretto especially gripping when taken alone. Worse, it is poetry, a dangerous ingredient in theater. The magic of *Four Saints* issues from a marriage made in heaven. Never have two artists so realized their individuality precisely by sacrificing it to a common cause. Stein and Thomson took not only talent but their very presence from each other. Alone, neither fashioned a work of comparable strength.

American he utterly was despite, or maybe because of, the removal from his homeland which gave him a new slant on his roots. For it was he who first legitimized the use of home-grown fodder for urbane palates. He confected his own folksong by filtering the hymns of his youth through a chic Gallic prism. This was the "American Sound" of wide-open prairies and Appalachian springs, soon borrowed and popularized by others.

At the start of World War Two, Virgil Thomson returned from Paris to begin his fourteen-year stint as critic for the *New York Herald Tribune.* And the rest, as they say, is . . . well, it's geography. Thomson single-handedly changed, for a time, the tone of serious American composition from the thickish Teutonic stance which had dominated since before MacDowell to the transparent Frenchness of those in the Boulanger school.

He was at his peak when we met in 1943. As his in-house copyist, for which I received twenty dollars and two orchestration lessons a week, my daily chores were done on the parlor table within earshot of the next room where—propped in bed, a pad on his lap, an ear to the phone—Virgil ran the world of music. When I arrived each day at ten, he would have performed his ablutions, and now, in clean orange pajamas from Lanvin, propped up and surrounded by an ocean of pillows with a sharpened pencil and a big yellow pad (he never learned to typewrite), he conducted the musical life of Manhattan from his bed. If it were Tuesday the phone would be off the hook as he scrawled (his handwriting was as infantile as his musical calligraphy) his Sunday sermon, which he would then, with no revisions, dictate by phone to his secretary, Julia Haines, at the *Tribune*. The subject of the sermon, he explained to me, could materialize from anywhere: the previous month in concert halls (he reviewed three concerts a week), crank letters from strangers, reactions to the state of modern song in France, or from a question Maurice Grosser put to him en passant. On other weekdays he would spend the morning hours on the bedside phone, mostly on business for the paper: making assignments to his staff of critics (which included Paul Bowles), or telling them his reactions to their reviews from last night. He might otherwise extend or accept invitations involving Oscar Levant or Sir Thomas Beecham (whom he loved) or Ormandy, or simply gossip with his Franco-American cronies, who included the art world as much as the music: the brothers Berman, Sylvia Marlowe, Philip Johnson, Tchelitcheff, Peggy Guggenheim. Since the bedroom door was wide open as I labored, naturally I overheard all this, often with a lifted eyebrow (I was the *bourgeois* he was pleased to *épater*), unless he specifically asked me to close the door, an academic gesture since his shrill voice carried.

On one such occasion his mother, Clara May Thomson, then aged seventy-nine and in New York for the first time, was present. She slept in a room down the hall but arrived at Virgil's each morning at 7:30 to help the cook—a large and humorless old-world Negro woman named Leana—shell peas or iron shirts on the other end of the table whereon I labored. Toward noon I was asked to close the door, and we all cocked our ears as Virgil dialed Paul Bowles.

"I have to bawl you out, Paul dear, so have you had your breakfast?"

"Breakfast at noon!" snorted both women with midwestern righteousness.

As for Paul Bowles being chided, it struck me as . . . as against nature that anyone could be in the driver's seat with Paul; Paul was just not accessible. I hadn't seen him yet since living in New York, but still thought of him with vague awe if not respect. Virgil's reprimand concerned what he called Paul's "pose," going around saying he didn't know anything about nineteenth-century German music, for this made mockery of criticism and by extension of the *Herald-Tribune.* Of course, Virgil had no love for, or careful knowledge of, German music either, but when a review of, say, a Brahms symphony was needed it was assigned to Jerry Bohm or Arthur Berger or, *faute de mieux,* Paul Bowles, who was admonished to do his homework. Meanwhile Virgil took his mother to all sorts of recitals, including one of John Cage's for prepared pianos. Asked her opinion, Mrs. Thomson replied: "Nice, but I never would have thought of it myself."

Were I to dare interrupt a phone conversation with a query about some illegible smudge, Virgil would remonstrate either by amending the smudge to look worse than before or by declaring: "That's baby stuff, baby. Don't bother Papa with baby stuff." "Baby" was one of his favorite words. So was "amusing," which in English rings more preciously than in French. Everything was amusing: Macbeth, a cherry pie, his mother's heavy overcoat. When he said to the stony Leana before she went out shopping, "If you see any vegetables that look amusing, buy them," she came back empty-handed.

In the afternoons Virgil, dressed, would receive in the parlor. Again I eavesdropped as he rehearsed his Violin Sonata with Joseph Fuchs, or served coffee to the staff of *View* magazine, which wanted an article from him, or chatted with his most frequent visitor, Maurice Grosser, friend and longtime lover from Harvard days, a topnotch realist painter of people (Jane Bowles), landscapes (the coast of Maine), and foodstuffs (mainly eggs and rounded fruits and vegetables like eggplants and pears, all vastly enlarged). Maurice, a Mississippi Jew, was in physical stature reminiscent of Morris Golde, sinewy, short, excitable; in mentality he was, arguably, the brains behind Virgil's brains. It was Maurice who took the raw sketches of Stein's *Four Saints in Three Acts* and superimposed a scenario which blossomed into the ideal libretto, even as

Alice Toklas wrote Stein's famous autobiography. And it was Maurice who fashioned Gertrude's loose, if inspired, prose about Susan B. Anthony into the tight scenario which became *The Mother Of Us All*.

The fashioning began in 1946, when Virgil was fifty, Gertrude seventy-two. When Gertrude succumbed to cancer on July 27, not living to see the new opera, Virgil, who by nature was an optimist though he never showed his emotions, seemed visibly shaken for weeks. He said: "It never occurred to either of us that we would die. Otherwise we would have written an opera every year."

As he had with *Four Saints,* Grosser organized Gertrude's vernacular of American political oratory into a singable theatrical vehicle, with a coherent plot involving feminism, the vote, and race relations. These events were intoned by historic characters (Susan B. Anthony, Daniel Webster, Constance Fletcher, Lillian Russell, Ulysses S. Grant), by real-life friends (Virgil Thomson, Gertrude Stein), and by a series of imaginary creatures (Joe the Loiterer, Chris the Citizen, Angel More, etc.), plus a dozen smaller roles taken by chorus members and by dancers. From the opening drum roll the sound is like *Four Saints:* always the plain phrases with their modernistic touches (triads used polytonally) soldering the Baptist-sounding hymns of the composer's Kansas City childhood. And always the point-blank verse of Stein's, so ideal to Thomson's setting. The same happy chemistry is at work, though less "abstract" than before, and American as baseball.

Twenty-five years later Virgil would compose his third and final opera, *Lord Byron,* with the youthful Stein-influenced poet-actor, Jack Larson. Larson's overall style is mock-heroic, and not unexpectedly a bit too Steinian for comfort. The music is pure Thomson. The faux-naïf notion of transporting Kansas City nostalgia to George III's London seems surrealistically amusing, but is quite unconvincing. What functions brilliantly for Susan B. Anthony cannot begin to sustain the passionate sweep of Lord Byron's character. As for the vocal lines, since everyone sings the same *kind* of music, there is a lack of differentiation that turns to monotony. The monotony was not bothersome in *Four Saints,* which followed no story, nor are saints expected to present contrasts, to "do" anything. But that was in another time and place, and what worked with Gertrude cannot work without her.

Virgil the author, as his ten books attest, was the world's most informative and unsentimental witness to other people's music. These qualities were enhanced by his addressing the subject from inside out—from the standpoint of the maker—and by his readability which owed so much to Paris where, in art as in life, brevity is next to godliness. Beside him, other critics were superfluous. They may have shared his perception, even exceeded his scope, but none boasted his knack for cracking square center with that perfect little Fabergé hammer. His lucidity was due no less to an innate clarity of mind than to a voicing of that mind through an ideal language of thrift: he spoke French in English. Since he knew what he was talking about and didn't waste words, merely to be in his presence was to learn. And merely to think about him is to risk being influenced, as these pale phrases attest, for no one out-Virgils Virgil.

Virgil the musician, over and beyond his affable innovation (based not on new complication but, ironically, on age-old simplicity), was our sole composer as convincing in song as in opera. His music cannot be assessed on the same expressive basis as any other music, even Satie's, since his more than any other depends on words. If Virgil never received a bad review (or, except for the Stein operas, a really good review), it's less because reviewers were intimidated by Papa than because they didn't know what to say about this seeming inanity. In fact, the inanity was sophistication at its most poignant. His every phrase is aria-in-a-microscope, built from but two or three intervals. The result differs from folksong only in the ambiguous accompaniment and eccentric literariness. The songs are rarely sung right, but despite their sparseness they do need to be heard to be believed. They are not *Augenmusik,* yet the critic's ear is not often given to listening to them, even in imagination. Thomson's unique urge was to codify simplicity, the way others have been urged to codify complexity. Thomson's composing gift never relied on interesting ideas, but on the uses to which dull ideas can be put. Displacing the ordinary, he rendered it extraordinary—that was his stock-in-trade. His music has little to do with romance or the grand statement, for it is as removed from the scene of action as cherubim are removed from the scenes they decorate. His music does have to do with joy, never carnal joy but the pure joy of merely being—again like cherubim (or saints). Thomson's lifelong effort would seem to have been to cleanse his art of *meaning,* in the Beethovenian sense, of sensuality or suffering or what we call self-expression, seeking instead, like pre-romantics such as Mozart, to delight.

It is true that Thomson was a pathfinder, that he wrote our first prestigious operas and film scores, that the prestige lay in the use of indigenous material, and that this material in turn was adopted by more "sophisticated" composers who gave it the slick American Sound. It is also true that Thomson's music, for all its originality, does not have very much to say. And is it so original? Outside his operas, did he accomplish anything not accomplished through the folkloric phantasmagorias of Charles Ives, or through the tongue-in-cheekeries of his idol Erik Satie? Ives aimed emotionally higher than Thomson and hit the mark. Satie composed in *Socrate* one of the most serious pieces of all time. Emotion and seriousness are not what we identify with Thomson's music, though finally they are the yardsticks by which all meaning is measured.

If in texture Virgil Thomson was American as apple pie, in "message" he was French as *tarte Tatin,* because he was not a specialist. During the decades of our friendship (sometimes warm, sometimes cool) I never thought of him as less than this century's most articulate musicologist and most persuasive opera-maker. Like all artists he was able to do what cannot be done. Through his prose he convincingly evoked the sound of new musical pieces, and through his musical pieces he continues to evoke the visual spectacle of all our pasts.

When I last beheld Virgil Thomson two weeks before he died, in 1989, he was ensconced as usual in that armchair near the piano, gazing at paintings by dear friends—Stettheimer, Arp, Grosser, Bérard—that had for so long hung on his east wall at the Chelsea. In the dreamy murmur that was now his sole voice (contrasting with the glib staccato that once so intimidated most of us), he announced: "Just sitting here, day after day after day, I realize how beautiful my pictures are." That is how I like to remember him—a general practitioner, in taste as in talent, never blasé, dying as he had lived, among an array of old acquaintances.

1989

Aaron Copland

Aaron Copland was the father of American music. American music, for the moment, will be defined as music penned by Americans after 1925, eschewing the up-to-then German traditions admired by, say, Griffes and MacDowell, stemming from the economical leanness promoted by Nadia Boulanger, then coming to a close around 1955 when the serial killers took hold with a featureless canvas that could in no way be identified as national. If Virgil Thomson was the first to borrow native Kentucky tunes and treat them symphonically until finally, like Poulenc in France, he composed his own folk music (so to speak—or so to sing), Copland improved upon the practice, embellished it, taught it, and made it his own. *Appalachian Spring,* with its stress on spare harmony and homemade folksong, its dearth of counterpoint, its scoring without much doubling, and its fairly simple hand-clapping rhythms, defined American music for two generations.

The first of his music I ever heard was *Quiet City* in 1940, and it bowled me over. Except for Chicago composers, Sowerby and Carpenter mainly, the notion of American Music hadn't quite taken with me.

Now here suddenly was Aaron Copland's gem, at once so French like all I adored with its succinct expressivity, yet so un-French with its open-faced good will. So I tried to find as many of Copland's records as possible, although except for *El Salón México* (and I had visited that nightclub during a trip south of the border with my father) there wasn't much available.

We first met when I was nineteen and a student at Curtis. I went to the West Sixty-third Street studio, which I recall as a single narrow room as long as the block and compartmentalized by shelves heavy with air-checks and acetates of his various scores. Aaron was affable, immediate, attentive, with that wonderful American laugh; in the four-plus decades since that day I've seen him behave with the same unaffected frankness not only with other young unknowns but with countesses and Koussevitzkys. He played me a tape (only it wasn't called a tape then) of *Of Mice and Men,* of which I was especially touched by the super-simple D-minor moment for solo strings illustrating the death of Candy's dog. I played him a juvenile trio, my Opus minus-one, which I still have in a drawer somewhere. We talked about whether tunes came easy, and gossiped about Mexico and Chicago. That was that.

In the summer of '46 I got a scholarship to Tanglewood and became one of Aaron's six protégés. The protégés were billeted in one huge stable in a Great Barrington girls' school (now a golf club), along with Martinů's six protégés, and Martinů himself. But Martinů fell from a garden wall during the first week, was badly shattered, and had to be replaced by Lopatnikoff. The twelve student composers had two lessons a week with their respective maestros, plus two group sessions, plus access to all kinds of rehearsals, notably of *Peter Grimes,* which received its American premiere there. It was the happiest summer of my life. Aaron lived in Pittsfield and invited me to dine once or twice, and to see *Señorita Toreador,* an Esther Williams movie that used *El Salón México* as background music. He also offered me scotch and sodas (he was never a drinker, but I was) which quite went to my head: Aaron was my teacher, after all. "Don't tell anyone," said he, "because one can't make a habit of inviting students out." But what did he really think of me?

I was always a lone wolf and never became one of Aaron's regular flock anymore than I became one of Virgil's, except that I worked as a copyist for Virgil, so I knew him better. Aaron had an entourage, so did Virgil; you belonged to one or the other, like Avignon and Rome, take it or leave it. I left it. Or rather, I dipped my toe in both streams.

Virgil's "Americanness" predates Aaron's. Virgil's use of Protestant hymns and, as he calls them, "darn fool ditties" dates from the twenties. Aaron's use came later, filtered through Thomson's. One may prefer Aaron's art to Virgil's, but give Virgil full credit: Aaron knew a good thing when he saw it. Although he's had a wider influence, he'd not be what he is without Virgil's groundbreaking excursions.

Isn't it interesting that this composer, raised as a well-off urban Jew, wrote exclusively about poorish rural gentiles? Like all artists Aaron was a child, but where some play at being grown up Aaron's childishness had a frank visibility that I've never seen elsewhere, except perhaps in Ravel, of all people. Someday I must expand a theory about their resemblance—in their target if not in their arrows. For although Ravel was lush where Copland was plain, both stressed the craft of *dépouillement*, of stripping bare. And has it ever occurred to you that in their "representational" music they seldom portrayed the adult world? Ravel with his toys, his Daphnis, his affinity for animals, was *L'Enfant et les sortilèges* incarnate. Copland's Common Man was an abstracted man, like his ballet personages who were eternal adolescents in the wide open spaces. He was forever drawn to the pubescent realm of *The Tender Land* and *The Second Hurricane*. Both men were urbane (they knew "everybody") but dwelt far from the madding crowd, Copland in sophisticated innocence, Ravel in naïve sophistication.

Aaron brought leanness to America, which set the tone for our musical language throughout the war. Thanks largely to Aaron (via Virgil, of course) American music came into its own. But by 1949 there started to be a give and take between the United States and Europe. Europe woke up where she left off in 1932, like Sleeping Beauty—or Sleeping Ugly—and revived all that Schoenbergian madness, now perpetrated ironically not through the Germans but through Pierre Boulez, who was a most persuasive number. The sense of diatonic economy inseminated in us by Copland was swept away in a trice, and everyone started writing fat, Teutonic music again. It was as though our country, while smug in its sense of military superiority, was still too green to imagine itself as culturally autonomous; the danger over, we reverted to Mother Europe. Aaron never really survived the blow.

In 1949 when I was living in Paris, Shirley Gabis (now Perle) and I invited a half dozen people over to hear Boulez play his Second Sonata, and Aaron came. At least one of us left the room in the middle, so discombobulating was the performance, but Aaron stuck it out with a grin. On the one hand, he was aroused by the nostalgia of his own Parisian past, when everyone tried to *épater les bourgeois;* on the other hand, Boulez was appealing and sharp as a razor, and Aaron would like to be taken seriously by the younger man and his mafia. Artists, even the greatest, once they achieve maximum fame, are no longer interested in their peers' reaction so much as in that of the new generation. Who knows what Boulez thought of Copland's music? The French have always condescended to other cultures. Except for Gershwin's, names like Copland and Harris and Sessions were merely names when I first dwelt in France, and are still (*pace* Carter and Cage) merely names there. Anyway, that same day, Aaron sat down and played his *Variations,* no doubt to prove he was just as hairy as Boulez, but the effect was one of terrific force and form, and, yes, inspiration, thrown at the hostile chaos of the enfant terrible.

It is interesting, too, how few vocal works there are by Copland. Beyond the two brief operas mentioned above, what is there? Well, the first extant manuscript is a one-page fragment named "Lola," composed at age fourteen. And there were a couple of songs from the late twenties, and some little choral pieces from the films of the late thirties.

Then in 1950, with the premiere of *Twelve Poems of Emily Dickinson,* which we had heard about for years but never heard, a curtain was raised. Bliss was it then to be alive, at least for us young composers — all twelve of us!—when every new work by Copland (or Stravinsky or Shostakovich or Britten) was greeted with ecstasy, and the land was still rich with the enthusiasm of first-times.

I came back briefly to New York in 1952 and visited Aaron in one of his hundred sublets (this one deep in the south Village). Patricia Neway was there, rehearsing the Dickinson songs which she was to premiere with the New Friends of Music. I was terribly interested (and, as a songster myself, maybe a bit jealous) that Aaron kept the verses intact without repeating words not repeated in context, and impressed at how sumptuously, even bluesily, melodic the songs were despite the jaggedly disjointed vocal line. He had already—hadn't he?—written the Piano Quartet, his first leap onto the tone-row bandwagon. But here now again was the pure old master, clear as mountain dew.

During the fifties we saw each other less, since I lived in Europe for that decade. But whenever he was in Paris I invited him chez Marie-Laure de Noailles, where I lived, or chez Marie-Blanche de Polignac, who "received" on Sunday evenings. I can still see him in these two extraordinarily beautiful houses, amid the fragile Proustian society. Renoirs all over the walls, breast of guinea hen all over the table, the dizzy scent of Lanvin perfume pervading the salons, and Aaron so down-to-earth with his famous contagious giggle, so plain, so—dare I say it?—Jewish, and at the same time cowboyish. For it's notable, maybe even something to be proud of, that the first truly important American composer is a Jew, yet a Jew who never, as Lenny did, wrote Jewish music. Except for *Vitebsk.* Always at these functions he was duly impressed, but anxious to get to the sonic core of the situation, meet whatever musicians might be there, or listen (especially at Marie-Blanche's) to Poulenc, or Jacques Février, or maybe Georges Auric playing four-hands with the hostess. Mostly, though, he was probably un-excited by the tone, anxious for something more current, more vital.

As Aaron's fame swelled during the sixties and seventies, his influence waned and he receded into his own world. Any "world feels dusty when you stop to die,/We want the dew then, honors seem dry"—as he depicted in his most beautiful song. But the honors that accrue to him ever more vastly appear so often to be simply praiseworthy, a touch standoffish, treating the man like a saint. Now, to be a saint, you must once have been a sinner, and I feel that it diminishes Aaron to avoid discussion of his various temptations. We all recall his friendly reticence, his hunger for gossip, although he himself was not given, as Virgil was, to gossip. Aaron never said nasty things to others, but I've seen him cool to people who wanted something out of him or who were too clinging. And I've seen him lose his cool, as when he nearly expired while listening to Auric's awful Piano Sonata, and actually swearing when it was over. Or when I referred disobligingly to Boulanger in *The Paris Diary,* he wrote me that he would simply not endorse a book that was so vindictive about someone he had always loved and needed. (That slap did me good and reversed many an exhibitionistic stance.) I've seen him elated, especially when a new piece was being played (you never get blasé about that first performance). I've seen him struck dumb by the beauty of a passing human being. I've seen him depressed, dark, near tears, about the plight of an arrogant friend we both loved. But he never actually talked about his carnal life, except elusively. His rapport with Victor Kraft was ambiguous, and in any case, pretty much deromanticized by the time I knew them both. It's not my place here to speculate on later loves—his generation even including Auden, was circumspect. Indeed, Aaron was the most circumspect person I've ever known, considering how he encouraged others to let down their hair.

I am thrilled, and I wish Aaron could be thrilled too, to discover how cyclic our world becomes if you live long enough. Recently I've heard any number of scores by young men and women in their twenties, scores which do more than emulate the wide-open spaces of Aaron's most beloved works—they actually sound (in timbre, tune, and hue) like steals from the master. Always admired by the masses, he's becoming readmired by fickle youth.

Nevertheless, I asked three members of this youth: "Is there any composer whose next work you just can't wait to hear?" They had to stop and think. They were not agog as we once were about how the Clarinet Concerto was going to sound, how the new Nonet was going to sound, or how *Inscapes* would be received. These were *events*. Aaron Copland wasn't the only one, but he was the chief one whose new works we were all avid to hear. I don't think it was because we were specifically younger. It's that the whole world was younger, there were fewer composers around, the repertory of American works was slimmer, so any new addition was a thrill. Aaron was the king and in a sense still is. There hasn't been another man since then from whom all young composers await each new endeavor with bated breath, and whose endeavor usually doesn't disappoint.

Samuel Barber

Even as you read these words, somewhere in the world Samuel Barber's *Adagio for Strings* is being played. As the most performed "serious" piece by an American, the *Adagio* dispels two notions of conventional wisdom: that what is popular is necessarily junk and that the late improves upon the early. If Barber, twenty-five years old when his piece was completed, later aimed higher, he never reached deeper into the heart, and he is still held most dearly for works composed before his fortieth birthday.

Forever weaving and reweaving their web around our globe, what do the *Adagio*'s strings sing to us if not a sad, brief perfection? The perfection is not that of, say, a sapphire, for the sound has no glitter, is not "expensive." Rather it is like some forgotten love letter retrieved intact from a cedar chest, penned with vast and tender elegance, yet vaguely irrelevant. If the irrelevance is itself irrelevant now (for what dates more than timeliness?), it nonetheless seems to be, along with the elegance, Samuel Barber's defining property.

I had the impression—we all did—that Sam Barber in his heyday was the only musician in a land of iconoclast cowboys for whom elegance was the defining virtue; when he left us in 1980 at seventy he took with him, for better or worse, a concept of craft stemming from that virtue. Now insofar as it means control and taste, is *elegance* quite the noun for Barber's art? Does one confound the product with the person, well wrought in shape but overwrought in content, coolly French on top but Brahmsian beneath? And insofar as it means aloof and unruffled, is elegance actually the term for the person, and is his product so inevitably suave? Listen again to the First Symphony, frantic and — if you will — ill-bred throughout its nineteen minutes, or to the trivial and vulgar *Excursions* for piano. Then think back to the man himself, as Apollonian a creature who ever stopped chatter on entering a room, as canny and cultured a companion as one could desire on his good days, yet with on occasion the cutting manners that only those born rich can get away with (or think they can) and with the *terre-à-terre* opportunism that every composer, rich or poor, has harbored since before Haydn.

Diary: Paris, 1950. Barber loathes the imputations of the serial elite. He persists in addressing the perplexed René Leibowitz as Mr. Ztwiobiel. "Well, if a composer can't recognize his own name in retrograde, how can his listeners be expected . . .".

1958. The day he won the Pulitzer for *Vanessa*, Barber came, along with me, to dine at Lee Hoiby's. "Have you heard," I asked, "that Poulenc's writing a monologue for Callas on *La voix humaine?*"

"Francis is an opportunist," said Sam.

"Still, what a swell idea."

"Because Maria's an opportunist too — she can't stand other singers on stage."

"But still, it's a swell idea. Admit."

"You think so because you're an opportunist. Everybody says so."

"Yes, but still — wouldn't you have wanted her for *Vanessa?*" And I got up, collected my coat, and left. Before the elevator arrived, Sam came out to the hall and sort of apologized.

"It's just," said he, "that you punctured me where I was most vulnerable."

One hears Sam in his songs as unmistakably as one tastes Julia Child in her recipes, not least because he was himself a true singer. Yet is firsthand knowledge a prerequisite of first-rate work? At parties Sam would, if coaxed, accompany himself—though never in his own music —in some dear goody of yore, "Pale Hands" being a favorite. What he mocked was precisely what he once most "felt," for his own early efforts were close to the bone of Carrie Jacobs Bond. Which explains their popularity on safe recital programs. Despite his classy choice of authors (Prokosch, Hopkins, Horan, Lorca, Rilke), his most famous songs lack profile; they could have been written by anyone. Anyone, that is, with a big technique. His melodies were pretty solid, and so were all other accoutrements of Sam's musical structure—harmony, polyphony, rhythm, and orchestration—as they obtained to various forms, small and large. His sheer scope was vaster than any American's of the time, including Copland's.

But if his modes of expression were varied, his language was not. Often highly chromatic but always deeply tonal, Sam spoke one dialect all his life. He did not evolve, as Beethoven or Stravinsky are said to have evolved, but, like Chopin or Ravel, sprang full blown from the head of his muse and spoke his conservative piece as persuasively at twenty as at seventy. It might even be argued that some of his later works (the *Piano Concerto,* the *Toccata Festiva* for organ) can now, like Prokofiev's, be heard as bombast and *remplissage.*

In the competitive rat race Sam was a loner, a not-quite-magnanimous aristocratic who never lectured or visited schools. Nor could he inure himself to the angry young. Sam was categorically intolerant of many a peer and of all the electronic and aleatoric children who, in their turn, found him anachronistic. Was he deluded in his tastes? Art is not about taste, nor need an artist be "right" about his contemporaries (that's a critic's job) so long as he is right about himself. Sam was pretty much right about himself from the start; he knew how to do what he wanted to do.

Between 1950 and 1958, we met often in Paris, usually chez Henri-Louis de la Grange, a mutual friend, though I took him also to Marie-Laure's, and they hit it off, more or less. Early in the decade I was seated on the terrace of the Flore with my girlfriend, Heddy de Ré, both very high on *fine à l'eau,* when Sam and Virgil and two or three others materialized at the table next to ours. For no reason I called Sam a shit, and for a year was ashamed at this gratuitous folly. I wrote a song for him—one of six ecologues on poems of John Fletcher, and mailed him a dedicated copy. He acknowledged this decently, and never referred to my misbehavior. He was a great solace, too, when I was in anguish about my Italian friend, P., whom Sam knew and liked.

In New York during the 1960s he came to dine chez moi two or three times. In the 1970s I don't remember seeing him except at parties, where he was icy. Like many, he liked at first, and then didn't like my *Paris Diary,* which caused a flurry—so innocent now it seems!—among those in the closet. Sam was outraged (according to Chuck Turner) because I recounted an anecdote he'd told me years before, maybe at Tanglewood. "When you get to Italy," he had said, "you'll find the Italians acquiescent. But even when they say I love you they still want to be paid. A friend of mine was hiking in the most remote region of the mountains above Torino when he came across a peasant boy who'd never seen the city. They made love. After which the boy asked for money." That's all.

If I declare that although I in a sense am among Sam's audience, I never quite cared for the person, nor did I need the music: both were too rarefied, unpredictable, neurotic, and, well, too *elegant* for me to deal with. No sooner is that last sentence written than I'm assailed by contradictions. If I do not need Sam's sounds, how to account for his ever-haunting "Anthony O'Daly" smiling through my most-sung song, "The Silver Swan," which no one has pointed out in the forty-five years since that swan was hatched? For what reason have I kept over the years those dozen letters I now reread, finding in each a generosity somehow mislaid?

In 1978 a disc was issued on New World Records called *Songs of Samuel Barber and Ned Rorem*. The liner notes by Philip Ramey included separately taped interviews with each of us answering parallel questions.

Ramey to Barber: "What do you think of Ned Rorem's songs?"

Barber: "I like one, 'The Lordly Hudson.'"

Ramey to me: "And Samuel Barber's [songs]?"

Me: "Quaintly enough, I find Barber's songs the weakest part of his otherwise strong output. They work, but they work in a turn-of-the-century way. They present few problems, and that's why singers sing them. Understand that I'm not criticizing Barber's language, only his tradition."

On this disc is Barber singing his own *Dover Beach*, recorded in 1933. Why am I covered with gooseflesh when the live voice of this dead acquaintance fills the room, as now it does, lending a patina of precious antiquity to the furniture?

If frequent contact plus sharing of victory and woe are what make for friendship, then I'm not the one to recall Sam Barber in any formal fashion. We moved in different circles. Also, being almost the only ones whose catalogues were colored by Song, that fact in turn was colored — at least for me — by a certain rivalry. One may question the propriety of one composer publicly discussing another, especially when that other lies underground.

Leonard Bernstein

During the terrible hours following Lenny's death last Sunday the phone rang incessantly. Friend after friend called to commiserate, and also the press, with a flood of irrelevant questions: How well did you know him? What made him so American? Did he smoke himself to death? Wasn't he too young to die? What was he really like? None of this seemed to matter since the world had suddenly grown empty — the most crucial musician of our time had vanished. But next morning it seemed clear that there are no irrelevant questions, and these were as good as any to set off a brief remembrance.

I was nineteen in early 1943 when we met in his West 52nd Street flat. Despite his showbiz personality he had, and forever retained, a biblical look, handsome and nervy as the shepherd David who would soon be king and psalmodize throughout his days. To me, a Midwest Quaker, his aura was Jewish and quite glamorous, while to him I remained always something of a reticent Wasp who never quite got the point. Everyone in Lenny's vast entourage felt themselves to be, at one time or another, the sole love of his life, and I was no exception. The fact that he not only championed my music, but conducted it in a manner coinciding with my very heartbeat, was naturally not unrelated to love. Years could pass without our meeting, then for weeks we'd be inseparable. During these periods he would play as hard as he worked, with a power of concentration as acute for orgies as for oratorios. In Milan, in 1954, when he was preparing *La Sonnambula* for La Scala, I asked him how Callas was to deal with. "Well, she knows what she wants and gets it, but since she's always right, this wastes no time. She's never temperamental or unkind during rehearsal—she saves that for parties." Lenny was the same: socially exasperating, even cruel with his manipulative narcissism (but only with peers, not with unprotected underlings), generous to a fault with his professional sanctioning of what he believed in.

Was he indeed so American? He was the sum of his contradictions. His most significant identity was that of jack-of-all-trades (which the French aptly call *l'homme orchestre*), surely a European trait, while Americans have always been specialists. If he did want desperately to create a self-perpetuating American art, his own music, even the Broadway scores, was a grab bag of every imaginable foreign influence. Night after smoke-filled night we could sit up arguing the point, for Lenny ached to be taken seriously as a sage. Nothing was ever resolved, of course, not so much because musical philosophy is an impotent pursuit as because he was less a thinker than a doer. Yes, he was frustrated at forever being "accused" of spreading himself thin, but this very spreading, like the frustration itself, defined his theatrical nature. Had he concentrated on but one of his gifts, that gift would have shriveled.

I last saw Lenny in May when, with two other people, we went to a dance program, afterward to a restaurant. His role, as always, was to be the life of the party, but repartee fell flat, the concerned pronouncements were incomplete, his breath distressingly short, and he disappeared like a ghost in the midst of the meal. A month later we spoke on the phone, not about health or music, but about the plight of our mutual protégé, a young Romanian student without a passport. Lenny could simultaneously focus on his navel and on the universe, even in his agony.

Was he too young to die? What is too young? Lenny led four lives in one, so he was not 72 years old but 288. Was he, as so many have meanly claimed, paying for the rough life he led? As he lived many lives, so he died many deaths. Smoking may have been one cause, but so was over-work, and especially sorrow at a world he so longed to change but which remained as philistine and foolish as before. Which may ultimately be the brokenhearted reason any artist dies. Or any person.

So what was he really like? Lenny was like everyone else, only more so. But nobody else was like him.

1990

Franco Zeffirelli

Thirty-three years ago Franco Zeffirelli made his directorial Broadway debut with Dumas's *Lady of the Camellias*, starring a weirdly miscast "method" actress, Susan Strasberg, in a plush adaptation by the young Terrence McNalley, and with music by myself. The play folded after four evenings. But in the preceding weeks I had ample time to examine the maestro at work.

Unlike other renowned jacks-of-all-trades—Cocteau, for example, who wrote the dramas he often produced, or Leonard Bernstein who composed the music he often conducted—Zeffirelli is not a creator. He is the ultimate recreator, an interpretor de luxe, responsible for everything about the play except the play itself. With *Camellias*, if he did not write the book, or indeed the music (although at his urging I piped a four-hand version of Weber's "Invitation to the Dance" through an echo chamber), he did design the sets and costumes, affix a viewpoint by relating the tragedy in flashback, and direct the entire goings on. I was awed by his energy, his scope, his sense of detail, his "democracy," and a bit contemptuous (was I jealous?) of his knack for beguiling every-

246

one with his Italianate charm; he would simultaneously supervise the installation of a Louis XV *begère*, correct the diction (in fluent but accented English) of an understudy, regulate the dynamics of the tape recorder, even sew on a button while, with a studied casualness, he fraternized with adoring stagehands.

We were both 39. But he was (still is) far more famous than any composer can hope to be. As figures of commerce and glamour, interpreters today outshadow those they interpret: tenors and actresses and directors are apotheosized, while authors and painters are comparatively invisible, with composers at the bottom of the heap.

His fame preceded him. I am not an opera buff in the sense of being more taken with singing than with what's sung. For me, bel canto emphasizes the gargoyles more than the cathedral. Yet in London, three years earlier, I heard—saw—an unknown Joan Sutherland, manipulated by Zeffirelli, make sense of Lucia's mad scene by cupping her hand to her ear, heeding her alter ego as echoed by the schizophrenic flute. The young Callas too, launched by the maestro, lent new meaning to Italian song, and changed forever the way the world responds to all opera, including American opera. Samuel Barber, who had devised *Vanessa* for her, was devastated when she turned it down. She was never to sing in English, her native tongue. Nor did Zeffirelli so far as I know, ever direct an opera in English, except for Barber's *Anthony and Cleopatra,* which opened the new Met in 1966. The director inadvertently subverted the score, which he considered chamber music, by introducing live mammals—were they camels?—amidst the supernumeraries, and a gigantic sphinx on a turntable which collapsed in mid-performance.

However, after the 1963 failure of *Camellias* when I never saw him again, he did direct a series of English-language movies, mostly Shakespeare, with a care for verse and visual nuance which perhaps only a foreigner can impose. His *Romeo and Juliet* (1968) is a Renaissance painting in motion, every frame a masterpiece in itself, even as it serves the ongoing whole. The music (by Nino Rota), mostly in slow or fast waltz time, and the speech, mostly in iambic pentameter, combine in a continual counterpointing of three against five, delicious to my American ear. His *Hamlet* (1990), with the successfully perverse casting of Mel Gibson as star, is witty and poignant in its treatment of language, virile and melancholy in its view of Danish royalty in decay.

If the Barber opera was an expensive dud, Zeffirelli two years earlier made a joint debut with Bernstein at the old Met, in a production of *Falstaff*, resulting in one of the happiest collaborations in Met history. The two men were profoundly similar, profoundly different. Each seemed flamboyantly self-involved and flamboyantly generous, each held an extravagant vision of artistic presentation yet with tight control, and each concurred, in his own Mediterranean manner, on the approach to British whimsy. Viewed from outside, their ascending careers had also been similar: each was internationally celebrated, highly paid and in constant demand, yet treated grudgingly, even sarcastically, by the press, at least on this side of the Atlantic, until well into middle life. But politically they were on opposite sides. Bernstein, forever left-wing, lent his name and his gifts to every imaginable radical cause. Zeffirelli, forever right-wing, even campaigned for the senate of the new party in Sicily, Forza Italia. (In a recent *New Yorker* profile he declared "that he would impose the death penalty on women who had abortions.")

If LB was progressive in championing new music, his own and hundreds of others, FZ's conviction in matters artistic is literally to conserve. What contemporary works has he directed? Eduardo de Filippo certainly, two Albee plays I believe, and a filmed remake of *The Champ*. But no Gershwin or Berg, no Beckett or Brecht, no studies of the downtrodden, like those of his chief mentor, Luchino Visconti. "These new operas," he has said. "It is a left-wing plot. . . . I am a totally understood artist. I am misunderstood only by the left-wing, who expect me to do something different every time." Yes, he centers on the tried and true with his personal focus for Shakespeare, Puccini, Da Ponte, Mérimée, Verdi. Other stylish directors are equally reactionary, but hide behind specious "relevance," updating everything except the music (why *not* the music?), while Zeffirelli simply makes a work more of what it already is. "You must be faithful to the author," says he. His aim is "to take the audience by the hand and make them revisit a lost planet. We cry and laugh for the same reasons the ancient Egyptians or 19th-century Romans cried and laughed. The passions of the human heart never change."

"Taste" and "opulence" are the nouns most often cited for his effect, though the nouns are in some way mutually exclusive, the one implying restraint, the other excess.

A few weeks ago we spoke, I in Nantucket and he in Positano, for the first time in decades. I was touched by his warm use of the second person singular, his constant interpolations of "luv" and "caro," his patience with my rusty stabs at his language ("You need to get an Italian lover," he suggested), and his eagerness at my invitation to dine on the evening of his arrival in New York. "But only if I do the cooking," he insisted.

Franco Zeffirelli arrives alone, but with enough fettucini to feed a regiment, though we will be only four. Also are plastic bags of sauce, one a sausage and spice mixture, another of basil and tomatoes just plucked from his garden in Positano. This fare he has toted from Rome, with a stopover in London, landing in New York last night. Today has been spent conferring at the Met. Tomorrow he will fly to Los Angeles to stage *Pagliacci* for Domingo, thence to Tokyo for a new production of *Aida* before returning here to rehearse for the opening of *Carmen*. Meanwhile, indefatigable, he immediately asks for the kitchen where for the next hour he will chop and stir and sample, while downing a stiff Scotch-on-the-rocks (he will also down a bottle of Campaccio, assuring us, "I've never been drunk in my life"), and commuting to the parlor where he does a quick imitation of Sutherland as Lucia trying to appear two feet shorter, at his direction, by squatting beneath her capacious skirt. Then back to the stove without missing a beat of the monologue about his two most compelling loves, Callas and Visconti: how the former's spirit was broken during her Onassis years; how the latter allowed him—Franco—to be held by the police relating to a robbery of which he was clearly innocent; yet how both were among the magic few of the true gods he has known. Indeed, he is now mulling a film script dealing with the unknown final month of the diva's life.

Franco is not onstage, playing the lofty star. He's been everywhere and knows everyone and is in fact a star himself, but like all stars he's also starstruck, like we lesser mortals. He does know his worth, makes his points succinctly, sometimes as if by rote. Nervous, voluble, disheveled, he remains handsome with a confidential twinkle of youth, has an appealing tic around the mouth, and chain-smokes needle-thin Superleggeras which he puts out in his undrunk espresso.

While grating the parmesan he explains that, of his triple-threat professions, opera and theater and film, opera is where his lasting contribution lies. He can afford this contribution because of the vast success of his Shakespeare movies wherein he has reintroduced high culture not only to England, but to receptive young innocents across the globe. Yes, movies are bigger than life, from outside in, by virtue of the medium, but opera is bigger than life from inside out. He doesn't particularly aim for grandiosity, it just comes out that way as the nature of the beast. As for straight plays, maybe he is least at home there, as witness the Dumas drama which he has directed in all three mediums, most persuasively as *La Traviata*. What he wants with opera is to intensify, not change.

He may well empathize with modern American theater, having directed, in translation, besides the Albee plays, productions of Steinbeck and Tennessee Williams, and filmed two "realistic" American soapers, *The Champ* (Faye Dunaway) and *Endless Love* (Brooke Shields), but his disinterest in American opera is resounding. Unaware of both *Four Saints in Three Acts* and *Nixon in China,* he nonetheless disqualifies them in absentia because "they are not in the repertory." When he ponders why neither *Wuthering Heights* nor *Streetcar* have ever been musicalized, I tell him how Carlisle Floyd composed a viable setting of the Bronte in 1958 and how André Previn is currently at work on the Williams. Hmmm, says Franco, toying with his necklace of gold amulets, gifts from the great, a blessed medal from the Pope, for example, and the letter *aleph* from Bernstein. "Ah, Lenny, Lenny, how I miss him. *He's* the one who would have written the great American opera."

Around midnight, as he is leaving, Franco hands me a video. This turns out to be his induction into, and his convocation address to, the valedictorians at the University of Kent in Canterbury Cathedral last month. His theme is commendably predictable (the riddle of how art can save an increasingly artless society) and his words are standard ("You kids are about to enter a cruel world"). But his mien is eloquent beyond words, as he stands there like a wistful boy in tassled hat and flowing robes. As with his beloved Lenny, one is now struck by how the Zeffirellian force stems not from diction but from action, not rhetoric but physical example, not intellect but instinct. Like all artists, no matter how glorious ("Beauty is but a flower/Which wrinkles will devour"), he seems vulnerable, even insecure, anxious for all of us to love and admire not only his hard work but his very being. The work has never displayed originality (anyone can be original) so much as . . . what? . . . a sort of sumptuous respect for the tried and true, a vertiginously accurate juggling with expensive toys.

1996

Frank O'Hara

Here we are at Fire Island where three weekends ago Frank O'Hara was struck and destroyed, quitting this world with the same intensity that he lived in it. The need for comment lessens, time passes, and Frank left a harem of literate widows each of whom has already composed epitaphs less compelling than those he wrote for movie stars. So no need for comment, but a great need for phoning Frank to get his opinion on it all! I've reread the 8 or 10 letters he wrote to me in Europe during the fifties (none after: we grew apart once we lived in the same city) and was impressed anew not only by his intelligent humor, but by how urgently he seemed to want me to be a good composer.

How many artists care, really, about their friends as artists, except for instruction? Frank, while he lasted, was the exception, until it killed him. . . . It always used to be my habit at gatherings to ask Joe LeSueur: "Who in this room will be the first to die?"

His poems were, among other things, conversational, elliptical. Frank died in the middle of a sentence.

"Oh sing us *Hôtel* again, Ned." The request was genuine, though spoken in inebriation, and referred to my notorious moans resembling a cow aborting which Frank kindly nonetheless found musically rewarding.

I did not choose my profession, it chose me. Since childhood it has grown between me and people. A strangling protection. My music is all one love-letter, but to whom?

Frank O'Hara knows this but reacts otherwise, calls his poem by another name: Lucky Pierre. That poem itself is gratified, being squarely between the poet and his love, instead of between two pages. And it exists, remains, can be referred to (which a phone call can't).

Yet Frank is estranged and growing more so. Because of—not despite—his art.

Strangling protection or Lucky Pierre, whatever you call art, that art takes, drains, thrives, empties us forlorn.

All's in a name. A rape by any other name would feel less good.

I believe in the word, even in two or three, in stringing them together. But I do not believe in writing. Not that it can't be done: it's been too much done. Ditto for notes. But simultaneous notes are more amusing than simultaneous words. Music has more potential.

If Winter comes can Spring be far—*behind?* But Spring's ahead and waiting. Winter overtakes, dissolves into, and is excreted by Spring.

Then do seasons arrive before or after each other, or spiral about, intertwining, contradicting time?

So where do we go from here? To boredom. There's no beginning and end, and boredom's integral to it. Though one can vainly ponder as to how boredom, as we know it, might be a part of Eastern Art and Music. Twain don't meet.

Toward the middle of *The Chelsea Girls* I turn to Jack Larson: "It's a masterpiece, isn't it? And shall we leave now?"

To make a masterpiece was not Frank's pursuit. A masterpiece is for the future.

X, robust and appealing, speaks with poignance about always having found him sexy. If Frank knew that now, he'd turn over in his grave.

The Candide theme (Herlihy's *Midnight Cowboy*, Genet's *Quérelle de Brest*, or Southern's *Candy*, versus Britten's *Billy Budd*, Bernstein's *Candide*, or the Purdy-Albee *Malcolm*) makes good reading but bad theater. The beautiful but dumb cipher-hero plunging down a narrow path causing distress and destruction to intelligent victims—whom he ignores as victims—is inherently undramatic, being unclimactic. Meanwhile, the unlikely play *Fortune And Men's Eyes* works musically and thus works theatrically (over and above its "theme" stolen from *Haute Surveillance*). The author's quartet is composed of solos for each instrument, duets and trios for the possible combinations, and ensembles for the whole with an ingenuity all true climaxes imply and comprise.

> . . . *in rooms full of*
> *strangers my most tender feelings*
> *writhe and*
> *bear the fruit of screaming.*
> —FRANK O'HARA, For Grace

We met on John Latouche's floor, December 1952, toward the end of my first trip back to America. Sonia Orwell was then new in New York, and John gave her a party. Vast carpet, Manhattan-type wit I'd forgotten, of course piano tinkling to support divine Anita Ellis whom I'd never met either, who clutched her red satin hem and threw those closed eyes to heaven screaming *Porgy!* while the room exploded with applause that only Streisand, second hand, commands today. Today, when half those guests of John Latouche, and John Latouche, are dead.

Pushed by John Myers, Frank edged toward me, and placing the ashtray among our feet, exclaimed in that now-famous and mourned Brooklyn-Irish Ashberian whine I didn't at first take to: "You're from Paris and I think Boulez is gorgeous." He meant, as they say, well; and I was surprised that a poet then already knew Boulez' sound over here; but gorgeous seemed hardly the word, even from that poet, for that composer.

Snow, and the year was closing. I sailed to France where Bobby Fizdale suggested I write something for two voices and two pianos. What words? Why, those of his friend Frank O'Hara. So a friendship was planted over the ocean which blossomed into our "Four Dialogues," originally titled "The Quarrel Sonata."

Here I'd hoped to quote whole letters. It can't be done in diaries—that's for grandiose epitaphs and homages he's everywhere receiving, more than his more famous peers, Jarrell and Delmore Schwartz. Nevertheless, from May of 1955, plucked from their generous context, come concerns about opera after witnessing my *Childhood Miracle* on Elliott Stein's libretto:

> Surely we must do an opera together. Something terribly sweet and painful, maybe? . . . . In the final trio I felt you lifted the work onto a new height where the music was inspired; before that, one felt admiration for your gifts and an awareness for the facility of the setting, but was more impressed than moved. . . . The libretto

worked very easily on stage, but it is not up to Elliott's other work which I admire tremendously. Not that a libretto should necessarily be a major literary production. But there are qualities of peculiar insight in his other work which would not be at all foreign to the stage and which he seems to have consciously avoided in favor of a non-dramatic gentle whimsy. . . . I feel that the audience cannot be given enough, particularly in a medium where the writer is confined by the greater importance of the musical expression. . . . Bringing your own extraordinarily sophisticated talent to bear on this subject, dealt with as sparingly as it is (it is almost a "least common denominator" of the situation), is like getting a cannon on stage and not firing it. . . . I am prejudiced by my longing to have you write the significant modern opera I feel about to happen in music. There is no social, dramatic or sensational contemporary situation you couldn't deal with in your characteristically beautiful fashion, I think, and that is true of virtually no other composer now, saving perhaps Marc [Blitzstein] who has other ideas and other gifts from the ones I'm thinking of. . . . When you think of yourself in relation to the work I imagine hearing from you (and remember this is because I love what we already have and don't mean to be overbearing or overstep the bounds of discretion between one artist and another), think of Manon and Louise and 3 Penny and Lulu. Why deal with a melting snowman when a cocktail party would be a great opportunity for great music? I don't mean to harp on modern subject matter; of course the subject counts for little or nothing sometimes. But it doesn't hurt a great gift to have a significant subject either, whether it is the liberation of Flanders or love à la Onegin. And I really believe that an artist cannot be in his best work more mild than the times. It harms the work's conviction. . . .

More mild than the times. . . . I do not, like Styron or Blitzstein, pretend to deal with the time's Big Issues. Yet by definition my prose and music are of, and hence concern, our day. Who can say that narcissism or the forgotten themes of romantic love are less timely, less indigenous to our health or malady?

But when Stravinsky states that "artists and 'intellectuals' can be as dangerous and foolish as professional politicians . . . about matters beyond their competence," smart Mary McCarthy concurs, but points out that artists do possess a higher intuition and are good at smelling rats.

Frank O'Hara smelled rats. And from the common rats about the house he made his poetry, as Auden had a generation earlier.

1966

Julian Green

The news of Julian Green's death at 98 reached me last July, just prior to a performance in Nantucket of a song by me on words by him. Fifty years earlier, when living in Morocco, I had read my first work of Green, a novel called *Moira*, and was stunned—like meeting my double in a trance. Narrated in compact Gallic language, the story treated of American disorder: sexual guilt of, and murder by, a horny inarticulate red-haired youth in a southern university. New world puritan frustration via the mother tongue of Mallarmé. Green spoke American in French, the reverse of, say, Janet Flanner who spoke French in American. We had an exchange of letters, and when I returned to Paris that fall we met. The meeting quickly veered toward a violent intimacy which lasted about ten months, during which I saw Paris through his eyes and the world through his pages.

Green's first novel, *Mont-Cinère*, came out in 1926 and changed the tone of French literature. The subject was family greed in our southern United States, the language was lean and somber. Similar juxtapositions occurred in this American's twenty-odd fictions over a period of sixty years, all but one composed in French. By 1951, when we met, he had also become, along with Gide, Europe's principal master of the diary, a format which, if no more "true" or "confessional" than novels or autobiography, is by its nature more immediate. So I took up my own diary again, influenced, in manner if not in matter, by his. By extension the influence must have touched my music too, though no one can explain quite how, at least not in words. In this same year was republished a brief memoir called *L'Autre sommeil*. Green was still in his twenties when it first appeared, but it speaks of his own death with a sadness that seemed . . . well . . . musical. I translated and made songs from three paragraphs. This is the music sung again last summer.

Green eventually wrote several modestly successful plays, one of which, *Sud*, was turned into an opera by Kenton Coe. In 1971 he was the first person of American parentage to be elected to the Académie Française.

Julian Green was not a Thinker, much less a philosopher. If he had a riveting gift for plot, even in such an open-ended structure as the diary, the gift came as a stream of consciousness. "If I have anything to say," he wrote, "I'm hardly aware of it. If I do bring a message, then I'm like a messenger who is unable to read and whose message is incomprehensible to himself; or rather, like a stenographer who cannot reread his work because he only knows how to write."

But he *was*, in a sense, a messenger. Like many a holy convert he was more Catholic than the pope, and his prose is permeated with a sort of hopeless hope that the world will be saved. Those perpetual obsessions with sin and the true way, with prayer and dream, with shop talk (Jesus talk) among clerical friends! If in his *Journal* Julian Green continues, through his specific belief in God, to miss more general points at every corner, in his fiction this very "miss" provides the Julianesque tonality, the singular Greenery. Surely if one-track-mindedness empties the spirit of humor, it does fill the mind with an explosive physicality which remains the *sine qua non* of all large souls. (Humor is not physical but intellectual, and multiple-track-minded.)

Such skepticism was apparent to Julian, who deplored my atheism, promiscuity, and what he termed "dangerous frequentations," not to mention an age difference of 25 years. He gave me his books, photographs, insight into a rarefied milieu, a plaster cast of Chopin's hand (which, to his horror, I used as a bookend), and, above all, confidences about his closeted yearning requited by his tactile love for a statue of Apollo. His stifled emotions, the very grist of his early novels, grew less repressed in the later years. "I don't care what anyone writes about me when I'm gone," he often said. And he often said too—quoting Pascal quoting God—"You wouldn't seek me if you hadn't already found me."

Are we drawn to a work because of what we glimpse of ourselves already there, or do we discover only what we bring? Was my personal feeling—which was less than love and more than love—for Julian the man impelled by the unbearably wistful expertise of Julian the artist? Or was the unbearable wistfulness already in me, minus the expertise?

Today the expanse of time since first we met seems slight, yet surely I have at least a musical voice that has nothing to do with Julian Green. Though by another turn of the screw, I wouldn't be me if it weren't for him.

1999

Allen Ginsberg

This morning I've been rereading Allen Ginsberg's early poems. Despite their unflagging energy, long lists of Whitmanesque "yawps," all-embracing compassion and stinging eroticism, I'm impressed anew at how melancholy they mostly seem. Listen:

> . . . all movement stops
> & I walk in the timeless sadness of existence. . .
> my own face streaked with tears in the mirror
> of some window—at dusk—
>   where I have no desire

Listen:

> . . . this graveyard
> this stillness
>   on deathbed or mountain
> once seen
>   never regained or desired

in the mind to come
where all Manhattan that I've seen must disappear.

Or listen again to the notorious opening of *Howl:*

I saw the best minds of my generation destroyed by madness
    starving hysterical naked,
dragging themselves through the negro streets at dawn looking
    for an angry fix

— followed by a thousand lines of depressing fervor that established
Ginsberg, at twenty-nine in 1955, as our most influential American
bard.

The verses recall my own mother, who spent her life as an activist
for pacifism and for all civil rights. When the world did not listen, she
gave up and died. Ginsberg never gave up. Yet with the years he became less and less the subjective poet and more and more the objective
sloganeer for the teenage minds of the 60s and 70s: mantras, flower
power, LSD, counterculture. But he was also crucial to more worldly
movements: gay rights, environmental protest, Buddhist solutions to
violence. Like Hemingway, he grew to be more guru than creator.

Though close, we never touched, being reverse sides of one coin.
If the whole coin depicted public avowal of homosexuality in a pre-
Stonewall era when people didn't say such things, his side portrayed
the magnanimous redskin, mine the paleface narcissist.

Was it in 1958 that we first met? I recall a drunken bunch of us piling
into a cab, lurching from Virgil Thomson's at the Chelsea to Kenneth
Koch's on Perry Street, with me seated happily on his boyfriend's lap.
Did Allen mind? "Not if Peter doesn't," said he, and began to sing:
"Where is the world we roamed, Ned Bunn? . . . who roamed a world
young lads no more shall roam." For the next four decades, whenever
he saw me, my name would spark those verses of Melville. During
those same decades two aspects of my first impression stuck: 1) Allen
was as generous *with* his lovers as he was *to* his lovers; possessive love

contradicts all-encompassing love. 2) Any occasion was occasion for song, song being poetry's primal utterance.

Cut to Tangier in 1961, when this long sentence appears in my diary on August 28:

> Allen Ginsberg, who breakfasts on eclairs in the Socco Chico, who inhabits a shack-penthouse at the Hotel Armor with Gregory Corso, who takes strong pills with William Burroughs (*The Naked Lunch* has power not through order but through accumulation only), and who announced "all" to the New York Post two years ago, in short the original obstreperous Beatnik, tells me middle-classedly to "hush" when I ask Paul, in the Mahruba restaurant, too loudly before other diners, if the dancing boy is queer.

The "all," uttered to a leering reporter, had been: "Yes, I'm queer as a two-dollar bill." Then why the pious reaction to my question about the dancing boy, since in any case the other diners didn't speak English? As to Burroughs, I found him then as I find him now, a sophomoric bore as a writer, and an unmusically surly lump as a man.

In 1966 were published the confessional *Five Years* of Paul Goodman, and my *Paris Diary*. With Allen Ginsberg we became America's three unapologetic queers. (France for years had Gide and Genet, Cocteau and Montherlant, even as Greece had Cavafy.) Yes, America has always had her outspoken "dirty" authors, but they inevitably wrote in the third person.

The difference as guru between Allen Ginsberg and Paul Goodman is that one catered to the feelings of the young while the other catered to their minds. Obviously Ginsberg won out.

Diary, 1973:
One musician's heart sinks on witnessing Allen Ginsberg, presumably oblivious to the TV cameras yet mugging like Dean Mar-

tin in slow motion, embedded among acolytes intoning with mindless de-energized redundant unison the stanzas of William Blake. Ginsberg acknowledges he's never studied music, that his settings of Blake are "in a C chord, C-major" (he means in a non-modulating Ionian mode; his tonic is actually B-flat), and that he teaches Blake by singing him "because Blake sang, you know— he was a literal poet."

Formal study would not make Ginsberg a better composer, only a discerning one. He needs more of an ear: his music may be fun to join in, as any college songs are for the tone-deaf, but it sounds colorless, uncommunicative, and wrong for Blake, who needs a rainbow blaze. To counter, as Ginsberg does, that although no-body knows what Blake's own music was like, since it was not written down, but that it was "probably similar to what I'm doing . . . [which] is sort of in the style of Isaac Watts" (a hymnodist who died ten years before Blake was born), is not only to strain the cre-dulity of his students, but also to *know* the past, and to assume that an ugly drone is as valid as the simplicities being droned. Even if we did know Blake's own settings, why set his poems now in the manner of his time rather than ours? Would rock music embellish these poems? Maybe, but rock has its own words.

Couldn't Ginsberg musicalize his own good verses instead? Of course, then he'd risk the inadvertent masochism of a Paul Good-man whose non-professional love for music leads him to believe he's a composer. (Though unlike Pound who turned to Villon—as Ginsberg turns to Blake—Paul sabotages his own perfect poetry.)

2 March 1974

Tomorrow in Kansas, premiere of *In Time of Pestilence,* six short madrigals on verses of Thomas Nashe. The choice of poetry for these a cappella morsels I owe directly to Allen Ginsberg, although he doesn't know it. During an interview with *Gay Sunshine* long ago, Ginsberg quoted the line composed in 1593: "Brightness falls from the air"; and this urged forth my song. Thank you, Allen.

Coincidence is not the word for fine minds functioning together while miles apart; it is the word for mediocre minds finding greatness—which is never. There is no coincidence. So I was not surprised to recall the phrase only last night, isolated painfully, as I reread *A Portrait of the Artist* after thirty years. "Brightness falls from the air." Stephan Dedalus recalls the words as he picks a louse from his neck, crushes it between his fingers, and lets it drop shining to the ground.

From the hamlet garden we plaintively watch trains go by. From the train window we enviously see hamlet gardens. Finally enclosed in the actual arms of the butcher we've dreamed about, we dream about the butcher. Go up in flames, go down in flames.

Over the years Allen and I corresponded regularly, if not copiously. We "spoke" solely of poetry as it obtains to music, and as its subject is gay (though neither of us used that word). I was cranky, he was patient. He never raised his voice. Saints don't raise their voices, they inform through example. Still, saints are a dime a dozen and never really change the world, while poets are rare as rubies and leave us in another dimension.

I prefer to remember Allen as a poet. As such he was—is—dangerous, because his style, conversational and direct (like that of Frank O'Hara who also at his death spawned mediocre imitators), seems deceptively simple, thus easy to mimic. Still, if there are a thousand faux Ginsbergs about, better that than a thousand Mother Teresas whose pieties have strings attached.

If Allen grew to be less the dreamer and more the rebel, he nonetheless, in 1973, accepted membership to the American Academy of Arts & Letters at whose conformingly prestigious dinner parties he ambled from table to table photographing fellow members. (These included, after 1983, thanks to Allen's prodding, the nonconformist Burroughs.) It was at the Academy that I most frequently ran into him, and with whom I felt most at ease gossiping about who "was" and who "wasn't" amongst the distinguished immortals. For after a certain age, the age at which they become professionals in a competing society, artists together don't talk art, they talk shop. Shop means fees, sex, and death, in that order.

Like all true artists he was one of a kind. The "kind" was bardic, didactic, personal, where the artist's presence is as crucial as his work. No one was better at this than Allen Ginsberg. One may hope that the best of what he has to say, despite his absence from our fickle society, will last forever.

1997

Tennessee Williams

By an early age most artists have stored up enough "life" to draw upon forever. Even the greatest have a finite number of themes which they vary throughout their careers. The variation is refinement, re-experienced experience, echo. Art manipulates echo by refashioning (or personalizing) works by another, or by oneself at another time. Still, there is a golden echo and a leaden echo, as one poet sang years ago, and as Tennessee Williams demonstrates today.

His style has always been personal despite proximity of excellent friends—"Southern" and otherwise. Yes, he does show a dash of the meanness, whimsy, blasé anger and pussycat anxiety of McCullers, Capote, Vidal and the Bowleses (Jane and Paul). He too blends sexuality with horror. But he has more fun than the others, and more ease with words.

His content too is his own. Or, to situate through analogy, mix Jean Genet with Isaac Singer. Though Williams is as Goyish as Singer is Yiddish, both share an affection for (indeed, extract their identity from) what lies directly under hand, even when that is neither a bagel nor bourbon but a dybbuk's sigh or Martian spacecraft. They render the fantastic usual and the usual fantastic. . . . Though Williams is as American as Genet is French, both are drawn to the glamour of injustice, and both call forth a similar *dramatis personae:* tough guys, black giants, mad queens, policemen, angels.

But Williams' social spectrum is broader than theirs. Singer emits but one ethnic tonality, from Lublin to Broadway. Genet, in his stories, embraces neither women nor the rich. Now, Tennessee Williams' drawl is no less persuasive than his cosmopolitan repartee, his women are real (reread *The Vine* to quell that canard about men in drag), and his geographies are international. Also he has as good an ear as any author today.

He does not, as they say, have an ear for music (musically he is unperceptive, even deaf to all but the most naïve moods), but an ear for spoken situations. That ear, plus his contagious sense of the vastly carnal, has made him famous in the theater, where such qualities are showbiz effects as much as artistic virtues. When distilled in the fiction they bring forth an artist with no further need of a stage.

What makes him him? The large scope and mimetic gift. He is the ventriloquist of the underprivileged, rich and poor.

By 1965 Tennessee Williams' major themes had been mutually nourishing for twenty years. Big and little tales and plays ricocheted off each other, igniting always apparently novel combinations of energy, as a kaleidoscope confects endless patterns from limited colors. *The Yellow Bird* joined *The Glass Menagerie,* then shattered into *Summer and Smoke,* which faded back into a little fable called "The Resemblance Between a Violin Case and a Coffin." Meanwhile one small story, "Three Players of a Summer Game," swelled into a large drama, *Cat on a Hot Tin Roof,* while another large drama, *The Milk Train Doesn't Stop Here Anymore* (starring reincarnations of the false poet from *Orpheus Descending* and the mad diva from *Sweet Bird of Youth*), was thrust back into a small story named "Man Bring This Up Road," only to reemerge as a play, again called *Milk Train,* which would receive still further polishing in a little prose piece, "The Inventory at Fontana Bella." The dead hustler of *One Arm*, reborn and heterosexualized as Stanley Kowalski, turned half-queer again in *Hard Candy*, became the character of Chicken in a story, "The Kingdom of Earth," took to the stage in *The Seven Descents of Myrtle*, where he married and lived content. The gorgeous rough trade, those likable whores, offensive grandes dames, despised versifiers, and fragile introverts were shuffled and renamed but remained intact and were treated with devotion. Fear of aging, need to travel, compassion for marriage, obsession with quickie sex, all this was perpetually intertwined with humane twists. Alone in his theater catalogue, like a white elephant with a cannon, stands the awkward *Camino Real*, which aims high at intellectual poesy but hits neither rhyme nor reason. Meanwhile among his short fictions—most of them diamonds—glimmer unidentifiable gems shaped like hearts.

American theater has little to do with mature philosophic analysis and much to do with the pure energy one finds in animals or children. When our dramatists try Think Pieces they give us either artifacts like *Tiny Alice* or propaganda like *The Crucible*. They never spark the theological fireworks of a Mauriac, a Montherlant, a Cocteau, a Claudel, even a Sartre; our public doesn't care about morality issues beyond pop melodramas like *The Exorcist*. We aren't raised that way. Neither are our dramatists, who, after all, form a part of their own audience. (In France, conversely, there exists no wholly lay audience.) Thus a mature vitality has not yet been directed toward our theater.

Tennessee's ability to write straight fiction was his trump card. His stories are so fragile that when absorbed into their creator's *oeuvre* they don't disturb the surface, nor do they pollute the depths as do the later plays. They scarcely smell of those gas leaks of compromise that seep into even his best drama and permeate the worst, like that corny Saroyanesque foray called *Small Craft Warnings*.

Although for seven years I had known Tennessee the artist, having attended the historic opening of *The Glass Menagerie*, I never knew Tennessee the man until the afternoon of November 1, 1952, when I woke up in his bed after a Halloween party at Jane Bowles's, the first of a dozen bleary meetings over a span of several years, here and abroad. Then in the fall of 1957 John C. Wilson hired me to compose the incidental music for *Suddenly Last Summer*. It's not certain how confident Tennessee was of me now as a colleague, given our previous blurred rapport. It *is* certain that once the rapport was on a professional plane we were never again at ease together; even in the best of times Tennessee was hard to talk to.

In 1964 I composed the score for the second version (the one with Tallulah) of *Milk Train*. The production failed, but our acquaintance succeeded because of what it taught me. If Tennessee socially was hard to talk to, sometimes appearing inarticulate, that's because he listened to you. He attended, intensely, or abstractedly, or impatiently, but always as though considering, "Can I use this?" At business meanwhile he was verbose, molding raw material with a paradoxically extravagant economy. Inspirationally he resembled both Schubert (who could write a perfect song in a single sitting) and Beethoven (who would belabor the details of a symphony for months). Before rehearsals for *Suddenly Last Summer* Tennessee slaved each morning with Herbert Machiz, trimming and padding in what seemed a hit-or-miss manner. What began as a rambling monologue for Anne Meacham ended as a pair of what can only be called arias for female voices divided by an hour's worth of exposition. A dozen references to the sky as "a great white bone" were shaved down to two. The original title, *Music in the Twelve-Tone Scale,* was dropped when I explained that the term meant nothing, either in itself or as reference to the contents of Anne's soliloquy. "But can't you at least write some background music in that scale?" the author pleaded; "I just love the sound of those words." His approach to music was not even instinctive so much as plainly visual, or at best, intellectual, metaphoric. For example, he asked that Anne's entrance be accompanied by Corrida trumpets; he *saw* what bullfights connotated aurally as connected to the dark death of his unseen demihero. We tried it musically, but the association was too personal, too "poetic," to work. In the end Tennessee left me to my own musical devices which, I admit, were influenced by those of Paul Bowles, who

had almost singlehandedly created what must be called "The Tennessee Sound"—that suavely aching underwater bluesiness we have
come to link with passive heroines. (Alex North used that sound too in
his music for *Streetcar*, later choreographed by Valerie Bettis, and Lee
Hoiby used it in his opera *Summer and Smoke*.) Tennessee also kept
out of my way on the set of *Milk Train*. Not so director Tony Richard-
son who dolled up the play to within an inch of its life with irrelevant
japoneries. My score, which could have as convincingly accompanied
a Kabuki pageant, was at least salvageable as a concert suite, which is
what we composers always aim for.

In retrospect neither *Suddenly Last Summer* nor *Milk Train* seem
politically solid. The one depicts the male homosexual as an inevitably profiteering mama's boy; the other portrays The Artist as Victim,
whereas all artists, in mirroring the very society that supposedly vic-
timizes them, necessarily have the last laugh. Did the music, by its
nature, soften or harden these dramas? I can't say. But Tennessee—although like many literary people he never went to concerts, or talked
about symphonies, or listened to records other than pop—did sense
that music was as crucial to his plays as to Shakespeare's: it tightened
the dream, gave logic to folly. Then are his plays what people like to call
musical?

The difference between Tennessee Williams and Edward Albee as
users of language is that one is a poet, the other a musician. Albee
has claimed to be more influenced by composers than by playwrights
(which doesn't mean he's more influenced by music than by theater);
in fact, he never personally knew any playwrights until he became—as
we say in America—successful, though he was acquainted with lots of
composers. Albee is a well-informed Music Lover, while Williams was
tone-deaf. Both have utilized moody musical decor for their less naturalistic plays. But when it comes to adaptations of their actual words
for singers, Williams lends himself admirably to song and opera, Albee
not at all. Williams' prose, being poetry, is easily set to music; Albee's
prose, being music, is impossible to set to music.

JH feels that Albee's weakness lies in avoidance of characterization.

A Williams drama, even at its purple worst, always shows wounded or laughing individuals moving through the mismanaged argument. Because they are individuals they lived (or died) yesterday and last year, too, and are brought back tomorrow and next year by their maker in other plays. They people his *oeuvre*. But Albee writes plot before personality; his characters live only in the actors portraying them.

Yes, Williams' stories at their best are better than his best plays because they necessarily avoid the vulgar paraphernalia that our theater seems to require: laugh lines, etc.

After *Milk Train* (which coincided with the death of Frank Merlo) encounters with Tennessee became sporadic and were never in the line of duty. The last time we met was at the Gotham Book Mart a few months ago. He acted vague. I was uncomfortable. Yet on reading his obituary last week I felt I'd lost a close friend. Thus it is when artists die.

1974

Truman Capote

When famous artists die, nine times out of ten their fame dies with them, particularly in our century when glory is extra to what is glorified. If this is true with, say, Gide or Hindemith, who were not products of the American publicity machine, but whose vast reputations relied on their physical presence on the planet, and whose works became all but unavailable the morning after their deaths, how much more true it is of pianists and actors and ballerinas and bestselling authors. Bartók was a rare exception in having died needy and becoming immediately rich posthumously. Likewise Sylvia Plath, maybe Jackson Pollock, and of course Scott Fitzgerald. Mostly, though, we strut our fifteen minutes on the stage, then vanish.

Truman Capote would have seemed—before he died—an ideal candidate for oblivion. Like Warhol, he was famous for being famous; but how many of the gawking fans, who witnessed him drunk and incoherent on talk shows, ever read a word he wrote? The last half of his life was so cheap, so dissolute, so vulgar, so public, that, like a sort of reverse Rimbaud, he renounced writing (while advertising himself as the greatest author since Proust), and vanished into the spotlight.

When *Other Voices, Other Rooms* made headlines in 1948, I devoured it between classes at Juilliard, finding it, as I still do, though dangerously influenced by, superior to Carson McCullers. (Superior because, unlike McCullers, each word, as with poetry, was unextractable, and the words together formed inevitable chains, like perfect wreaths of roses, which in turn formed themselves into paragraphs, pages, chapters.) The notoriety lay, of course, less in the surprise that the book was good literature (even rarer then than now on best-seller lists), than that the back cover was adorned by a photo of the author gazing at us, doe-eyed 'neath yam-colored China-doll bangs, from a prone pose on a Victorian settee ("it assumes I'm more or less beckoning somebody to climb on top of me")—scarcely the stance of our Hemingways hitherto. If in real life he was not so cutely passive, he looked every bit as infantile—physically, that is—although his utterances, in that much-mocked voice, were always pointed, disarmingly honest and, I suppose, adult. Still, Truman wasn't like you or me. He was a conspicuous sissy, and not one bit ashamed. When I had asked Bowles how such a specimen coped in the actual world, he said that, well, Truman didn't often venture far from his geniuses and dowagers, but when he did (showing up in the Casbah maybe, or on the Lower East Side, or indeed in the plains of Kansas where a decade hence he would be documenting the Clutter murders), he was the source of disbelief rather than of scorn. Fame and chutzpah were his shields. He graced the odd side of Quentin Crisp's coin: being unreal, neither man posed a threat, but whereas Crisp as defiant victim got bashed now and then, Capote as defiant lord seemed immune to battery. This was clear in Paris where I saw him every day. *Other Voices* had just appeared there, under the weak title of *Domaines hantés*, and I served as translator during interviews (like many good writers—and composers, too—Truman Capote lacked the gift of tongues) which were conducted in places like the

Deux Magots, where strangers gaped approvingly. The rest of the time we talked.

What about? Not art, certainly. Do professionals after twenty ever talk esthetics (exhausting both their energy and their secrets) rather than money, sex, and contracts? Nor did we talk music, since Truman like most literary types knew nothing of that. (His impression of Jennie Tourel: high heels and silk pyjamas, even when hiking through mud at Yaddo. His impression of Esther Berger: "I think she's sweet"— I lifted an eyebrow—"like a cobra.") Mostly I listened as he improvised around, for instance, his "dear acquaintance," Denham Fouts, an American who in the late thirties slept with just everyone—Jean Marais, King Farouk, the Maharajah so-and-so—everyone, that is, except Hitler. "Had Denham Fouts yielded to Hitler's advances there would have been no World War Two, and Denham would not have had to slit his wrists in the bathtub of that Roman pensione." Truman talked of the long poem he was making, *The Postman's Lantern*, which would surely be settable to music (where is it now?). He speculated on why Paul Bowles stayed for so long in Morocco, then put it down to the available sex. He was stirring in a description of Jack Dunphy, who had left his wife, dancer Joan McCracken, to live with Truman forevermore. Jack's modest but true gift as a playwright Truman praised to the skies, but he praised too Jack's wise eyes, pale hair, and virile nape, and claimed to *need* the color, taste, and smell of each segment of Jack's body. Still, I seldom saw them together. Truman's life was compartmentalized. The two men were as unlike as Topsy and Eva.

In early November Truman left for Sicily and I returned to Africa. In March 1951 this was mailed from Taormina to Marrakech:

Dear Ned, Your card was forwarded to me here where I have been for over a year working on a novel. Am leaving in three weeks for Venice and late in July sailing home. Would so like to see you; I hope you *will* come back to N.Y. I hope you are *working*. I think of you often. My love to Marie-Laure—my love to you

et mille tendresse [sic]
Truman

In N.Y. my address is still 1060 Park Avenue

But our paths didn't cross until two years later when he turned up again in Paris. Meanwhile, his reference to "sailing home" impressed me (most expatriates in those days repudiated America), and his emphasis on "working" influenced me; a short story collection and *The Grass Harp* had just come out, and I read them with pleasure and envy at his knack for unstilted metaphor and structure, virtues I sought to impose on my music. On 28 November 1953, he came to lunch in Marie-Laure's blue marble dining room, and told us he was taken with the rich because they *were* rich—he wanted to *use* what made them tick, if in fact they ticked by being rich. Ostensibly he swapped his fame for their wealth. But did the rich ever in fact coolly sign checks to him? and can it be seen, looking back, that he ever "used" all that research in his books? He was vicarious in the sense of being a prudent watcher, moralizing about, without participating in, the global gangbang (nonpolitical department). On 17 December he dragged me to one of those loud caves in Saint-Germain-des-Prés (sober, I loathe nightclubs—the din!) where we sat for hours watching the young dance the Java. He said, "You have an innocent profile, at least from the right."

He never came to France again, not while I lived there. In New York we met from time to time, generally tête-à-tête, though sometimes with his famous flock. I do treasure an evening with Dietrich, another with Gloria Vanderbilt. Still another in a Third Avenue cinema, theoretically watching *To Catch a Thief,* actually refereeing an onanistic exchange between a male couple in the row ahead, after which we supped at Johnny Nicholson's now-defunct café where, over a chocolate soufflé, I heard about the chores of celebrity. "Yesterday, five minutes after my new phone had been installed, and nobody could possibly have known the number, it rang, and a voice said, 'This is Speed Lamkin.' Talk about opportunism!" (Speed Lamkin was to have a brief run as the poor man's Truman Capote during those distant years.) I remember also the first television production of a Capote oeuvre, "A Christmas Memory," and Frank O'Hara's guffaw when Geraldine Page appeared on the screen, looked mistily out at the country dawn, and uttered the script's first line, "It's fruitcake time." In 1959, with Valerie Bettis, I composed a dance called *Early Voyagers*, based on *Other Voices, Other Rooms*, which toured the U.S. with the Washington Ballet Company. And so forth. If Truman and I weren't quite friends we were staunch pals, always casual and mutually respectful.

But the nature of our rapport was to sour horridly.

On the eve of my fortieth birthday in 1963 Glenway Wescott gave a dinner party. There were five of us, with Truman doing most of the talking. Luridly he recalled his recent stint in Kansas, detailing for our amazement the qualities of mind and body of two young murderers (one of whom he was clearly in love with) standing trial there. He was making a book out of it—a nonfiction novel, he called it—"but it can't be published until they're executed, so I can hardly wait." Truman's position vis-à-vis those poor boys was admittedly unprecedented; he'd spent more than a year living near them on death row (and would eventually return to Kansas to witness their execution). Still, I remember asking myself later that night if he had quite the right attitude. Did he believe what he said? Or was I—as he called me, when I objected to his repeated use of the word "nigger"—a hick, who missed the finer points. (Truman was not a racist, but he did possess a personal vocabulary.)

On 14 April 1965, Patrick Smith and Richard Hickock were hanged. Immediately *The New Yorker*, in four long installments, published Capote's account which came out as a book at the end of the year under the title *In Cold Blood*. Even before the first printing the author was said to have earned, with subsidiary rights, etc., two million dollars. In February of 1966 I sent this letter to *The Saturday Review* which printed it:

Capote got two million and his heroes got the rope. This conspicuous irony has not, to my knowledge, been shown in any assessment of *In Cold Blood*. That book, for all practical purposes, was completed before the deaths of Smith and Hickock; yet, had they not died, there would have been no book. The author surely realizes this, although within his pages it is stated that $50,000 might have saved them—that only the poor must hang.

Auden, in his libretto *Elegy for Young Lovers,* portrays a poet who, for reasons of "inspiration," allows two people to perish, and from this act a masterpiece is born.

Now I am suggesting no irresponsibility on the part of Capote other than as a writer: I am less concerned with ethics than with art. Certainly his reportage intrigued and frightened me, and certainly he presented as good a case against capital punishment as Camus or Koestler. But something rang false, or rather, didn't ring at all. His claim to an unprecedented art form gives cause to wonder.

An artist must, at any cost, expose himself: be vulnerable. Yet Capote the man, in his recent work is invisible. Could it be that, like the Ortolan-eaters so admirably depicted in Janet Flanner's recent *Paris Journal,* he is hiding his head in shame?

(The Ortolan reference is to the tiny yellow sparrows which, according to old French engravings, are roasted alive and consumed, bones and all, "with napkins hoisted like tents over [the eaters'] heads to enclose the perfume, and maybe to hide their shame.") A month later Kenneth Tynan took up my tack in the *New York Post,* Truman retaliated—and became more famous. I was not invited to his fabulous party at the Plaza, the high point of which was reportedly the entrance, not of such guests as Tallulah Bankhead or Candice Bergen or Janet Flanner herself, but of the law enforcement contingent from Holcomb, Kansas.

In 1967 I and three other composers were honored at the American Academy of Arts and Letters. I duly noted the occasion in my diary, and concluded the entry thus:

What I shall remember, however, is not the glamour of the ceremonies proper but the appearance during the earlier informal festivites of Truman Capote, with dark blue shirt and coral tie, as he approached me with an uncharitable glint in his eye. Beginning softly, he crescendoed to a point where a crowd gathered, and finished off with frenzy: "I've liked what I've read of yours lately, Ned, etc. etc., I didn't see it, but friends told me you'd written something in *Saturday Review* against my book. Now I worked hard. You didn't go through what I went through. I produced a work of art, and you have no right to attack it. . . ." This! twenty-eight months after the fact.

Anyone has the right to attack a work of art, especially when the work is self-advertised as documentation. An author who claims his facts are unassailable because they're art wants it both ways: Don't hit me, I'm a lady.

I never saw Truman again. Two years later I was doing a "signing" at the Gotham Book Mart for my new *Critical Affairs*. Truman was invited, and apparently got as far as the shop downstairs. Andreas Brown, who runs the Gotham, later said that Truman picked up the book, found his name in the index, read the reference, and decided not to come upstairs. I had written:

Truman Capote, in adapting for other mediums his goodies of the past, gets a lot of mileage from a comparatively meagre output. His art becomes his life. Like record producers, he glories less in creation than in distribution. But distribution is *the* art of today. Nor will there be, in any case, posterity for anyone.

Time passed. I didn't think much about Truman, there was nothing much to think. He appeared oftener on the tube than in type, talking about writing rather than writing; what he declared was, in essence, that he was good and "they" were bad, but he offered no proof. I did, however, enjoy two or three visits from his biographer, Gerald Clarke, for whom I dredged up scenes of childhood. Suddenly one morning in May of 1976 a friend phoned and told me to rush out and get the current *Esquire*, for in the second installment of *Answered Prayers*, called "Unspoiled Monsters," Truman Capote had immortalized me. (He is writing here of "the leathery little basement bar" in the Hôtel Pont Royal:)

Another customer of this bar, whom I met there and who was friendly enough, was the Vicomtesse Marie-Laure de Noailles, esteemed poet, a *saloniste* who presided over a drawing room where the ectoplasmic presence of Proust and Reynaldo Hahn were at any moment expected to materialize, the eccentric spouse of a rich sports-minded Marseillais aristocrat, and an affectionate, perhaps undiscriminating, comrade of contemporary Julien Sorel: my slot machine exactly. *Mais alors*—another young American adventurer, Ned Rorem, had emptied that jackpot. Despite her defects—rippling jowls, bee-stung lips, and middle-parted coiffure that eerily duplicated Lautrec's portrait of Oscar Wilde—one could see what Rorem saw in Marie-Laure (an elegant roof over his head, someone to promote his melodies in the stratospheres of musical France), but the reverse does not hold. Rorem was from the Midwest, a Quaker queer—which is to say a queer Quaker—an intolerable combination of brimstone behavior and self-righteous piety. He thought himself Alcibiades reborn, sun-painted, golden, and there were many who seconded his opinion, though I was not among them. For one thing, his skull was criminally contoured: flatbacked, like Dillinger's; and his face, smooth, sweet as cake batter, was a bad blend of the weak and the willful. However, I'm probably being unfair because I envied Rorem, envied him his education, his far more assured reputation as a coming young fellow, and his superior success at playing Living Dildo to Old Hides, as we gigolos call our female checkbooks. If the subject interests you, you might try reading Ned's own confessional *Paris Diary*: it is well-written and cruel as only an outlaw Quaker bent on candor could be. I wonder what Marie-Laure thought when she read that book. Of course, she has weathered harsher pains than Ned's sniveling revelations could inflict.

My first reflex was to dissolve in disbelief. My second was to retaliate, not so much in my own defense as in Marie-Laure's—she was dead and couldn't fight back, but I was alive and could. Still, fight back I didn't—not because as a Quaker I was wont to turn the other cheek, but because my lawyer, Arnold Weissberger, explained that his business was to keep clients *out* of court; also, that the Pulitzer Prize (which came to me the following week) would deflect public focus from Truman's bitchery.

Between 1977 and 1982 I kept a column in *Christopher Street* wherein the next paragraphs, separated by years and lodged in apposite contexts, glimmered.

I've occasionally admired the Coctelian rightness of Truman Capote's off-the-cuff repartee, and for years have retained in my treasure chest of wish-I'd-said-thats the following from one of his long-ago interviews: "When I throw words in the air I can be sure they'll land right side up." This noon, thumbing the Goncourt journals, I come across this from Gauthier: "I throw my sentences into the air and I can be sure that they will come down on their feet, like cats."

Suicide as an art form. Mishima at his peak dies publicly for what he feels to be truth. Truman Capote at the ebb of his power kills himself publicly for what he knows to be non-truth. Whereas Mishima grows ennobled, Capote shrivels (if a toad puffed up with hot air can be said to shrivel). His sketches of others are ultimately harmless, but the unwitting self-portrait is putrid as Dorian Gray's. All that Truman touches turns to fool's gold. A book may or may not be a work of art, but it's not for the writer to say so, or even to know so. An artist doesn't "do art," he does work. If the work turns out as art, that's determined by others after the fact. Art and morality aside, Truman's work can't work. A work which names real names but whose author is fictitious? An author must be true, his characters fictitious.

Today Truman's is a name uttered in hushed tones by the likes of Cher and Johnny Carson: he's the poor man's thinker, *le savant des pauvres* who are mostly quite rich. Not that the real intelligentsia is contemptuous, they just have nothing left to say. Truman sold his talent for a mess of potage.

On Dick Cavett's show Truman Capote, looking like that extraterrestrial embryo from the end of *Close Encounters,* posits the same defense of his upcoming nonbook as he posited last year and the year before: "Well, Marcel Proust did the very same thing." One might quickly reply: Yes, and so did Hedda Hopper. Every writer— or interpreter or conversationalist or archeologue (to avoid the word "artist")—depicts reaction to milieu; there is literally no other material to work with, on or off the earth.

Those extracts are as much as I've ever said in print about Truman Capote. However pertinent, they grieve me today. Were we kindergartners flinging mudpies? Is there a special ethics to friendship with public figures? Truman was confected of three disparate characters: private person, public person, writer. Are friends still friends when they publish what they feel about each other's professional claims or social fame? Truman hurt me, I did the same to him. Now it seems silly, benign, reparable, and it's too late. Last summer when his picture appeared on the front page of the *Times,* "Truman Capote Is Dead at 59; Novelist of Style and Clarity," I felt a sense of pride and of loss. Pride, because America cared to mourn a poet as it celebrated politicians. Loss, because, like Marie-Laure, Truman could no longer fight back.

After his death I reread most of his published work. He often speaks of the datedness of others, making his own datedness loom larger still. Of course, everything dates: Bach and Tolstoy date no less than jitterbugs and hula hoops—or you and I. Our exquisite viewpoint toward love and death this morning is, by virtue of afternoon trials, reslanted and thus dated—though maybe more intense—this evening. All things date: they date well or they date badly. I went through the early stories with the hoped-for exhilaration of finding long-lost friends. They're very 1940s, all about coy adolescents, doppelgängers and little else. Split personality was the rage after the war. Technically though (especially the remarkable "Children on Their Birthdays") the tales are flawlessly professional in that they're neither too short nor too long, the sentences sound inevitable, the images apposite. *The Grass Harp* cloys. *Other Voices* holds up (maybe because it's about queers? and they were the long-lost friends), although Gore V. contends that the most ravishing vision therein—the little country train being so slow that butterflies float dreamily in and out of the windows—is swiped from McCullers. But I never saw it in McCullers. *The Muses Are Heard* remains original, informative, funny. So does the 1956 etching of Brando. The rest seems dispensable. Still, what remains is his alone, an oeuvre tinier than his reputation, about the size of Duparc's in song, Beardsley's in pictures, Jane Bowles's in fiction.

Jane Bowles is nowhere mentioned in the printed interviews (although Truman contributed a preface to her Collected Works); nor is Bill Archibald, who wrote the film script for *The Turn of the Screw*, which Truman signed for his "name" value and then took credit for; nor is Harold Arlen who, as composer, was solely responsible for *House of Flowers*. Like most American literary types Truman knew and cared nothing about classical music (though his instincts are elsewhere sound: "Streisand's great fault as a singer, as far as I'm concerned, is that she takes every ballad and turns it into a three-act opera. She simply cannot leave a song alone"). As for his last projects, notably the snippets from *Answered Prayers*, he forever reviewed them, instead of writing them—telling us what to think instead of letting us decide. The fault with *Answered Prayers* is not that it's gossip, but that it's cheap gossip, and Truman must have known this on some level of his consciousness. We learn nothing potent about the world's most interesting hearts and minds to which Truman alone had access, only their dirty little secrets. We never *are* told how the rich tick.

I weary of my efforts here. We are forever wishing our artists were something else, rather than what they are. It is too easy to say that

Truman frittered his gifts away. The very frittering *was* his gift. The very fact of him, even in those first bright years, was never what our academics deem "serious," but who cares for them. Like Sibelius, like Rossini, Truman ceased composing long before he died, and was what he was.

He might not be quite out of my heart, but Truman is off my chest.

1994

Envoi

All endings are sad, even the end of pregnancy. I resent my friends' wives who rob me of my friends, who end the meaning of this friendship. And all change too is sad, even a change for the better. Stars' meanings alter as we come near, but *we* never change really—though nothing stays truth in a third person's mouth.

What's new for the old is old for the new, so how do we know where we are? I mean, the old are new yesterday, the young today. A child, not having been born, can't see this. Yet an old person feels newer today than yesterday when he was younger. So things get newer as they grow older, because today is younger than yesterday.

Old's the opposite of new, but also of young. Old people are more recently old than the unborn, more newly old, newer, constantly on the crest of the wave, advancing, nearer to that future from which the young are distant. Antiques grow ever newer—new hags, a new crone. Newborn babies are all wrinkled with age.

Last month is older than today. Is today younger, or only newer? The past, now old, was when the world was young. So we become younger and younger as we continue on and away from that old time when the world in flames was brand new, and so very agèd it now seems. And we are newer, being more recent. . . . Memories of the future, the ancient future.

Oceans are old and they don't wrinkle. Now Marie-Laure corrects me: "Darling, oceans are nothing *but* wrinkles!" Well, I could wish forever to be nailed to those waves.

He is looking older and unchanged. (I am afraid of looking older if not changed.) . . . But neither would I look changed and nobody has ever been changed and nothing ever changes, which is why fairy tales are about the turning of ducklings into beauties and pumpkins into coaches, and why children now take drugs—to ignore what seems to be an alteration in the world outside them.

I want so to notate these joys of the past, but hesitate, for fear the very words may themselves become memories to break the heart in later years. . . . I feel happy. Unhappy only that all must change. Glad that nothing changes. I live so as not to be anonymous; how many say this? are they more content? Why must I evolve? Books don't—why must I? But books *do,* depending on the reader's age and the time he lives in. They change too in rereading, generally for the worse; when they change for the better it's not, unfortunately, because the reader is smarter, but because the book is older.

Styles, like skin, change every seven years but with such overlapping that we notice nothing. If only we could shed like snakes! or, like caterpillars, emerge from cocoons as butterflies into a new season of joy. Nothing again will ever be new, though every homecoming necessarily indicates a change. But the same voyage will always be new. Nothing is waste that makes a memory.

The hand that wrote me the burning letter is dead. Old letters die but we still remember. Finally we don't remember anymore. All passes. Beauty too. Masterpieces last longer (longer than living) though seen newly by new eyes, but they also disappear. Even continents, which are here the longest, must finally be washed away. The most exciting crotch won't stay that way, nor this paper, nor this ink. Will it all be back like our flying saucers in a universal circle?

Books have ends. But there's no denying the fact that the older I get the more past I'll have. The speed of that past, like the speed of the things of the earth, increases with the world's age, accumulates with the hysteria of a falling boulder.

It's painful, occasionally dangerous, to share a tender experience, for the future so quickly becomes the past where we find ourselves alone again. But without this sharing, how live? By molding silently that which the public will eventually snatch away to share among themselves? These sentimental sharings nonetheless take place every day despite us, and are accumulated in a nebulous attic from which we withdraw them in our old age and laugh.